SOCIOLOGY OF RELIGION IN INDIA

Important Books of Similar Interest Published Recently

Encyclopaedia of Sociology of Politics, in 3 Volumes
Edited by Motwani and Saksena

Encyclopaedia of Sociology of Religion, in 3 Volumes
Edited by Nayar and Nayar

Encyclopaedia of Tribal Religion, in 12 Volumes
Edited by S. M. Channa

International Encyclopaedia of Anthropology, in 12 Volumes
Edited by S. M. Channa

Encyclopaedia of Ethics and Logic, in 10 Volumes
Edited by Piet and Prasad

Landmarks in Indian Anthropology, in 74 Volumes
Edited by Several World Famous Authors

Untrodden Fields of Anthropology, in 2 Volumes
By A French Army Surgeon

SOCIOLOGY OF RELIGION IN INDIA

Edited By

V. G. Nayar

&

M. G. Nayar

COSMO PUBLICATIONS

2001 INDIA

Chapter-1

The Guru as Religious Type

Chapter-1

The fighting excursion[1] is sparked off by three questions: Whether the Hindu guru falls into any of the categories listed by G. Van der Leeuw in his work *Religion in Essence and Manifestation*; whether the word *śiṣya* can be rightly translated as 'disciple'; and, finally whether Kierkegaard's analysis of the Socratic-style teacher could be extended to the Hindu guru. Under 'founders' Van der Leeuw includes the reformer, teacher, philosopher and theologian, exemplar and mediator. The one which might seem to come closest guru idea is 'teacher', indeed popular usage identifies 'guru' with 'teacher'. The Vedic literature, including the Upaniṣads and the Smritis, deals with *ācārya*-gurus. The *ācārya*-guru gives *dīkṣā*. At this stage preceptional instruction is not a new plus ultra but is to be combines with ritualistic observances and yogic practice. There must however be a 'fitness' on both sides. The guru should have the Sāstras at his finger-tips (he must be *śrotriya*, able to 'cull' them as one culls flowers), should practise them and be able to impart them. Such a man will be in a position to judge the fitness of the pupil and impart instruction to the worthy. The disciple must be teachable, he must have a tranquil mind, and he must draw near of his own accord. Significantly, the *ācārya* does not go in search of pupils. He is the lodestone which attracts. Indeed the fitness of the pupil for instruction is measured in no small part by his ability to seek out the teacher who can help him most. The guru corresponds, it would seem, neither to Van Leeuw's preacher category nor to the teacher category. The preacher goes forth 'with a message'. His business is with proclamation par excellence. The teacher is "an instrument of salvation" but he "neither imparts salvation nor announces it".[2] The teacher as instrument of power, particularly through his word, no doubt possesses authority. That Van Leeuw has in mind the Buddhist tradition rather than the Hindu is evidenced in his comment that "the original potency, which is indeed the basis of the teacher's status also, continually compels the disciples to forget the absolute sufficiency of the doctrine in favour of their teacher".

The Hindu guru, however, does not transmit doctrine. His function is otherwise as we shall see later. Following H. von Glasenapp, Van Leeuw is, however, right in saying that "the Hindu guru is very often revered as divine by even the most free-thinking sects; or, as dev-guru, he becomes the actual object of worship". But what he says next gives us pause. I quote: "His disciples follow the teacher: their response is the result of a summons: 'Follow me'"[3] He goes on to speak of disciples as imitating the master, adopting, propagating his teaching and generally assimilating his way of life, that of the hallowed teacher. Now following or imitating is foreign to the Hindu idea by reason of its incompatibility with svadharma. The guru's function is traditionally that of putting the learner on a path which he has to follow for himself. The initial awakening, in which the guru has a part to play, is followed by further stages to be attained. A paradox is involved, though, in that although the guru's task begins with initiation into a way of life, the relationship with the initiate is so close that the guru[4] is almost bound to become a focus of devotion. We might say that in so far as Van Leeuw links the teacher with the imparting of 'doctrine', the Hindu guru is hardly a teacher of this kind. We need to make a distinction between doctrinal and non-doctrinal instruction and to associate the Hindu guru with the latter.[5] That such instruction involved a modicum of self-giving on the part of the guru is referred to by Bipin Chandra Pal as follows: the guru "reveals that much of himself to his disciple as is suited to the requirements of the inner life of the latter".[6,7] This author gives a reason different from the one suggested earlier as to why the guru is not an exemplar in the way a religious saviour or founder would be. He says that following in the steps of the guru or doing what the guru would do in the circumstances is rules out on the ground that this would amount to an "attempt of the lower to override his own proper law and adopt that of the higher".[8] While this includes the *svadharma* argument, the point of the objection is rather this — that it would be wrong to emulate those at a higher stage of development than we are ourselves. This brings to mind the common root of the Sanskrit word for disciples and the word for governing and ruling. While the instructor in secular subjects, or indeed in philosophy, could be argued with (indeed the intelligent pupil is shown as full of questions, *vide* Yama's complimenting Nachiketas, *Katha* 1.2.9), the searcher after liberation is not in quite the same position.

The difference in connotation of the Latin-rooted 'disciple' may be recalled. Webster's dictionary spells out the meaning thus: "One who receives instruction from another; a learner, especially one who accepts the doctrines of his teacher and assists in preaching them; a follower." The doctrinal point, we noticed earlier, was taken up by Van Leeuw. Disciplehood in the context of Christianity refers to the twelve who were chosen by Christ and of whom the following three things could be stressed: They were His companions; they witnessed to His word; and they were sent forth to preach the Gospel. 'Disciple' and 'apostle' are used interchangeably in the Gospels, and the term 'apostle' means specifically one who is a messenger. In Hebrews 3.i. the word 'apostle' is further attributed to Christ Himself in the sense that He was sent from heaven to publish the Gospel. In the first century, the primitive church used the word apostle for other ministers in addition to the twelve, and the Greek church applies it to the seventy disciples of Christ as well as to the twelve. While there may be some analogy to witnessing and spreading the message in the case of Buddhist disciplehood, these ideas seem foreign to what was and is involved in being *śiṣya* within the Hindu tradition. We need then initially not to be guided by connotations of teacher and disciple in other traditions but to examine the guru/*śiṣya* relationship within the Hindu tradition. The relationship concerns first of all the concept of *dikṣā* and secondly that of *sādhanā* and how it is to be attained.

In Vedic times the 'profession' of *ācārya-guru* was confined to Brahmins. The *omkāra mantra,* moreover, could only be given to a Brahmin. The initiation conducted at the *upanayana* ceremony was the prototype for initiation of other kinds, so that the word guru was applicable, say, to the teacher of dancing, music, etc. There was also the further extended sense is the object of *sevā* (service), the dust of his feet is to be taken, taboos are to be observed re touching, and in general the behaviour of 'inferiors' is strictly formalized vis-á-vis them. Gurudom then was not only ascribed to those who had special knowledge to impart to those who wished to learn, but it was tied up with a hierarchical pattern of society where behaviour at different rungs was strictly regulated. The passivity of a certain kind of pupil is sometimes attributed to this tradition in much the same way that Kant decried the pupil who listens to everything that the teacher has to say. In the modern era the Brahmos have not been alone in speaking critically of this aspect of *guruvāda*.

The characteristic role of 'spiritual' gurus (as against instructors in various 'secular' subject) is that of awakening certain powers in the initiate. Differences in the powers to be awakened can be noticed as the idea evolved over long periods of India's history. The Vedic type involved the awakening of the faculty of discrimination so that the soul realizes its separateness from *māyā* [the twofold power of avidyā, namely *vikṣepa* (distortion) and *āvaraṇa* (concealment) has to be overcome through gnosis]. The *dependence* on gurus seems to have increased as time went on. And yet that a man can attain 'self-recognition' without the help of *dīkṣā* was also recognized. Patanjali discussed this under the rubric of *pratibhājñāna*. The Śaiva writers were alive to this possibility and distinguished different types of grace corresponding to different types of *pratibhā*. Analogies used in referring to the guru's role include these: the puff which removes ashes from cinders and makes them glow, and the water and manure which nurture the seed of *pratibhā* into full growth.[9] Whatever be the guru's role it was understood that this must be supplemented by ethical living, faith, and yogic practices which bring about control over the self and sometimes control over external nature through *alaukik* means. Recognition of differences of temperament was associated with the need for different paths. The lateral proliferation of types was accompanied by a vertical proliferation of staged steps of ascent.

The idea of a progression in the relationship of guru and pupil is seen notably in the *Bhāgavadgītā*, where the original relationship between Krishna and Arjuna is presented as that of friendship, and advances to that of Lord and devotee, the greater relationship including the earlier form. The concept of progression is also built into the notion of a line of succession from master to pupil. It is the gurus who transmit *paramparā* (tradition). Popular parlance has it that to know a man you must know who his guru is. Following the *Bhāgavata* the Vaiṣṇavas have an elaborate classification of the devotee's progress in ten stages. In this connection it is said that Chaitanya reached the eleventh and twelfth stages, that is, beyond the union of Rādhā and Krishna. This raises an interesting question about the difference between guru and pupil. The guru is characterized by *siddhi* (realization), and the pupil is characterized by his pursuit of *sādhanā*. But once the notion of progressive stages is admitted the way is opened for a turning of the tables, for a one-time pupil to acquire guru status vis-á-vis his former guru. There are indeed stories of such reversals. This fits in with the śāstric belief that there can be no satisfaction greater than that of being outstripped either by son or pupil. Another somewhat 'liberal' aspect of the guru idea may also be mentioned. For enlightenment to be tied up with devotion to a guru provided a way of realization apart from knowledge of texts, a way, this is to say, for the illiterate and for those of lower castes. Indeed from the Middle Ages onwards the caste of the guru seems to have been less and less important. The *mantra*, significantly, is heard, and not read. It belongs to the oral tradition, and not to literature. It could therefore be communicated to an unlettered man.

The *mantra-dīkṣā* idea is developed in detail in the Tāntric literature.[10] In imparting a *mantra,* the guru awakens the wisdom latent in man through his *guru-śakti*. In fact dependence on the guru is greatest among the Tāntrikas, complete surrender on the part of the initiate being required. The notion of potency operates on both sides of relationship. The guru's words possess power (the bīja idea), and this awakens the *kuṇḍalinī-śakti* in the disciple. The guru is himself both a recipient and a transmitter of grace. At the same time it is believed that God (as *antaryāmin*) is the guru par excellence. To this extent the Tāntric guru is something of a mediator. Both claims seem to be made, that the guru has intuitive knowledge of Brahman (i.e. he possesses wisdom) and that he is a 'realized soul'. In either case the guru is a channel of *śakti*. To those who would point to the excessive dependence involved, the Tāntrikas reply that *śravaṇa* is followed by *manana* and *nididhyāsana*, and that after initiation the disciple is in no small sense put on a path which he must follow for himself and on which he must be a light unto himself (through *antarātman*).

The *sadguru* takes the disciple even further along the path. The classification of different gurus has been done variously by recent thinkers, Sri Ramakrishna spoke of the highest guru as one who is content with seeing the successful result of his teachings in his disciple's life.[11] Contact with a *sadguru* is supposed to endow the disciple with some of the former's powers. Thanks to this contact, the disciple stops accumulating new *karmas* and the *sadguru* bears the *karma-phala* of many of the old *karmas*. This brings in an element of vicarious suffering[12] into the guru concept. But in spite of the guru's grace in helping the disciple to overcome *saṁskāras* and *vāsanās* the individual still has to make his own effort, that is to say, the operation of *guru-śakti* does not obviate the need for yogic practices etc. A further mode of operation of the *sadguru* is in influencing all (both inanimate objects and people) with whom the disciple comes into contact. All this brings a gradual process of divinization. But, interestingly enough, unlike the Advaitins who aim at 'realization' in terms of identity, the Vaiṣṇavas regard the progression in a different way, with *Brahmajñāna* at a lower stage, followed by union with the *antarātman* through yoga, and devotion to Bhagavān coming as the highest stage *following upon* liberation. Although relation with a Mohānta guru may be commonly regarded as indispensable, the second stage (direction by Caitya guru) and devotion to Bhagavān take the initiate further. That liberation is possible of attainment is assumed throughout. The existence of 'realized' persons capable of being gurus is the presupposition of the whole process. Some of the Tāntrikas, for example, maintain that liberation is possible in three births to one who cultivates the *siddha-mantra*. The language of 'realization' is not hospitable to the idea of further progress in spiritual life — this may be said both of the Advaitin and those following the mediaeval and later cults. In this respect the Buddhist, in spite of the *anatta* doctrine, is more adventurous in conceiving a succession of stages or dimensions of spiritual pilgrimage, an endless and not-to-be-guessed-at process of graduation. It can also be noted that the instructive role of both guru and *sadguru* does not amount to a total act of self-giving.

The guru instructs according to his insight into the disciple's need. A doublesided insight is required, that which guides the disciple to the 'right' guru, and the latter's insight into the congeniality, worthiness, etc., of the disciple.

Among recent religious figures, Ramana Maharshi did not have any guru, but believed that the *sadguru* is none other than the Supreme Self which abides in the heart. For Ma Anandammayee also the guru is not indispensable. Apart from his political mentor Gokhale and Raychandbhai, the guide of his youth, Mahatma Gandhi (whose religious thought has many interesting features although he could not properly be described as a religious figure) may be said to have had no guru. He was often impatient with those who 'idolized' him, protesting that he was only a humble aspirant for Truth and had not yet attained it. That those who themselves had no gurus should be regarded as gurus by others is of course ironical. The student of comparative religion will also notice that the religious aspirant in the traditions referred to above are in quest of a supreme religious experience rather than a Supreme Being. The philosophic quest of relief from *dukha* is a religious quest too. Much of the ascesis, therefore, is cast in terms of getting rid of hindering elements such as *vāsanās* etc. We also notice a difference between those who stress gnosis as the qualitative character of the desired experience and those who speak of love. The Tāntrikas link control over oneself with control over nature and therefore associate *alaukik* powers with gurudom. All this suggests that the *guru/śiṣya* idea has developed in manifold directions over a period of centuries, but that the guru is not classsifiable in any simple way under Van Leeuw's categories of teacher, mediator, or exemplar, although there are elements of each of these in the conceptions of the Hindu guru. That it was capable of still further development in Buddhism and Sikhism witness to its importance in the religious life of the subcontinent.

The Socratic Analogy

In his *Philosophical Fragments,* Kierkegaard charcterizes the Socratic-style teacher in ways which bear some analogy with the guru concept. Kierkegaard addresses himself to the question: "How far does the truth admit of being learned?" The Socratic answer is phrased in immanentist terms. The truth is *in* us. Bretall[13] in his short introduction uses the language of realizing "our true selves". On such a view the teacher's role is not to communicate the truth, but to bring to birth what is already latent in each man. To be unaware of the truth amounts to error, to ignorance. The remedy is gnosis. All these are tied up — the initial condition, the remedy, the teacher's role in it, and the 'healed' condition. There is perhaps no explicit suggestion that the teacher on this view is a fellow-seeker, although this would seem to be the implication of Plato's *Dialogues*. Socrates is a seeker to the last, and possesses a humility which is perhaps unique in the annals of the Greco-Roman world. Plato suggests, with the enthusiasm of the devoted pupil, that Socrates' mission was a divine one (vide *The Apology*). But what Socrates does for his pupils is on a strictly human level, in fact the maieutic kind of help is the noblest that one human being can offer another. There is, indeed, an utter absence of pretension in the Socratic pedagogy. Socrates is not the practitioner of a skill, a techné. He had no high opinion of those who treated philosophy as if it were a techné, a skill to be acquired. Each individual stands alone in his dignity, and if this is so, the teacher is a mere occasion, not an 'authority'. Each man is a light unto himself. The teacher asks the question and sparks off the self-examination which leads to a discovery of the truth. He provides the reminder which stimulates recall. Revelation, on such a view, becomes redundant. All moments of time have equal significance. The highest wisdom is less the 'attainment' of the truth than the awareness of ignorance, for he who claims to know and is in error has no means of correcting himself. The one who is aware of his own ignorance is thus the wisest of all.

For the purpose of this discussion no excursion will be made into the theory of recollection or the problem of time, both of which are critically important in the context of the argument between the Socratic and the Kierkegaardian. The focus will be on two matters: the immanence of truth and the role of the teacher. There are both points of agreement and disagreement if we compare Kierkegaard's presentation of the Socratic-style teacher with the mainstream-Hindu guru concept. In both it is assumed that what was not *in* us could not possibly be acquired.

Immanentism is combined with monism on the Advaitin view, but not, of course, by Socrates who makes a big point of avoidance of speculation. The truth is *for* all, but not that all *are* one. Socrates does not go into the 'obscuring elements' which bring about ignorance, in the way the Hindu thinkers do. 'Forgetting' is the reason given for our ignorance. The 'world' is not looked upon as a general drag on ethical or religious endeavour. Whereas the Hindu guru is such by reason of avowed expertise (being 'God-realized', 'self-realized', and the like) no such claim is made by Scorateṣ. The Hindu guru gives instruction, whether by way of mantras or otherwise, but Scorates eschews anything of the kind. Yet we have the significant similarity that both the guru and Socrates attract by the lodestone of their personalities, by the impression that they 'have something' which others do not have. Neither go out to 'seek the lost'. In both cases, moreover, neither the *śiṣya* nor the philosophical pupil need a 'new organ', the organ of faith. But there is a noteworthy distinction. The Hindu guru is the dispenser of grace and as such can be spoken of as a focus of enabling power. For all the similarity in terms of both being 'gnostic' and not 'redemptive' models, in so far as the guru is associated with *śakti* (even in some measure in the non-Tāntric forms) there is no hint of anything analogous to this in the Socratic teacher. Socrates' daimon guides him, but there is not outpouring of power vis-á-vis those who come to learn from him. Socratic fallibility is progressively mitigated through the dawning of knowledge in place of ignorance. Socrates is an 'awakener', and so is the Hindu guru. But both Socrates and his pupils are seekers from first to last. There is no element of authority either in their relationship or in the 'weight' of their experience. Indeed they are in quest nor of a supreme experience, but of the truth. This is conceived in terms of *vision* in the Greek manner, rather than in terms of an existential *anubhūti* which has through the ages been the goal of the Hindu religious quest and which goes under the name of *sādhanā*.

SOME ANALOGIES AND DISTINCTIONS DERIVED FROM THE CHRISTIAN EXPERIENCE

The Christian understanding of redemption and salvation is at first sight so different from both the 'gnostic' model of Socrates and the 'liberation' model of the Hindus that contrast rather than comparison would seem to be the order of the day. If one were to single out the core beliefs of Christianity (something which does not fall within our terms of discussion here) this would centre on the person of Christ Himself and His conception of a redeemed humanity to be brought to fulfilment in God's own time. On both points, the uniqueness of the Christ-figure and the conception of a new society, we have nothing for which the guru concept can provide any analogy. Gurus are ipso facto many, and their function is to awaken individuals and not to bring about transformed communities. Gurus receive service (*sevā*) rather than give it.[14] As Kierkegaard forcefully insists, the Christian is he who is *in* the truth (not that truth is in *him*) and this he can only be through the saving power of the one who is the Way, the Truth, and the Life, i.e. Christ Himself. What is required is not knowledge, not even belief (in any doctrinal sense), but acceptance.

We may begin with the difference between the outward man and the inward man (Vide II Cor. IV. 16) which can be regarded as the Christian reaction to the immanentist theme. The outward man, that is Adam, is contrasted with the inner man (Christ). The new man is to be 'put on' in the language of Coloss.III, 9-10. Now the concept of the *creature* is crucial here, for the divine potency is seen in the whole created order, in unregenerate man, and in the perfect life of Christ. The language of immanence, in so far as it is present, is such via the implicate of creaturehood. The Church Fathers discussed this in detail in terms of the 'nature' of man, and what the words 'image' and 'likeness' might mean. Man is made in the image of God in terms of his intellect. Up to the time of the Cambridge Platonists reason was regarded as the candle of the Lord, and it is indeed this that gave rationalism its weighty credentials. The intellect as 'human spirit' is to be distinguished from the Holy Spirit which is identical in substance with the Father and the Son. The early Hellenistic Fathers avoided extreme immanentism in skilful ways. For example, Clement of Alexandria writes: "By nature we are adapted for virtue, not so as to be possessed of it from our birth, but so as to be adapted for acquiring it."[15] Justin wrote of the germninal Logos

(Logos spermatikos) according to which the Logos is active in all men, imparting to them whatever goodness and knowledge they possess. But while the Logos works in others as a seed, He works in Christ as a whole. The Logos assumes shape and becomes man in Christ. The philosophical respectability of the language of growth and becoming (a major contrast here with Hindu thought, or at least Advaitin thought) via Aristotle enabled the Fathers further to explicate the theology of man and his capacities. Irenaeus understands 'man made in the image of God' as a being capable of fellowship with his Maker. Needless to say, this implies neither an identity of being nor a merely gnostic (in the sense of 'cognitive') relationship. The former is ruled out thanks to the doctrine of creation. Irenaeus writes: "Created things must be inferior to Him who created them."[16] The pattern of spiritual growth (and growth must be stressed) is an ascent towards the perfect, 'approximation to the uncreated One...'.[17] The matter is summarized succinctly in the following passage:

> Now it was necessary that man should in the first instance be created, and having been created should receive growth; and having received growth, should be strengthened; and having been strengthened, should abound; and having abounded should recover (from the disease of sin); and having recovered should be glorified; and being glorified should see his Lord.[18]

A fine analogy from the craft of the potter follows:

> Offer to Him thy heart in a soft and tractrable state, and preserve the form in which the fashioned thee, having moisture in thyself, lest, by becoming hardened, thou lose the impressions of His fingers.[19]

Irenaeus' 'recapitulation' concept embraces both the 'historical' dimension of the redemptive process and the Alpha-Omega idea which was familiar to first- and second-century Christians. Jesus, as man, through 'recapitulation' perfectly fulfilled what God had intended man and his entire creation to be. Irenaeus puts it thus: "The word of God, Jesus Christ our Lord, because of his immense love for us, became what we are, in order to enable us to become what he is."[20] Both Jewish eschatology and Aristotelian metaphysics found the notion of completion and fulfilment intelligible, the one by means of the idea of the goal of the temporal process, and the other through the idea of a full development of potency into actuality. The Kingdom of God was precisely this - a process at work through the ages, illuminated paradigmatically in Christ's life and to be brought to fulfilment through the working of the Holy Spirit. The Alpha-Omega analogy illustrated the same point: Creation is Alpha, moving towards Omega, and Omega is contained within it. The redemptive work of God is thus exhibited throughout history - past, present and future. A Greek Orthodox scholar makes this clear: "The Messiah is called *tsemach* (seed) and the very notion of the Messiah derives from the Pleroma.....the world is 'unfinished', 'embryonic', so as to further and direct that synergy of divine power and human power until the Day of the Lord wherein the seed attains its final fruition."[21] As to what the new heaven and new earth would be like its main feature would be that men would remain perpetually in communion with God and with each other. That the 'divinization' of man would take time is intrinsic to the Christian idea. The images used are not those of identity, but of sharing, of being members one of another, of being branches of a vine tree–an interdependence so organic that to be cut off is death, and to be one of the 'members' is life. Such a sharing amounts to 'realization' on the Christian view, if the word 'realization' is at all to be used.

A few other related themes may be briefly referred to here. The apostles or original disciples were said to be invested with the power of the Holy Spirit. Their work, however, was less to instruct than to *testify*. Their witness would result in an adoption of others into the new society, or Kingdom of God. The path was not a solitary path of self-perfection, but a sharing in a way of life, having 'all things in common', with Christ as head. The real instructor, as the Protestants stressed, was the Holy Spirit. The believer is 'inwardly taught' by the Holy Spirit, as Calvin put it. What we have then is an inner accretion made possible through Divine infusion. If the early fathers stressed the role of the church as a 'treasure-house' of truth, in Irenaeus' phrase, Protestants centuries later were no less insistent on what Calvin called "the sanctification of invisible grace". As for those who have progressed far in their spiritual pilgrimage it was of these that the eighteenth-century New England divine, Jonathan Edwards, spoke: "The grace which is in the hearts of the saints, is of the same nature with the divine holiness, though infinitely less in degree."[22] It is Edwards, too, who makes it clear that what God brings about is something *new*—"that which could be produced by no exalting, varying or compounding of what was there before, or by adding anything of the like kind".[23]

No conclusion can emerge from such a brief look at the three separate ways of regarding man's pilgrimage—the Hindu, the Greek, and the Christian[24] for even these have their own inner diversity. But the Hindu view seems distinctive for its belief in certain 'realized' souls who are fit to initiate others into spiritual life, and the Socratic form of the Greek view of its paradoxical notion of the ideal instructor as he does not instruct (there are analogies here to some aspects of Gautama Buddha's own practice). The Christian thinks in terms of a Divine process of education where men, all men without exception, are pilgrims in this life, with the promise of a new order into which we can be initiated now, and which offers more than we can ask or think in a future order of being when God's Kingdom will fully come.

NOTES

1. I shall be concerned with the Hindus, and not the Buddhist or Sikh, concept in this chapter.
2. *Religion in Essence and Manifestation*, p. 228.
3. Ibid., p. 229.
4. Latter-day reformist criticism of *guruvāda* is no doubt directed at this extreme dependence which the critics regard as slavish.
5. Instruction through *mauna vyākhyā* (silent discourse) is also most important in the Hindu (also Buddhist) tradition. A hymn attributed to Shankaracharya speaks of "*Mauna vyākhyā prakatita parabtahma tattvam yuvānam*".
6. Bipin Chandra Pal, *Character Sketches*, p. 69.

7. Jean Daniélou had made the point that there is a concept of degrees of spiritual growth in Christianity, the business of the *didaskalos* (teacher) begin to give each aspirant the food he needs. Thus, to the sinful, Christ appears as a Redeemer, to the sick as a Healer, and so forth. *Origen*, p. 47.
8. Bipin Chandra Pal, *Character Sketches*, p. 70.
9. Vide Abhinavagupta's *Tantraloka*.
10. Vide *Sanata-Kumāra-Saṁhitā*, *Gautama-Saṁhitā*, *Nārada-Pañcarātra*.
11. *Śrī Śrī Rāmakrṣṇa Kathāmṛta*, I, p. 68.
12. An idea developed further in Mahāyāna Buddhism.
13. A *Kierkegaard Anthology*, ed. by Robert Bretall, The Modern Library, New York, 1936, p. 153.
14. Christian theologians in India who utilize the guru idea point out that Christ has come to serve and not to be served. Vide James Massey, 'The concept of guruship in the New Testament', in *The Nature of Guruship* ed. by Clarence O. McMullen, pub. for the Christian Institute of Sikh Studies, Batala, by ISPCK, Delhi, 1976.
15. *Stromata*, Book vi. Chapters 11 & 12.
16. *Adversus Haereses*, iv, XXXIX, 1.
17. Ibid., iv, XXXVIII, 3.
18. Ibid., iv, XXXVIII, 3.
19. Ibid., iv, XXX, 2.
20. Ibid., V (Preface).
21. Paul Evdokimov, *L'Orthodoxie*, Paris: Delachaux et Niestlé, 1959, p. 84.
22. *The Works of Jonathan Edwards*, London, 1817, Vol. 4, pp. 105-6.
23. Ibid., pp. 107-9.
24. A Christian interpretation of the guru idea can be found in Swami Abhishiktananda's "Guru and Disciple" and

passim in the book edited by Clarence O. McMullen mentioned earlier.

Chapter-2
The Concept of Sevā

Chapter 3

The Concept of Self

Chapter-2

The way in which the different communities in India employ the concept of *sevā* admits of interesting comparative treatment. It seems to be a concept, moreover, which secular-minded welfare societies can make use of, perhaps in some transformed fashion. What follows is only an inadequate sketch of a subject which I feel merits fuller study.

The word *sevā* is used in ordinary language in a sense which is not too far from the religious (likewise the daily gesture of greeting bears a common root with the concept of obeisance to God). For example we say, 'Can I perform any service for you?' The very query suggests what Gabriel Marcel has called 'being available' or 'open' to the other. The notion seems to arise from a context where not only men, but, at one pole gods, and at the other, animals too, are the object of men's acts of service. As far as the latter is concerned, in an agricultural community there is a relation of mutual service between men and animals. To watch cattle being tended is at once to be reminded of this. The land too has to be looked after if it is to bring forth fruit. In these cases we have a kind of symmetry which serves men's interests no doubt, but which is yet not wholly of the order of interest. We are familiar with the way in which urbanization breaks the links between men, the land, and animals and the consequent loss of roots which this involves.

In the family the members serve each other, certain personal services developing on the younger members in accordance with the hierarchical structure of the traditional Indian family. These are a preparation for a total structure of relations where man's bonds with others are related to bonds with tradition, with gurus, with the wider community, and with God. The very gods become domesticated when each home has its shrine. Outside the home, in the forest schools, teachers were served by students, and teachers in turn served students through imparting instruction to them. This institution, as also the *āśram* idea, fostered *sevā* between members of a special group. *Dan* which was considered to be a form of *yajña*, was directed towards certain people, e.g. the custom of giving charity to Brahmins. All this, of course, was capable, as any institution is, of misuse. The very idea of 'giving' can become part of a sort of balance of accounts where merit is weighed against demerit. Even poverty in the form of beggarhood can come to receive sanction for the occasion it provides others for accumulating merit. Here it must be noted that the practice of philanthropy as a conscience - saving device is by no means confined to ancient times.

Indian religious thought contains not only the polarity of renunciation and attachment but that of renunciation and service. The latter is not to be identified with the polarity of faith and works of which Christianity speaks, but is no less difficult to analyse. Renunciation has as its core the sense of a leaving behind of self-centredness. But this in itself need not lead to a turning to 'the other'. In fact the turning towards another presents a special problem to the *sādhak* since such turning is, at the 'normal' everyday level, accompanied by attachment. But Hindu and Buddhist writings on this subject, therefore, lay special stress on the need for disinterestedness in the *sevak*. In other words, a distinction is made between the service which springs from attachment and which (to use Kant's term in another context) might be pathological, and that which springs from the religious consciousness, whether this be of the Hindu, Buddhist, or Jain variety. One particular cultural factor is also relevant here, that is, the value say on the life of the *sanyāsī* or, in the Buddhist tradition, the value set on the monkhood. The institution of *sanyāsa* amounts to the freedom given by society to certain of its members, who are temperamentally so inclined, to opt out of that very society. In all periods of India's history the *parivrājak*, the wanderer or pilgrim, has evoked the admiration of the common folk, and absence of ties has been regarded as at least one mark of holiness. So that whereas the bonds of mutual service related the laity in their daily living, the religious 'specialist' was characterized by an absence of such bonds. The institution of monkhood is of course quite different from that of *sanyāsa*, the common factors being that of religious specialization and absence of familial ties (except in those cultures which accept monkhood as an intermediate stage between that of the student and the householder).

The Buddhist belief in the interdependence of all life provides a basis for what could be an ethico-religious world-view centred on the concept of *sevā*. The Vedantic idea, likewise, could have fostered such a world-view. The historical reasons why this did not in fact come about cannot be entered into here. *Dānaśilata*, the obligation to share, which is incumbent on the laity and the monks alike, needs more precise definition. Is the surplus to be shared, or one's very all, however little it may be? Some other questions arise too. If individual *sādhanā* may at times lead in the opposite direction from *sevā* in the Hindu tradition, the quest of equanimity in the Buddhist tradition may have a similar result. The metaphysical walls of *karmic* isolation, moreover, offer resistance to the project of helping another man on his way. Whether *karuṇā* goes beyond the attitudinal level is another problem for scholars to consider. However there can be no doubt as to the nobility of the ideal of Bodhisattvahood. The seventh-century poet Santideva writes: "I would be a protector of the unprotected, a guide to wayfarers, a ship, a dyke, and a bridge for them who seek the further shore; a lamp for them who need a lamp, a bed for them who need a bed, slave for all beings who need a slave." Ethical and religious injunction fuses. The devout Buddhist is to be benefit to others by means of his example, his detachment, and by avoiding occasions of fanning resentment.

The Vaiṣṇavas included *sevā* as an element in devotion, and the latter in turn is a return to, and at the same time a transformation of, the old idea of service as *yajña*, or as worship. But here (as in the case of *Gesinnungsethik* in general) the subjective pole of experience, or at most the polarity between devotee and God, tends to encourage an intensity and exclusiveness of relation where service of the Lord may fail to ripple out in the direction of service to others. Here again cultural factors would enter into any attempt at assessment of the range and limits of the impact of what purported to be a dynamic movement in India's religious history, especially an assessment of to what extent an inward disposition succeeded in externalizing itself in activities of a practical kind.

It is in the Sikh religion that the mutual involvement of service to God and service to man is stressed in a pronounced and most explicit manner. Great importance is attached to the householder's existence and this expresses the belief that life is meaningful precisely in terms of our relations with others. If all labour, the evil of begging will be removed. If pilgrimages are avoided the unity of the home will be preserved, as likewise the growth of sects of devotees, who become a burden on society, will be stemmed. Guru Nanak says: "A place in God's Court can only be attained if we do service to others in the world." (*Sri Raga,* M. 1.) In his *Japji* he speaks of 'loving attachment', by implication distinguishing this from the 'attachment' which had been the target of criticism in the classical philosophical tradition. Serivce is enjoined in many a passage, of which this is but one example: "I have learnt by the light given in the Perfect Master; Recluse, hero, celibate or sanyāsī–none may expect to earn merit without devoted service–service in which lies the essence of purity." Service, moreover, bears the special meaning of service to the poor (as against, say, ritual service to the Brahmins). Guru Angad warns that "Alms-gifts, penances and sacrifices are equal to selfishness". Guru Arjun provides penetrating criticism of the man who follows the *jñānamārga* when he says that service of God and humanity 'destroys the darkness of ignorance, purifies and develop a sense of discrimination' (*Sarang*, M.5). The mutual involvement of reverence, love and service continues even in the highest stage of perfection, for the ideal individual continues to practise service, charity, equality, forbearance, brotherhood, non-stealing, and to work hard. The ultimate test of spirituality is that such a man can awaken society in the promotion of these values and that such a society will in turn provide a foundation in which such personalities can freely develop. The *Var Asa* is devoted to an account of the stage through which a man becomes a *sevak*, showing how services is the outcome of devotion to the Name.

To turn to the Semitic religions, both Judaism and Islam refer explicitly to 'service'. The Psalmist writes, "Service the Lord with gladness", and a succession of prophets worked out in their various ways what love of God and love of man involves. The idea of *khidmat* is highlighted in the Qur'ān and duties to

God and man set forth. Remarkable in this connection is the following. If there is any failure in the performance of duties to God this may be pardoned by God Himself. But failure of duty to a fellow-man can only be pardoned by him against whom the sin of omission has been made. In the Christian tradition the concept of love is so interpreted as to include service. In the Old Testament the injunction "You shall love your neighbour as yourself" is found as early as the Book of Leviticus (ch. 19, v. 11). The powerful image of the suffering servant runs through both Old and New Testaments. Christ's saying, "He that is greatest among you shall be your servant" (Matt. 23. 11) is exemplified by Him in the washing of the disciples' feet. St. Paul shows how neighbourly love is an expression of what we have ourselves received. The injunction 'feed my sheep', can be taken as either an injunction to serve the spiritual needs of others or an injunction to provide concrete benefits. The actions of Christ Himself show an awareness of both sets of needs, as is evidenced, say, on the evening when the five thousand were fed. The paradigm of service for the Christian is found in the mystery of the Incarnation, e.g. He "emptied Himself, taking the form of a servant, being born in the likeness of men" (Phil. 27). Christ preached that service to the needy was service to God, "Inasmuch as ye have done it unto one of the least of these My brethren, ye have done it unto Me" (Matt. XXV, 35-40).

Nineteenth-century religious reformers in India had a rich and varied tradition to draw upon. They could draw on the Vedāntic idea of the oneness of all men, as Vivekananda did. Krishan's injunction in the Gitā to 'worship Me in all beings' could be interpreted in a more concrete and practical way than had hitherto been the case in India's previous history. The concept of *Daridranārāyaṇa* in Vivekananda's thought provided a basis for service quite other than what had been found in the concept of compassion in earlier Indian ethical systems, both Vaiṣṇavite and Buddhist. It was in 1884 in Dakshineswar that Sri Ramakrishna had said: "Compassion for being? Will you, little man, bestow compassion on beings? You wretch, who are you to bestow compassion? No, no; not compassion for Jīvas (souls) but service to them as Śiva (God)." Vivekananda interpreted this in his own way: "He who sees Śiva in the poor, in the weak, and in the diseased, really worships Śiva." Service received a new dimension in Vivekananda's understanding of it as *work*, and as both means to, and symbol of, "God-realization". He went so far as to say that "Liberation is only for him who gives up everything for others." Vivekananda turned from the rarefied vertical relationship between man and God (or, to use language more consonant with his tradition, turned from the brooding awareness of the identity of *Ātman* and *Brahman*) to the horizontal relationship, for how can man love God whom he hath not seen unless he love his brother whom he hath seen.

Another recent landmark in the development of the concept of *sevā* is to be found in Mahatma Gandhi's life and thought. The best way in which a man can be of service to others is to make them aware of their own non-violent strength. This awareness is both enlightenment and the leverage of action. The ideal society would be one where each would stand on his own feet, being neither exploiter nor exploited. At the same time it would be a society based on mutual aid where all served each other's needs mutually, as in the ideal village republic. No one class would be the natural servants of another. There would be no beggars to be the recipients of *dān*, for it is a sin to make others a condition of one's own acquisition of merit. In so far as those who are the victims of a wrong must themselves undertake satyāgraha in order to change the heart of the exploiter, each man bears his own burden. But he does not bear it alone. There can be not only individual satyāgraha, but collective satyāgraha too. In the ideal society, service would give way to sharing, to giving, each man contributing his talents, however small, to the common pool. The 'oceanic circle' idea suggests the transforming influence such men and such communities would have on society in the wider sense, and even in the world at large.

Finally, how can the concept of *sevā* be rethought in terms of our contemporary needs? We have seen how *sevā* was originally a part of religious duty, how it tended to presuppose an unequal relation between benefactor and beneficiary, and how in its least spiritual form (paradoxically) it was regarded as a means to the acquiring of merit. Today a welfare state provides certain services for its citizens, and in order to this the state is vested with power to exact dues (taxes) out of which all will be served in proportion to their needs. Such a state centres round the concept of 'rights' — that each citizen has the right to be provided with a certain among of goods and services. The reverse side of this is, no doubt, that each should contribute by his works to the common weal. The feeling is, however, prevalent in many quarters that in our time the correlation of rights and duties is often lost sight of. Some of this is an outcome of the politicization of our life. What can the older concept of service contribute to the new kind of society where power tends to be centralized and services centrally administered? The small village community of the past was based on the ideal of a non-competitive society where each man served others by utilising whatever talents he had in the following of his hereditary occupation. If there was a sharing of wealth, there was also a sharing of poverty. If so happens that today the concept of the welfare state has been implemented most in societies which are increasingly secularized — that is to say, where the sphere of the sacramental is progressively diminishing. Undoubtedly in such societies, from one point of view, the area of free choice, the possibility of non-traditional forms of behaviour, is thereby immensely increased. At the same time the willingness to serve others' needs with no consideration either of interests or of the acquisition of merit, is something for which the secular society finds it difficult to offer motivation. The moral philosopher has always carefully distinguished the ethical from the religious impulse, insisting on the autonomy of the former. The new demythologized and contextualized ethic which expresses a reaction against the past is avowedly individual-centred. But there is little motive power in it for turning attention towards others' needs. The springs of action, to use a phrase belonging to an earlier generation, tend to run dry.

The new conception of *sevā* which could leaven such a society would be based on mutuality, on sharing, on *dān* in a new sense. This is by no means the same thing as philanthropy of which this century is seeing no lack. There is a need, as Gabriel Marcel has phrased it, to "multiply the bonds" which link us with others. The concept of *sevā* can find expression in new patterns of behaviour if it be reinterpreted in terms of 'caring' where 'caring' includes 'caring about' and 'caring for'. A society which was able to actualize the idea of 'caring' in this sense would have no ecological problems, no underprivileged citizens, and would not have acts of violence as a part of its day-to-day happenings.

Chapter-3

RELIGION AND 'SOLIDARINESS'

Chapter-3

The alleged decline of religion in the west

It is common knowledge that sociologists like Weber who stressed the social function of religion showed concern in their lifetime at the extent to which belief in religion seemed to be on the decline in western industrial societies. What cohesive factor was there, they asked, which could take the place of what held traditional societies together? Some of them, no doubt, showed an ambivalence of attitude of "eastern" societies. Crocodile tears could be shed over industrial backwardness allegedly attributed to other-worldliness (overlooking the phenomenon of colonial exploitation) while at the same time an envious glance could be cast at the participatory ethos of traditional societies.

The main factors reckoned to be responsible for religious scepticism in the West are: (1) the growth of a scientific outlook; (2) the impact of other cultures; and (3) distress leading to a disbelief in the possibility of a beneficent deity (traditionally discussed under the rubric of 'the problem of evil'). There may be many other factors too.[2] At any rate scepticism does not seem to have brought about social disintegration and the jeremiahs among earlier sociologists seem to have been over-apprehensive. This suggests that although religion, inter alia, does have a cohesive function, if its functioning atrophies there are other factors to step in and take its place. The image of a sophisticated sceptical society falling apart at the seams was a bogey. The army, the bureaucracy, and the party are only too ready to step in and save the day.

However, it is only fair to mention three other considerations. Firstly, western social liberal societies run on a considerable amount of 'spiritual capital' derived from traditional religion. This is tied up not so much well with cohesiveness as with things like belief in the value of the individual (derived from Greek, Jewish and Christian sources), the possibility of a just society, social responsibility - all matters which are susceptible of a secular interpretation. Secondly, secular humanism is paralleled by apocalyptic-type new-look sects which are extremely cohesive in themselves but which diverge in a radical way from the mainstream ethos. This is particularly true of America. A third consideration concerns modernistic theologies (not necessarily demythologizing ones) which in one way or another try to keep theological thinking 'in line with the times'.

I mention the foregoing in order to point out the difference between the western situation (to generalize) and the Indian. There is nothing currently in India parallel to 'the decline in religious belief'. The impact of the scientific outlook is for the most part honoured in the breach rather than in the observance. As for the impact of other cultures, local exigencies force us in on ourselves and we are not in a particularly outward-looking period of history. The local culture does not see any incompatibility between distress and belief in a transcendent order. For generation *dukha* has been taken to be an inherent characteristic of the human condition. The new factor is otherwise. It is none other than politicization of corporate life at almost every rung - something which has *both* cohesive and divisive import.

The secular image

The historical reasons behind India's adoption of a secular mode of statehood are too well-known to need more than a brief mention. In the context of the two-nation theory it was necessary to show that free India was a country in which people of many faiths could live together in peace. Impartiality between people belonging to different communities became an article of policy. There is always a gap between policy and practice, and so it is not surprising that there are still peculiar lapses such as the performance of Vedic ceremonies at public functions, the protection of backwardness through non-interference with personal law, and so on. In fact the difficulty of pursuing a secular state policy in a non-secular society has been progressively felt since Independence. The characteristics of a secular society have been listed by D. L. Munby[3] as follows: "A secular society (1) is not committed to any particular view of the cosmos or man's status in it; (2) is pluralistic and not sacral; (3) does not 'attempt to enforce belief or to limit the natural expression of belief'; (4) recognizes the need for common aims, but allows its organizations and institutions to have limited goals; (5) tries to make the various aims as concordant as possible; (6) is a society 'without official images'." It would take a detailed study to work out the applicability or inapplicability of these considerations to Indian society But, to begin with, some of Munby's points can be disputed. For example, a society can be multiple-sacral (vide point 2). Disallowing the slaughter of a particular species of animal which others think to be necessary for food would fall under point 4 as an example of failing to make one's goals limited.

When we look for possible sources of dynamism, neighbourliness, etc. in non-secular thought systems such as would be of service in promoting the goals of a secular state (national integration is only one of such goals) we are really asking for something rather exceptional, it can perhaps now be seen. We are, to begin with, trying to enlist forces which in themselves have little or nothing to do with 'national' concerns. That attempts to enlist 'religious' sentiments in aid of 'national' goals can often backfire is familiar to us all. One has only to think of the Khilafat movement to have an example of it.

Problems of national integration[4]

It is as well at this stage in the discussion to have an idea in our minds as to what the current problems of national integration in India are. Only too often the impression is created that a certain sort of unitariness or 'solidariness', which is after all incompatible with federal statehood, would nevertheless be desirable, and that failure to achieve it is the mark of failure to achieve national integration. National integration has to do neither with centrism nor with uniformity. It rather stands for a healthy interaction where disparities of wealth are at a minimum and cultural diversities do not result in separatism. (John Stuart Mill's definition of a healthy society comes to mind - one where diversity is not merely contained, but welcomed.) Integration may operate at the political, economic, and social levels. The adult franchise is reckoned to provide the main level of political unity, articulated at state and lower echelons of power. Economic integration is the goal of state policy if it be identified as the purpose of the successive Five Year Plans with their strategies for providing employment and the like. Social integration is a function of many factors in which the operation of political and economic determinants should not be underestimated. When we think of problems of national integration we often have one or other of the following in minds: (1) the integration of scheduled castes and tribes into the mainstream of national life; (2) the relation of the majority community with minority communities; (3) inter-State questions; (4) the relation between hill and plains people; (5) the relation between town and village people. These are all matters which involve political, economic and social components.

Now, to ask how religion enters into these issues is to ask a major question regarding the religious component in culture. The institutional aspects of religion are a segment of culture alongside other segments such as the family, the economic order, and so forth. These both compete with and reinforce each other. But religion is also a dimension of the other aspects of culture, e.g. it enters into the daily routine work of rearing a family, deciding whether a child should attend school prayers, etc. There are occasions when the religious dimension obtrudes in interactive situations so as to bring about the confrontation of communities, resulting in conflict. This is most likely to happen if there is economic disparity between the groups concerned. I may mention an example from pre-Independent India. One of the first things Gandhi did when he went to Noakhali was to institute a fact-finding survey of land-ownership in the region. Finding that more than 80 per cent of the land was owned by a fraction of the population, he said in no uncertain terms that the problem of the region was basically an economic one and not at all religious. The same was the case at the time of the Patuakhali Satyagraha much earlier. We cannot expect the religious pool of ethical ideas to come into effect while there are still vast discrepancies of wealth between man and man. There can only be an efflorescence and happy diversity of cultural aspects such as language and literature, religious belief and practice, and the arts, if the basic grievances that the poor have against the rich are tackled first. In the absence of this the chances are that any particular community will remain at the level of *reaction* vis-á-vis another and fail to reach the level of response. Let us also not overlook the fact that there are aspects of integration where religion hardly comes into play. In this category we have for example the integration of competing productive systems, the integration of tribesmen in the wider community (say, in Orissa, Andhra Pradesh, or the N. E. region), or in measures to end land-alienation and other forms of exploitation and various initiatives in the public and private sectors to strengthen the weaker sections.

The religious component in contemporary Indian culture

Lest the findings should seem rather negative, we shall now turn to some examples of the religious component at work in present-day Indian society. I choose only five cases.

(1) Vinoba Bhave's attempt to bring about a non-violent revolution in land-ownership through persuasion may be mentioned first. In so far as his work fell into a transcendental framework of thought (at Paunar he spoke publicly in favour of a combination of science and spirituality) we may concede its 'religious' character. It was integrative in intent in so far as it was aimed at bringing about a more equitable distribution of land resources. Grassroots level projects of this kind certainly contribute their mite towards national integration.

(2) The incorporation of some of the tribes into the Hindu fold is a matter which Indian anthropologists have been studying for several decades. In certain places in West Bengal there are castes which are probably tribal in origin and whose members are entrusted with the worship of local gods or goddesses. Even high caste people offer worship to these local deities through the help of the so-called lower castes. This throws light on the integrative pattern of growth of Hindu civilization and its powers of absorption through the process of sub-stratification. At the same time it must be said that the adoption of the mores of one community by another need not necessarily be regarded as an *integrative* phenomenon. For example, a caste-like hierarchy among Muslims in some West Bengal villages is evidence rather of a new emerging class formation under the pressure of industrialization and urbanization.

(3) In the North-Eastern hill regions we find a phenomenon of a different kind. Under the impact of Christian missions there has been an impetus towards westernization along with a sense of individual rights which goes along with it. New productive systems are growing up alongside the old. At the same time, partly for political reasons and partly for fear of being drawn into the pushes and pulls of the plains' economy there is a new assertion of cultural identity among the tribal people in this region. The tendency is integrative in so far as separate tribal identities merge their differences in the interest of a wider unity. It can, of course, lead to something rather different if there is a sense of neglect by the Centre, and so on.[5]

(4) The revivalist encouragement of rightist factions has been a familiar feature of recent political history. It has a precursor in last-ditch revivalism in nineteenth-century India. It is interesting from a sociological point of view in that it shows how religion can be an extremely conservative factor in political life.

(5) The retreat into God-man cults[6] by some of the middle classes is yet another curious contemporary phenomenon. Whereas salvation-cults and movements in many of the Third World countries (including Central and South America and Melanesia) have arisen among the wretched of the earth and consequently had a strong 'revolutionary' appeal,[7] twentieth-century cults in India have on the whole been centred among the privileged who see no particular reason for social commitment and who are indeed perhaps disillusioned with politics.[8]

While the first three may be regarded as having a positive relation to national integration, the last two (or at least the fourth) seem dysfunctional in relation to it.

Barriers, Frontiers and balconies

It seems true to say that in the 1980s, religion need not present a major barrier to solidariness at the national level, i.e. to national integration. Behind communal incidents (we cannot deny the occurrence of these) we can find political and economic factors at work and evidence of the activities of the few who fish in troubled waters. It is under the pressure of such factors that communities may acquire a 'frontier' mentality with reference to each other. If the 'religious' leadership fails to curb communal passion then conflict ensues. As against this there are always men of goodwill who are brave enough not to side with the wrong-doers and who incur the wrath of their co-religionists. Chaman Nahal in his brilliant novel about Partition entitled *Azadi*, tell of the aged Muslim at prayer, begging Allah to forgive his brethren as they make a parade of unfortunate women in the street outside.

The balcony idea is perhaps a halfway point for the ordinary man who has no very close relations with men of another faith but is close enough to watch, close enough not to 'react', yet not close enough to respond. We should not underestimate the number of fields in which the transition from balcony to arena has been made, where indeed the distinction may never have obtained, e.g. among weavers, fishermen, musicians, and above all among children for whom all are intrinsically akin as playmates. Are we to say that in these cases religion is providing an integrative factor or that a sense of common humanity triumphs? The latter interpretation seems more correct. The barriers now are of a different kind: economic inequalities, casteism, an anomie born of extreme poverty, and a fast increasing regionalism which is the heritage of the creation of linguistic States.

Religion as integrative ethos

In asking of religion or religions that it/they should provide some sort of integrative ethos we are engaged in a somewhat academic exercise. In a pluralist society are we asking for some sort of common denominator conception which might excite intellectuals but which would be quite unintelligible to the man in the street? In many parts of the world it has been nationalism which has been the 'religion' which has led men to throw off their yokes. But nationalism is a poor matrix for norms of individual and public behaviour and it is not surprising that the euphoria of newly independent nations wear thin after a few decades and the integrative force of nationalism can scarcely maintain itself without the stimulus of alleged or actual threats from outside powers. If both states and society are to be concerned with the general welfare some common aims and images seem to be needed. Religions, either in the sense of historical traditions or personal faiths (to follow W. Cantwell Smith's distinction), seem unable to provide such images at the national level in an environment where men believe different things; nor perhaps should it be otherwise in a secular state.

And yet mutuality and harmony, concordant discord, requires a perspective which can lead us from reaction to response. If the channels of communication are kept open (and not clogged by economic-political sources of friction) we should in the course of time be led both to an understanding of what is common and to a respect for what is diverse. There are enough concepts of stewardship, pooling of talents, neighbourliness, care and service[9] in the various religious traditions to inspire us all. There are already voluntary institutions at work which show in action how religious principles can be brought to bear on race relations, delinquency, problems of the old, and care of the young. The channelization of spiritual impulses into constructive social outlets, in the words of one religious tradition, is God's work. It is seen, for example, in a wonderfully, concrete form in the life-work of Mother Teresa and her associates. Along with this an intellectual task faces the leaders of various communities with the need to disengage the essential from the non-essential in religion, the *upādhis* which stand in the way of seeing the other man as a brother. It is not a task that can be performed ab extra, but only by men of faith within the respective traditions themselves.

To move from reaction to response is to move into a network of relationships, of links between being and being, that does not stop at frontiers. Writing on love, Anders Nygren[10] characterizes it as spontaneous and 'uncaused', indifferent to human merit or worthiness, as creative, and as opening the way to fellowship with God. The Gospels present the idea of the impossibility of loving God in the absence of love of one's brother. They do not underestimate the difficulty of loving the brother whom we have seen. It is often our neighbour whom it may be most difficult to love. And yet it may be that in the resources of a non-secular society there are powerful funds of simple goodness without which a secular state would hardly be able to function. There is no doubt that Gandhi believed that this was so in this land of villages. He also much liked the teachings of the *Hitopadeśa* - the individual sacrificing himself for the village, the village for the nation, and the nation for the world. Education can foster these springs of goodness so that the strong feelings roused by holy places, rituals, taboos and social conventions and all those matters which highlight our differences no longer have sway over our lives. So far, educators have been playing safe by dropping religion from the curriculum altogether so that children are often ignorant of the meaning of each other's festivals. And so an opportunity is wasted, for it is above all the times of celebration that can be shared.

Religion should not be 'used' by the state. But the spiritual resources which nurture man's inner life and link him in fellowship to his neighbours are resources which lead to ever-widening unities. It is also the case that it is our religious life that is most likely to teach us that the oceanic circle[11] of unities cannot stop at national frontiers.

NOTES

1. The title utilizes a term coined by R. C. Zaehner in contrast to A. N. Whitehead's stress on 'solitariness'. The substance of the chapter was presented at a seminar on "Religion and National Integration" in Benares Hindu University in November 1976.
2. Some additional ones are mentioned in Chapter III. Of course a transformation of traditional belief need not amount to scepticism.
3. *The Idea of a Secular Society and its Significance for Christians.*
4. National integration has been the topic of a great deal of discussion of government and other levels in recent years in India.
5. The Jharkhand movement presents a complicated case where new unities tend to spilt up into sub-nationalisms

under the pressure of various factors such as treatment meted out to other communities (e.g. scheduled castes), wooing by State and Centre politicians, and so forth. The 'indigenization' of Christian communities in this area is the further phenomenon to be studied in depth.

6. Vide Peter Brent's *God-men* and V.K. Mangalwadi's book *New Gurus* (Vikas), 1976.

7. Vide Vittorio Lanternari's *The Religious of the Oppressed.*

8. Vide Chapter VI.

9. Vide Chapter IX.

10. *Eros and Agape*, Vol. 1, Part I, p. 46 ff.

11. A Gandhian concept of ideal decentralized social organization, seen in terms of concentric circles, with the individual at the centre - a model directly counter to the pyramidical one where power is lodged at the apex, i.e. the state. Vide my *Gandhi's Religious Thought*, Macmillan, London, Notre Dame Press, and Macmillan, India, 1983.

Chapter-4

THE UNIVERSALIST THESIS

Chapter-4

The universalist thesis, in recent years associated with the name of S. Radhakrishna, has in fact a long pedigree. Not all those who spoke of universal religion, and/or made claims for Vedānta in this connection, were talking about the same thing. That all religions are the same, whether in the short or long run, has never been maintained in a crude form. The thesis has always had a certain subtlety. Wherever 'sameness' is under discussion, however, philosophers have regarded the matter as falling within their territory, and there is no doubt that questions concerning 'aspects', 'essence', 'what really is the case' have metaphysical overtones. But the historical stages through which the thesis itself passed and the very considerable differences between those who were attached by the theme need to be sorted out before the philosopher can profitably intrude with his 'what do you mean by...?' approach. I shall only briefly mention some of the major figures with a view to showing that they were not all maintaining the 'same thing'.

One of the earliest and perhaps still the most convincing exponent of the thesis was Raja Rammohun Roy. The works in which the theme of 'universal religion' was developed were the *Tohufut-ul-Mowahedeen* published in Persian in 1803 and the pamphlet on *Universal Religion* published in 1829. The former bears the stamp of the impressions gained on his travels when he found "the inhabitants of all countries agreeing generally about the notion of one Being, the source and governor of all that exists..... Turning towards one Eternal Being is a natural tendency of the human mind." That the ways in which men conceive of God and worship Him differed was patent, but Raja believed that there was an underlying core common to all religions, i.e. belief in one Eternal Being. If he had been more informed about Buddhism than he was his thesis might have been considerably modified. But, as it was, the ground for his thinking that there is a fundamental untiy of all religions (which isn't the same thing as saying that all religions are one) is the evidence of monotheism which he found in the religions with which he was familiar, that is Hinduism, Christianity, and Islam. Shiv Nath Shastri summarizes the position thus: "The sum-total of the Raja's teachings.....is that the doctrine of the one true God is the universal element in all religions, and as such forms an article of faith of the universal religion of mankind; but the practical applications of that universal religion are to be always local and national. As a herald of the new age he held up before men a new faith which was universal in its sympathies, but whose cardinal principal was that 'the service of man is the service of God'." Ramananda Chatterjee spoke of him as believing in pure theism and in the moral government of the universe, and goes on to say, "He did not reject any truth to be found in any scriptures or in the teachings of any prophet or saint, he revered and accepted truth from all quarters: but at the same time he did not accept any book or teacher as infallible." This assessment perhaps project an eclecticism which would hardly allow for genuine diversity of religious belief, a diversity which the Raja was always senstive to. Brajendranath Seal puts it rather differently, saying that in the prefaces to the Vedānta abridgement and the translations the Raja moved from comparative religion to 'universalism'. He sees him as recognizing that none of the religions are a *part* of the truth, but that each is *the* truth specially and ethnically expressed. This truth should not be degarded by elaborate and *tāmasic* (anti-social) rituals, and religious symbols should be 'adequate' to the truth. The historic religions move along their own lines to a universal ideal or centre of convergence, and this ideal is the ideal of Universal Religion. The last part of this assessment, the convergence point, is lent support by the booklet on *Universal Religion*. But it is important to remember that Rammohun was thinking of a situation which could come about in the future. The rediscovery of the pristine was a task set for future generations who would find in religion a unifying and not a divisive force. Recognizing as he did that each historic religion grew in its own way, two important consequences followed. There could be no question of the 'sameness' of each historic tradition. But, equally important, as each tradition grew in accordance with the exigencies of time and place (and this of course includes the interactions stressed by the diffusionists) each generation needed to purge what had grown up, to prune and purify, so that out-of-date superstitions and prejudices could be got rid of. Behind the arguments of *The Precepts of Jesus* were the convictions, first, that doctrinal controversies stood in the way of acceptance of the ethical teachings of Christ and that such controversies, especially those concerning Trinitarianism, should be put an end to; secondly, that Christian moral teaching, shorn of myth and miracle, could have a universal appeal, and, the addendum is significant that "they alone were a sufficient guide to secure peace and happiness to mankind at large." Here the utilitarian spirit of the early part of the nineteenth century can be easily detected. One further comment is necessary vis-á-vis those who later were to advocate Vedānta in the name of universalism. The Raja's view on religion cannot be divorced from the context of social reform. When he first embarked on a Bengali translation of the Vedānta the Raja had as his express aim the disproving the scriptural warrant for idolatry. He wanted to provide the man in the street with weaponry against rites which encouraged superstition and obscurantism. He did not appeal to the Vedānta in the name of recalling men to impersonal Brahman but to a simple theism which could appeal to the learned and the unlearned alike. This is what Bipin Chandra Pal referred to in 1901 when he said that Raja Rammohun Roy was against the Abstract Universalism (sic) of the popular Vedānta "which really is the parent of idolatry", the idea behind that those who cannot attain unto the path of the *jñāni* will console themselves elsewhere.

Eclecticism is an epithet which better fits Keshub Chunder Sen than it does the Raja. He reacted against Advaita Vedānta, saying that "Hindu pantheism in its worst form is proud, being based upon the belief that man is God" and got together a *Ślokasangraha* culled from many sources. It was some years after his meeting with Ramakrishna Paramahamsa that he proclaimed the Church of the New Dispensation, "which is the deposit of all ancient wisdom and the receptable of all modern science, which recognizes in all prophets and saints a harmony, in all scriptures a unity, and through all dispensations a continuity which abjures all that separates and divides, and always magnifies unity and peace, which harmonizes reason and faith, *yoga* and *bhakti*, asceticism and social duty in their highest forms, and which shall make all the nations and sects one kingdom and one family in the fullness of time." For all this imposing programme of synthesis, Keshub Chunder's thinking had an unmistakable Asiatic bias and to this he made frequent reference in his lectures. Another characteristic of his conception of universal religion is that it centred on religious *leaders* and *founders*—personalities rather than texts. Men such as Socrates, Buddha and Christ are "God's manifestations to each one of us". Each stands for certain ideas, but since all ideas are universal and eternal, they do not contradict each other. Each religion contains an aspect of the truth (cf. the Raja's belief that each religion is *the* truth in an ethnic grab), and so it follows that "we must then freely honour all of them, and gratefully accept from each what he has to deliver instead of binding ourselves as slaves to any particular persons as the only chosen prophets of God". Keshub Chunder's New Dispensation, like the Baha's movement, claimed that all religions were valid paths and at the same time that there is another path which 'includes' all the others and is therefore more 'adequate'. Add to this a nationalistic fervour which had made itself heard in no uncertain way in the last quarter of the nineteenth century in Bengal and we have what Farquhar refers to as "an extraoridinary mixture of ideas." Keshub Chunder's pot-pourri is not only an example of the synthetic spirit which Brajendranath Seal attributed to the ancient Hindus, but brings in a theme which was to continue in subsequent formulations of the universalist thesis by Hindu writers—the theme of rationalism. The synthesis contained a basic contradiction—that between a universal essence, an underlying unity which can be found in all religions, and the quiddity of "the religion of the Hindus". Christianity lost its root as a sect within Judaism before it became a "world religion". To rediscover 'Jesus the Jew', is now a task more easily embarked on by the Jew than by the Christian. But Hinduism has always been the religion of the Hindus—indeed one utters a truism in so saying. Were some educated Hindus trying to make of Hinduism a world religion whose devotees would extend beyond India's frontiers? There was no such attempt as far as Raja Rammohun Roy was concerned. Keshub Chunder's is a different story. At a time when some Indian Christians gave the impression of siding with the colonial power on the one hand and being "apart and separate" from the Hindu community on the other, some of the Hindu intelligentsia tried to incorporate elements from Christianity into their own faith. The lasting incorporations were not theological, however, but rather meliorism and activism which found an outlet in social channels, in fact elements belonging to liberalism rather than to christianity as such. That 'reformation' should be linked to nationalism was not a new phenomenon in the history of religious communities Europe's experience had been likewise. What should not escape notice is that Keshub Chunder's language occasionally betrays a cultural imperalism which is the negation of 'universal religion', certainly in the sense in which Raja Rammohun Roy understood it. In a sermon entitled "Bijatiya Bidhan" (Foreign Dispensation), he said the following: "As long as the Aryan blood runs through our veins we will protect our national religion with our might and shall not be denationalized.... The Bengal-born New Dispensation will one day be spread all over the world but everyone will have to admit with gratitude that this religion grew in Bengal and it is Hindu in character."

The contradiction between 'universalist' and 'national' was to become even more marked among those who popagated Vedanta in the decades that were to follow. The history of Buddhism extended beyond India's shores, indeed the Buddhism that remained in India was largely vestigial. But until the advent of Swami Vivekananda Hinduism was the faith of the Hindus as Judaism was the faith of the Jews. The parallel is not of course exact as the Jews were deprived of a homeland in the modern era until farily recently. One answer to the riddle of outward-looking Hinduism of which the New Dispensation was a rather curious variant, might be found in a desire to return the compliment in the countries of those who had come to India in order to propagate their faith. The 'export' of Hinduism is of course a more recent phenomenon, and it can be noted that the western 'converts' to Hinduism are looked at askance by the orthodox genuine article.

From Bengal we may next turn to a thinker of a rather

different kind in Maharashtra, Visnubava Brahmachari. His case for the "universality of the Vedic religion" seems to go as follows: (1) Vedic religion is the true path. (2) "Nothing exists which is not contained in the Vedas." (3) "Veda means knowledge; it is a part of God himself." (4) In ancient times everyone received religious teaching through Sanskrit. (The argument given is that the Indo-Aryan languages show great similarity.) (5) All should therefore be brought back to the Vedic religion. He used the term Veda in an extended way, including in it both the Gītā and the Purāṇas. It is clear, though, that he did not hold with the many-path view of religion according to which all are equally valid. The propagation of the Vedic religion which he felt himself called upon to undertake, was presumably directed to Hindus who had wandered from *sanātan dharma*. And yet there is strand in his thinking suggesting a more radical view. Like the thirteenth-century thinker Jñāneśvara, he shows evidence of insight into the social implication of *Tat tvam asi* — an implication which Swami Vivekananda in particular was to make the cornerstone of his philosophy. Herein lay a paradox in Brahmachari's standpoint. It ill befits a thorough-going monist who recognizes a divine spark in the merest blade of grass to look upon some fellow-creatures as *mlecchas* as Brahmachari did. The point about *sanātam dharma*, however is its *timelessness*. The Vedic apologist has to decide whether he will insist on universal validity in respect of space as well as time. The propagating impulse that we find in Visnubava Brahmachari, or later in Dayananda Saraswati, shows a reaction that was as much national as religious; a reaction against the proselytizing activities of Christian missionaries who, in the minds of many, could not be dissociated from the colonial power.

Universalism certainly seemed to be in the air towards the end of the nineteenth century. Annie Besant's Theosophical Society made frequent use of the phrase 'universal religion' in their publications. This is how she defined it:

> The common doctrines of all religions, that which has been believed everywhere, at all times, and by everyone, form the body of doctrines promulgated by Theosophy. These are: The One Existence – the One God-manifested in the universe under three Aspects.....; the hierarchies of superhuman

> Beings—Devas, Angels, and Archangels; the Incarnation of Spirit in matter of which Reincarnation is the human phase; the Law of Action and Reaction, 'as a man sows, so small he reap'; the existence of the Path to Perfection, and of divine Men; the three worlds—physical, intermediate, and heavenly- and the higher heavens; the Brotherhood of humanity. These are the leading doctrines of Universal Religion.

The alternation of upper case and lower case letters leaves the reader somewhat out of breath. That the above can claim to be "common doctrines" of all religions was never substantiated by the theosophists themselves. They are not even common to the religions of Indian origin. Indian reactions to this melange of ideas ranged from a sense that theosophy had, if nothing else, brought certain Indian ideas to the notice of the western public, to Swami Vivekananda's feeling that Annie Besant gave a wrong impression about Hinduism to foreigners. There were, however, many who felt that to stress the occult element in 'eastern' religions was untimely when scholars, both western and Indian, were anxious to project a 'rationalist' image of Indian philosophy and religion. Reformers, moreover, were keen to sift the wheat from the chaff and it hardly helped their cause if enthusiasts of foreign origin were in a state of uncritical euphoria about everything on the subcontinent.

With Sri Ramakrishna Paramahamsa we come to a thinker-saint, a *sādhaka*, whose pronouncements, whatever we may think of them, stand foursquare on the basis of his own religious experience. Anyone who approaches his contribution to the theme under discussion encounters first of all his attempt to enter into the spirit of different religions, to 'realize' them as the language of Hinduism would have it. The famous passage in which the 'same goal' form of the universalist thesis occurs runs as follows:

> As one and the same material, viz., water, is called by different names by different peoples - one calling it 'water', another 'vari', a third 'aqua', and another 'pani', even so the one sat-chit-ananda (satcitananda), the Everlasting Intelligent Bliss, is invoked by some as God, by some as Allah, by some as Hari, and by others as Brahman.

The idea was not that all religions are the same, since disciplines, devotional practices and religious languages obviously differed. The fact that each attempt to enter into another religion involved a separate *ascesis* would be at least one evidence of their distinctness. But there are problems none the less. It is perhaps only if one analyses the religious life into two elements, discipline or technique versus goal that the kind of claim that the Paramahamsa made *can* be made. It requires, in fact, the kind of view that looks on the goal as the attaining of a certain state of *consciousness*. If the goal is regarded in other terms, say, entering into a relationship with a transcendent Being, to take one example, then the path will be specific to that goal; indeed, in this example, path/goal language becomes inappropriate, for the way is the truth and the life. Some way say, moreover, that although a man of exceptional sympathy (I use the word in the Schelerian sense) might glimpse what it would be like to be a Christian, a Muslim, etc., this would not at all involve his actually successively *being* a Christian, a Muslim, etc. But since we need constantly to remember that Ramakrishna was a *bhakta* and not a philosopher we might still raise a further question about the comparability of mystic experiences, a question to which, needless to say, we shall not find an answer. The peculiarity is that in this case the experiences belong to one and the same man. Two points arise: first, whether a Hindu could undergo a Christian or a Muslim mystic experience, and, secondly, even if it were possible, whether the experient would be in a position to remember and compare one experience with another, and then, even more radically, even if he could, if he could be spoken of as "the same man". These latter issues are not entirely germane to the universalist thesis, except that Ramakrishna, like some of his predecessors, often seems to be saying that mystics experience the same thing or the same sort of thing (these are of course 'not the same') so that you get a kind of 'universal religion' at the highest possible rung. In order to go further in this direction one would need to know what is meant by 'same experience', 'same religious experience', etc. As long as we have diverse experiments we have, presumably, diverse experiences. To be able to say that the content was similar would require a degree of communicability usually taken to be rare as far as mystics are concerned. To speak of a universal experience among mystics would be to speak of something which we could hardly identify. In any case it would be a notion distinct from the notion of 'universal religion'.

With Swami Vivekananda, the neo-Vedāntin, we are again in a rațional approach to universal religion, but which is so along with regarding Hinduism as the "mother of religions" and, within Hinduism, assumes that Vedānta is the core. No doubt it was his special gift to see the Vedāntic oneness as bearing a pointed to our obligations to our fellows. Swamiji did believe all religions to be equal as Mahatma Gandhi did (this is a still more recent interpretation of universal religion). He also believed that a regenerated Hinduism had a special message to give to the world (we have referred to this attitude as 'returing the compliment'). But he attributed to the Hindu this belief: "we accept all religions as true". If this were so, then the question of purifying Hinduism or speaking of 'true Hinduism' should not have arisen. He did moreover speak of Hinduism as "the true religion", revealing his nationalist bias rather than any well-thought-out conception of what truth in religion amounted to. One standpoint than can be glimpsed in one of his writings is that Hinduism is true *because* it accpets all religions as true. This would give a further twist to the universality claim made for neo-Vedānta. It would also provide another shaky logical base for the truth of Hinduism. Moreover, unless Hinduism be synonymous with Vedānta (which it is not) it would not provide a premise for concluding, "It is Vedānta alone that can become the Universal religion of man." In any case *becoming* the universal religion of man and already *being* it are not the same thing. Barring these philosophical traps there is no doubt that it was the message of service which the Swami wished to place before India, and that he believed it to be essential in the sense that through it India would be able to become a nation on the move.

A specifically *Indian* interpretation of the universalist thesis was also presented by Dr. Bhagawan Das in his book entitled *Essential Unity of All Religions*, first published in 1932 under theosophical auspices. A well-balanced review of the book appeared in August 1940 in the *Calcutta Review* by Professor Sushil Kumar Maitra, commenting that "The work has a primarily practically aim, and is written with the express purpose of preparing individuals and nations for the building up of a better, more spiritual world, based on fellowship, sympathy, and understanding." The non-theoretical aim of the author is in fact made clear in the book in spite of the weight of erudition which runs through its several hundred pages. Dr. Bhagawan Das hoped "to reconcile religions", "to promote religious brotherhood and to find an alternative to the Russian experiment". He shows real concern with the promotion of peace among the different communities in the subcontinent and in the world as a whole, and believes that religion which has often been a divisive force in the past need not and should not be such. He writes, "Religion, to justify itself, must be of help and service everywhere." The book contains classified quotations from the scriptures of the various faiths, pointing out common features under the headings of the intellectual, emotional and volitional elements in religious experience. An effort is made to "ascertain what is most indubitable, most in accord with the best service, and, more than all else, is most approved and agreed in by all concerned, and most likely to promote good-will and active sympathy between all human beings". This near-Benthamite approach to religion we encountered before. Likewise a stress on the Asiatic character of the 'major' religions and their 'substantial unity'. The author discerns a vital role for religion if it is so understood. He indeed tries to find in religion "a continuous organic unity", the realization of which can promote human brotherhood. As he puts it, "To recognize that Unity in the Essentials of all Religions is to promote the cause of civilisation" (p. 16).

To see where all this fits in our map of those who support some form or other of the universalist thesis require a sifting out of the major theses, and this is now offered in point form.

(1) It is possible to distinguish the essential from the non-essential in religion. This is a third alternative to rejecting all religions *or* accepting all religions (p. 71).

(2) All are "in essence exactly the same" (p. 752).

(3) The majority-principle should be followed in determining what the essentials of all religions are: "the new proclamation, of Universal Religion, has to be made on 'democratic' lines, i.e. the lines of 'majority rule'.......".

(4) "The Essential Religion.....is eternal, universal, impersonal, all-pervasive, unchanging, in *substance*....." (p. 87).

(5) "....the same fundamental truths have been received by God in different scriptures, in different languages, through different persons both in different nations" (p. 82).

(6) "Religions are many and of many forms and formalities; the Universal Religion is one" (p. 92). Use is made here of the water, light, fire, etc. analogues.

(7) The quintessence of 'religion' or 'religiousness' is "The feeling, and the implicit and explicit recognition of the omnipresence of the larger Self; and of one's particular smaller self being a part, and subordinate to, It, as a cell or a tisssue in an organism"......(p. 107). The language of self and Self is continued in many other passages of which here are a few:

(i) "When man has found God, his own Eternal and Infinite Self, and has thrown away his smaller self, he has himself become the Truth, the Life, the Way, and no longer needs any other way to God. Whichever track we try, we always come round to the one and only way - of merging the small self in the Eternal Self, the dew-drop in the Sea" (p. 113).

(ii) "....the concept, feeling, sense, of a common I, a single I, running through all bodies, and vitalizing, energizing , moving, controlling them all.....is the very heart, the foundation, of all the religions" (pp. 171-172).

(iii) "All religions therefore pre-eminently proclaim Recognition of the Universal Self as the one sure guide in all situations"...... (p. 449).

(iv) "Realization of Self in all as God in all, and consequent service of God, is perfection and completion of religion" (p. 759).

(8) The different religions differ in emphasis: "various religions and sects, philosophical schools, civilizations and epochs, emphasize various aspects, facets, parts of the same One Universal Way and Life and Truth; through all necessarily expound, implicitly if not explicitly, all the aspects; for these

are inseparable (p. 119).

(9) "The one basic Truth is that man is in essence one with God" (p. 122).

(10) Differences between religious are mostly in connection with practices. "Yet those differernces are only apparent" (p. 573).

(11) India has a mission as far as religion is concerned: "to inaugurate a new Reform, a Reincarnation, of the Eternal Universal Religion, in the shape of a Scientific Religion" (p. 764).

It will only be possible to comment briefly on some of these points which the author supports with a wealth of learning, bringing to light indeed several remarkable resemblances of sentiment, imagery, etc. among the various quotations he cites. The task of sorting out the essential from the non-essential in religion is very understandably a leading theme in reformist thought in nineteenth and twentieth century India. The challenges presented by Christian missionaries, secular liberalism, and the preasence of large minorities in the country professing beliefs different from those of the majority community kept thinking Hindus on their toes. Added to this was a national pride which constantly burst out in the colonial situation and which often went to extreme lengths in vindication of India's ancient culture. Dr. Bhagawan Das at his best combines the resurgent nationalist bias of his times with an internationalism which seeks for brotherhood beyond national frontiers.

The thesis which Dr. Bhagawan Das presents under point (1) is really an educationist's thesis. The "elements of Essential Religion" in all the great religions are to be fed to the younger generations "instructing them that the husks are useful only for preserving and storing the grains in, and not for eating and assimilating" (p. 72). Dr. Bhagawan Das, as a distinguished educationist, really believed that if students had access to the 'core' thought expressed in the various scriptures this would result in a certain breadth of perspective and largeness of heart. In spite of the many commissions on education which probed the implications of secularism in free India, this was not a suggestion that was ever taken up in the 'aided' schools, or even in the others. One may wonder, however, whether a purging of all historical elements, of a rooting in the lives of the great founder-figures, make for a singling out of what is essential in any one religion, let alone in all religions in their great variety. Religion can as well, and perhaps better, be understood through the lives of these figures as through the formalized teachings found in scriptures. The task of isolating the essential from the non-essential in any one tradition is difficult enough. The Catholic and the Protestant, for example, would not agree with regard to the Virgin Birth, nor would Hindus agree on *varṇāśramdharma*. The lowest common denominator of agreement may not be the best way of discrimating 'essences', even if it were concedd that it would be possible to seek out essences with but scant reference to history. The phenomenologist's use of the word 'essence' is of course different, for on this view even the 'accidental', the *upādhi*, would count as essence in so far as it was a content of experience. But it is interesting to reflect that even this latter use of the term accommodates historicity with difficulty. An existential understanding of world-views, whether religious or otherwise, would not set about the task by distinguishing seed from the husk, but by entering into the total like-world as far as possible. In this approach, as on the phenomenological one, the totality of strands in their interconnection and context would constitute the phenonemon 'religion'. 'Meaning', in both the phenomenological and existential ways of understanding a religious world-view is not something which can be culled through an intellectualist sifting of grains from husks. The line of thought which discriminates the essential from the non-essential is, in short, inherently judgemental or theoretical. That judgement is involved is seen in the criteria which are offered for distinguishing the essential from the non-essential. The criteria are: (1) "what is most indubitable"; (2) "most in accord with the best science"; (3) "most approved and agreed in by all concerned"; (4) "most likely to promote good-will and active sympathy between all human beings" (p. 70). The criteria are most interesting ones. But as soon as we start looking for what Leibniz called "compossibility" we come up against difficulties. If indubitability is seen with the eye of faith this is something which each tradition understands in its own way. Take, say, the question of rebirth. This may appear indubtiable to the Hindu, but an open question or definitely something that is *not* so, to a man of another faith. Reference to scientific considerations has for many people in modern times raised a myraid questions. It is unlikely that this would enable people to decide between the truth claims of various religion or more provocatively, it is not at all certain that the verdict of science is particularly *relevant* to the determination of, say, whence we have come or what we may hope for. The majority-principle point was referred to earlier. A mere counting of heads may well result in an 'unexamined' set of prejudices. Even to qualify this, as Adam Smith does in the context of ethics, by speaking of 'well-informed' judges, would be to beg the question. The fourth point underlines the utiliarian bias which appears in recent times in functionalist analyses of religious phenomena. There is a sense in which it is patently true to say that it is obvious what is "likely to promote good-will etc.". It is certainly possible, negatively, to determine what will *not* "promote good-will etc." It is, however, from a purely pragmatist viewpoint, more likely that a man would be influenced by what is likely to promote good-will from the teachings (plus the example of the lives of the relevant founder-figures) of his *own* tradition than by a common denominator formula put together by well-meaning scholars.

The three alternatives which Dr. Bhagawan Das poses: rejecting all religions, accepting all religions, and distinguishing the essential from the non-essential in religion, are not as clear as they appear. "To reject all religions" can itself stem from an ideological position which resembles religion in respect of conviction and commitment. Some would say that Marxism comes into this category. To accept all religions may mean (1) to grant equal validity to all religions and personally to be committed to one, (2) to grant equal validity to all religions (with a proviso like 'for all who like that sort of thing') but to withhold from commitment to any one. This is a position which the logically-minded may indeed regard as untenable but which is held by many modernists who follow the principle of 'live and let live' but who do not themselves feel particularly 'affected' by the various conflicting claims. The very conflicts themselves are often regarded as off-putting on such a view. To 'accept all religions' on either of these interpretations of the phrase, cannot be therfore be eliminated as "impracticable" (vide p. 71).

My criticism of the 'sameness' asserted in point (2) in the list of the main theses will follow from the discussion of the concept of essence given earlier. If, for historical reasons, it is not possible to separate the essential from the non-essential, the thesis about sameness will not stand. Wilfred Cantwell Smith's distinction between tradition and faith is illuminating here. Neither the tradition, nor the faith, can be the 'same' in people who belong to two different major religious presuasions. There can be 'similarity' of both tradition and faith in people belonging to similar sects, e.g. the family resemblance between non-conformist patterns of belief and behaviour, or the similarity of the contents of Vaiṣṇava hymns in various Indian languages. Dr. Bhagawan Das overstates his thesis by speaking of religious as "in essence exactly the same" (p. 752).

We now move on to his characterization of "Essential Religion" in terms which would be acceptable only to one major living religious tradition and moreover only to one philosophical school of thought attached to that tradition. The language of self and Self, which he reckons to be common to all religions, has no application in the Judaeo-Semitic group of religions, in Buddhism and Far Eastern religions, or in the so-called 'primitive' religions. The quotations listed under point (8) can hardly be advanced as satisfying the four criteria laid down earlier. They represent a sincere expression of one particular, and highly philosophical, strand in Hinduism, but can in no way be taken to be "the very heart, the foundation, of all Religions" (pp. 171-172). Part/whole language appears on p. 107, merging of the self in the Eternal Self (p. 113), and the language of 'realization' on p. 759 - all matters on which there is a major divide between the Advaitic style of philosophico-religious thinking and the rest of the Hindu corpus of thought and life-style, to say nothing of the distance between this style and religious thought outside the Hindu fold.

The next question concerns what the difference between various world-views amount to [the classification under point (8) includes many different categories all together]. The difference, we are told, is one of the emphasis. Each emphasizes aspects, facets and parts of the "same One Universal Way and Life an Truth". But if there were only one way then there would be no question of anyone's changing his faith, something which we are told is quite feasible: "It is equally indisputable that anyone and veryone can withdraw his faith from any religion, and put it on any other, whenever he likes; can put off one and put on another at will" (p. 71). Whether in the interests of brotherhood or whatever, Dr. Bhagawan Das is reluctant to admit the difference between religions. As far as practice is concerned, the differences, we are told, are only 'apparent' (p. 573) and as far as prayers are specifically concerned, "essential parts of all are almost exactly the same" (p. 573). One gets the impressions that, in order to obviate the barriers that have from time to time in history separated religious *communities* the author is anxious to establish the *sameness* of the basic truths of religion. But it is difficult not only to substantiate the thesis of a common denominator in all religions, but to see how the isolation of such a content would promote the cause of human unity. Universalists of various brands have never been happy about the exuberant *diversity* of religious belief and practice. They are rather in the position of a gardener who in displaying his blooms adds the comment, "Yes, they are all flowers." The book ends with a suggestive comment, in theosophical vein, about India's mission as far as religion is concerned: "to inagurate a new Reform, a Reincaranation, of the Eternal Universal Religion, in the shape (sic) of a Scientific Religion" (p. 764). Sri Aurobindo had already maintained that the idea of the unity of mankind in the Godhead was India's special contribution to the thought of the future, and the linking of science and religion was to reappear later in Vonoba Bhave's speeches and writings. In the meantime, though, what Dr. Bhagawan Das showed was more the essential unity of *man* (something which can be illustrated by reference to almost *any* cultural phenomenon) than the essential unity of religion. One can also note that whereas some Christian thinkers explored the notion of *continuity* between the religions or saw the work of the Holy Spirit within the religions and in the 'non-religions' as well, a thinker like Dr. Bhagawan Das, from within the Hindu tradition, was no less sensitive to the challenge of religious pluralism. It is also an ironic reflection that when tribals were being increasingly absorbed into the Hindu social framework, and when *within* that framework people could acquire higher status and climb up the social state through conformity to Brahminic ritualism, some Hindu scholars were anxious to establish the universality of 'core' Hinduism, indeed to stress its modernity, and to maintain a 'sameness' that would most certainly have been repudiated by their forefathers.

It is time to consider the thesis as presented by S. Radhakrishnan with whose name it has been specially associated Radhakrishnan's 'universalism', expressed in a number of writings over a long-period; is based on two main planks, a metaphysical standpoint which could be described as a modified Vedāntism, and a conviction, based on his work in the national and international spheres, of the need of bringing into being a world-consciousness which will be able to overcome differences of nationality, religion, etc. The main places in his writings where this twofold thesis has been stated will now be briefly viewed in chronological order. The thesis in its most provocative form is to be found in *The Hindu View of Life* (1927, p. 23), where he claims that the Vedānta is "not a religion, but religion itself in its most universal and deepest significance". In *The Heart of Hindusthan* (1932, p. 88) he speaks of the same fundamentals in all religions: "that God is; that man stands in some relation to God; and that intercourse of some kind is possible between God and man who has in him the desire to be in harmony with God". Pluralism is accommodated in a similar manner in *East and West in Religion* (1933, p. 19) where the religions are said to be "tentative adjustments, more or less satisfactory, to the same spiritual reality, after which the human spirit feels and by which, in some manner, it is acted upon." The thesis develops further in *Eastern Religions and Western Thought* (1939, p. 2) where the question is not only one of metaphysics but the "obligation to treat the world as a unit". The eastern religions are believed to be specially relevant to the task of giving "a soul to the growing world-consciousness" (p. viii). A new humanism is on the horizon and mysticism "is likely to be the religion of the future" (p. ix). In 1947, in *Religion and Society*, he pronounced that the historic religions must transform themselves radically into a universal faith, and he expresses a preference for a religion of contemplation which would be a free of dogma: ".....when we take to the religious life of contemplation we are brought together.......The hardness of the ego melts, the tentativeness of the creed is revealed, and the intense focussing of all souls in one utter being is grasped" (p. 53). That the "perennial philosophy" is the "philosophy of ultimate religion", indeed of "religion as such", is the common thread in all these ways of presenting the universalist thesis. That the prennial element is something specifically Indian is found not only in *The Hindu View of Life* but in the subsequent works as well, including *The Bhagawad Gita* (1948, p. 12) which he claims presents "not merely Hinduism but religion as such, in its universality". In his *Fragments of A Confession* (1952) the central core of religion is said to be the "eternal religion behind all religions". From his earlier writings this common core would seem to be, on his view, nothing other than the Vedanta. The chapter on "The Meeting of Religions" (*Eastern Religions and Western Thought,* 1939), although writtern much earlier, contains a clearer statement which runs as follows: Hinduism accepts "every aspect of God conceived by man, and yet preserved its unity by interpreting the different historical forms as modes, emanations, or aspects of the Supreme". We can, and should, look forward to "a great dream of a world society with a universal religion of which the historical faiths are but branches. We must recognize humbly the partial and defective character of our isolated traditions and seek their source in the generic tradition from which they have all sprung" (ibid., p. 347).

The thesis, from the above, runs something like this. Metaphysics is concerned with "pure and universal" religious experience. Philisophy so conceived is centred on contemplation, on vision, and is not to be distinguished from religion. This moreover is synonymous with "religion of the Spirit". The various historic religions present various aspects of God. As such they are partial, and so defective, although we are also told that the "tentative adjustments" that each religion makes are "more or less satisfactory". The religion of the future is likely to be a contemplative one, a religion of essence, purged of "formal structures", which is indistinguishable from Vedānta which "is not a religion, but religion in its most universal and deepest significance", and which therefore does not share the "partiality" of the historic religions.

The thrust of the argument depends a lot on the conflation of philosophy and religion to be found in the Vedāntic viewpoint, for if it be metaphysics which can take us out of partiality of 'aspects' into timeless insights and if this be synonymous with the core of Hinduism then the latter is thereby rescued from the fate of the historic religions with their 'formal structure', 'defects', etc. Like Dr. Bhagawan Das, Radhakrishnan claims for Vedānta a core or essence status not only within Hinduism but among the family of religions, and this seems to be based on the unstated premise, thatthe "impersonal" is more fundamental than the personal, the timeless more fundamental than the historical. One could set about discussing this in many ways. For example, even if it could be established that Vedānta is the essence of Hinduism this would by no means show that it was the essence of religion as such. To interpret Hinduism in terms of one of its philosophical schools, as Joachim Wach said in his contribution to *The Philosophy of Sarvelaplli Radhakrishnan* (edited by Schilpp), is to forget that Hinduism has a history. Wach was writing on the methodology of the comparative study of religion in the light of a sensitive awareness of the genuine qualitative differences between the various religions. Any claim to the study of certain universal features of the various religions should be capable to illustration by reference to any of the so-called 'primitive' cults, or major religions (as for example Rudolf Otto does). But, once the historicity of religions is granted, essence language becomes inappropriate. This inappropriacy has been pinpointed most of all, in recent years, by Wilfred Cantwell Smith. In his inaugural lecture at McGill University in 1950 he said the following: "It seems to me that progress in the study of religion can come when we bring ourselves to forget about the nature of religion and attend rather to the process of its contemporary development." He expressed the hope that "comparative religion may become the disciplined self-consciousness of man's variegated and developing religious life". To shift from the talk of universal or major religions to the talk of 'living religions' reminds us of their variation and development by D. G. Moses, while retaining the belief that "ultimate truth is one" and giving special emphasis to the cognitive element in religious experience.

With Ananda K. Coomaraswamy we return to the view that it falls within the philosopher's territory "to demonstrate the common metaphysical basis of all religions and that diverse cultures are fundamentally related to one another as being the dialects of a common spiritual and intellectual language; for whoever recognizes this, will no longer wish to assert that 'my religion is best', but only that it is the 'best for me'. In other words, the purpose of religious controversy should be not to 'convert' the opponent, but to persuade him that his religion is essentially the same as our own." The two halves of this statement are by no means synonymous, for the principle of 'best for me' is hardly equivalent to the principle of 'essential sameness'. However, there is more to come. He goes on to say that there is not "any other ground whatever upon which all men can be in absolute agreement, excepting that of metaphysics, which we assert is the basis and the norm of all religious formulations". After recognizing the common ground "it becomes a simple matter to agree to disagree formulations are no more than paraphrases of one and the same principle". All this is reminiscent of Bhagawan Das and Radhakrishnan (he makes frequent reference to the former) in respect of the confident belief in the possibility of metaphysical agreement, and the feasibility of distinguishing the essential from the non-essential (with 'dogmas' allotted to the latter category) in religion. Familiar also is the belief that East and West can meet on the basis of "the purely intellectual wisdom that is one and the same at all times and for all men, and is independent of all environmental idiosyncrasy". That the prennial philosophy can have different forms is admitted in his book *Hinduism and Buddhism*: "The Indian tradition is one of the forms of the Philosophia Perennis, and as such, embodies universal truths to which no one people or age can make exclusive claim." He believed that recognition of the prennial philosophy can make for world peace. Elsewhere Coomaraswamy went further than this. "But it is not only in Philosophy and Religion —Truth and Love—but also in Art that Europe and Asia are united: and from this triple likeness we may well infer that all men are alike in their divinity." He concluded his homage to Shakespeare by witnessing "to the intellectual fraternity of mankind": saying that "it is that fraternity which assures us of the possibility of cooperation in a common task, the creation of a social order founded on Union". That the task is a practical one is admitted in his confession that "What is really needed is a point of view which is practical rather than scholastic or sentimental." But, for Coomaraswamy, as well as for Rabindranath Tagore, another consideration is also extremely important. To both men, religious experience most certainly had an aesthetic dimension that overflowed all boundaries of creed or even of cultural allegiance. When both witness to the "unity at the root of things" they are not only allying themselves with the prennial philosophy, for others had done that, but with the living rhythm which is known most of all to the creative artist. There is yet another stream of thought which flows with full vigour in Rabindranath's thinking (as it does, no doubt, in Sri Aurobindo's) and that is humanism. Universalism was not for him a thesis; rather the realization of unity and harmony was for him a poet's intuition, an intuition that was ever tuned to the message of the particular.

At a public meeting in Calcutta on 29 August 1921 Tagore ended his speech with these words: "In this new dawn shall we not remember Him, who is one (*ya ekah*), who is without distinction of colour (*avarṇaḥ*), and who with His multiple power makes true provision for the inherent needs of each and every class (*vahudhāśakti yogat varṇāṇānekān nihitārtho dadāti*)? Shall we not pray to the Giver of wisdom to unite us all in right understanding (*sa no buddhyā śubhāya samyunantu*)?" Tagore somestimes used thesitic language, as in this passage, and sometimes Upaniṣadic language. For example, in *The Religion of Man* he writes that in the depth of our being "there dwells the Eternal Spirit of human unity beyond our direct knowledge". He adds that maybe the "ideal truth does not depend upon the individual mind of man, but on the universal mind which comprehends the individual". We share in the Super-Soul "in all our true knowldge, love and service, and whom to reveal in ourselves through renunciation of self is the highest end of life".

The concept of 'surplus' which he culled from the Atharvaveda, provided entry to a host of new possibilities. The infinite perspectives of human personality include religion,

religion as relatedness, a power "in the hidden depths of our being". Tagore seems to be grafting an element of futurism, of possibility, onto an ancient Upanisadic root when he speaks of the Universal Man. He writes, "In our soul we are conscious of the transcendental truth in us, the Universal, the Supreme Man." In science we had "the rational mind of the Universal man". The 'surplus' is the fount of imagination, of memory, "the spirit of love", in fact of every dimension of freedom. Above all it was the spiritual kinship of mankind which was universal. He foresaw a future of boundless possibilities for the human world, a boundless which reflected the boundless elements in nature which he loved so much—the sea and the sky. Tagore's 'universalism' was, in many ways, far more of a 'horizon' concept than what it was for some of the earlier thinkers we discussed. The sense of horizon can, no doubt, also be glimpsed in Raja Rammohun Roy and Sri Aurobindo. But no one before Tagore had dared to root this in the Upanisadic vision of *what is*. In terms of the Indian tradition this was as starting a combination as combining Parmenides and Bergson in the western tradition would be.

It would not be correct to discern a concealed Christology in his notion of "the universal person who is human all the same". His source of inspiration is the songs of the Bauls with their troubadour celebration of God as brother, as comrade, as the apple of one's eye, heart of one's heart. In fertilizing a philosophical tradition with a folk one in his poet's way, he brought an eschatological element, a ray of hope into a climate of thought where hope had hardly been philosophically or artistically respectable, an element of joy here and now where joy had been reserved previously for a *turiya* state of consciousness. This larger life of freedom and creativity to which all men can have access is what Tagore meant by universal religion.

Sri Aurobindo's universalism is yet again different, not a thesis, but a system which owes not a little to his own understanding, a selective one, of the cultural history of India. The futurism of one strand of Raja Rammohun Roy's thought and the 'world-soul' concept of Radhakrishnan are both shared by Sri Aurobindo. He has great hopes of India's role in the commonwealth of nations: "It is she who must send forth from herself the future religion of the entire world, the eternal religion which will harmonize all religions, science and philosophies and make mankind one soul."

Since the universalist thesis presents, with considerable variations, a particularly Indian response to the fact of religious pluralism, mention must also be made of Mahatma Gandhi's angle on this issue. His belief that men see truth in fragments prevents him from the kind of universalism which advocates a single "aspect of the truth" in the name of universal truth. This is what he says: "Does not God Himself appear to different individuals in different aspects? Still we know that He is one. But Truth is the right designation of God. Hence, there is nothing wrong in everyone following Truth according to his lights. Indeed it is his duty to do so." Religions must "submit to the test of reason and universal assent" so that no religious doctrine be accepted which conflicts with morality. The 'same goal' language is used by Gandhi, without, however, buttressing it with metaphysical arguments. The basis of the 'equality' of various religions is their imperfection, and the ground of the latter is that "if we are imperfect ourselves, religion as conceived by us must also be imperfect". Hence we have the person-centred conception of religion of a Cantwell Smith with a difference. "All faiths constitute a revelation of Truth, but all are imperfect, and liable to error." Overcoming the defects of one's own religion would then be overcoming one's own weakness of faith, and presumably, talking into account Gandhi's life-work, purging traditions and institutions of the accretions which accure to them.

The following passage is an important one in this connection: "Even as a tree has a single trunk, but many branches and leaves, so there is one true and perfect Religion, but it becomes many, as it passes through the human medium. The one Religion is beyond all speech." The "universal and absolute truth" is said to be beyond the "dust of creeds and faiths". There is a link between his conclusion that all religions are true and yet all religions have some error in them and his insight into the value of such a belief as a regulative principle in our dealings with our fellowmen. Furthermore, not profession of belief in the last analysis, but *right action* was the mark of the godly man, in Gandhi's view.

The above survey presents some curious features in terms

of the history of ideas. In pre-Independence India a strong element of Hindu patriotism was expressed by those who advocated "universal religion". This continued even in free India. We noticed, however, two incongruities — the projecting of one philosophical style of Hinduism as the essence of what has been described by P.D.Devanandan[49] as a "federation of religions", and secondly the claim of the truth of this 'essence' not only for Hindus but also for those outside the Hindu fold. Indian idealism and nineteenth century western idealism fused in some minds and talk of parts, aspects, etc. became familiar. The distinction between the essential and the non-essential was often employed so as to classify all that was *distinctive* of any particular tradition under the latter category, i.e. the 'unique' was the 'non-essential'.

It was, moreover, remarkable that so many great minds should have imagined that religion could be unifying factor in the world when it was, in fact, economics more than any other factor which would show that unity was individible. Those who were interested in religion and those who observed the operation of the trade cycle did not appear to meet. The convergence thesis, as presented, say, by Teilhard de Chardin is in many ways an alternative thesis to the main thrust of the universalist thesis— the convergence point being seen, since Teilhard is a Christian, in the person and work of Jesus Christ. The idea that there can be concordant discord is a third possibility which gives no special weight to the universal and the common any more than any special beauty may be said to characterize voices singing in unison. Such a concordant discord can still present the combined witness which is perhaps expected of religious men especially in this century. Such a witness, rather than the hypothetical coincidence of insights of contemplatives of different traditions, would be universal religion in a new sense. Of all those whose writings we recalled, this would chime in most of all with thinking of Raja Rammohun Roy and, in a harmonizing key, with that of Mahatma Gandhi, both of whom never failed to identify in religion an immense power for the transformation of social and political life.

Chapter-5

MYTHOLOGIZATION AND DEMYTHOLOGIZATION

Chapter-5

In what follows we shall examine the hypothesis that the history of Hinduism shows a pendulum swing between mythologization and demythologization, and in this connection introduce two concepts which seem to have some explanatory utility, namely those of 'spiritual landscape' and 'remythologization'.

We need to begin with looking at the basic pendulum metaphor which we will be using. Pendulum terminology is sometimes appropriate when there is a marked oscillation between views, terms, states, or whatever the units to be compared may be. The phenomenon shows itself as distinguishable from progression, or from rebounds and reactions, being a pattern of change which is regularly repetitive in an alternating pattern. An example is provided by David Hume in *The Natural History of Religion* where he mentions, according to one of the theories he presents, that societies have a tendency to oscillate between polytheism and monotheism. Whether or not pendulum termonilogy can be applied in the periodizing of history seems to depend on various factors among which two stand out in importance. Let us say that a hypothesis is made to the effect that A characterizes period X, followed by B characterizing period Y, followed by A characterizing period Z, and so on. Question marks can always be raised whether the cluster of factors A which characterizes period X is in fact the same or similar to the cluster which characterizes period Z. Hard-liners can maintain that since period X is ipso facto termporally distinct from period Z the factor can never be "the same". To deny that there can be *any* similarity would, however, preclude us from ever making any generalizations at all about history. But there can be a different objection - an objection about importance. Say, the characteristics A detected in period Z are no doubt identifiable, but are not as important as characterizes P, Q and R. To associate period Z and A, if this be so, would be to make an error of stress, a top-sided assessment, an infelicitous judgement of importance. Yet another objection can conern periodization itself. Have we identified periods, X, Y and Z justifiably? The way we do it obviously hangs together with our clusters of characterizations. Then again, period X may be a matter of five centuries, Y may be one century, and Z may be a few decades. Would the pendulum hypothesis be affected by such discrepancies of time scale? We can further ask how often the swing needs to take place to qualify for classification under the rubric of the pendulum effect. The symbolized sequence of three stages given just now may not suffice. Current usage of the term in connection with elections presupposes two clear conditions — polarization of the factors compared, and a stable pattern of oscillation over a period of time. Where pendulum language is use, in other words, it is done so where the phenomena have a high range of predictability, something which averges out statistically. Perhaps this is to go too far. And yet those who use pendulum language in the context of the history of ideas would be the first to derive grist for their mill from phrases like 'in the long run', 'other things being equal' and other locutions used by those who think statistically.

Now clockwork analogies fascinated eighteenth-century thinkers on account of their fascination with the regularity according to which chronometers operate. The possibility of their running down, not being wound up, or otherwise going out of order was a very real one to men who could conceive of the frightening possibility of a *malin génie* at work. But to use the pendulum metaphor as a heuristic hypothesis does not commit us, in the twentieth century, in any way to the paraphernalia of the deistic world-view. We might detect a pendulum effect over a certain period and then find that the pendulum has stopped. Grandfather clocks often do. We could, of course, ask why it had stopped. Nor would our finding that it could not work any more make us deny that it had worked all right in the past.

The discussion will be confined to Hinduism, although Buddhism shows the highly interesting phenomenon of an initial swing away from Hindu myth to demythologized ethico-religiosity in the Buddha himself, followed by a new remythologizing by his followers. Whether a subsequent demythologizing can be said to have taken place after this depends on how one interprets the *dharmakāya* idea. All this is a theme for a separate occasion.

We turn then to Hinduism. One can be held up endlessly over the definition of myth, the stumbling-block of the mythic content of would-be demythologized forms of religious thought and so forth. There is, though, I think, little disagreement occasioned if one says that religion in Vedic times was strongly mythical. The content of the demythologized gives more pause, for whereas in a western context demythologized means "theologically purified" in some way or other,[1] in Indian religions it has meant something rather different, viz. either a shift to the philosophical, or a shift to monotheism. This way of putting it will cover the transition from the Ṛgveda to the Upaniṣads and the shift from the Purāṇic cults to the unitarian ethos of the Brahmo Samaj. The richness of the Vedas has been the subject of detailed study by generations of Indologists. Noteworthy from our point of view is the way Vedic religion centred on hymns, some of which were connected with rituals. The word 'hymn' is somewhat misleading if it is thought of in its modern context of congregational worship, for the Vedic verses were incantatory and invocatory. They were neither in the vernacular nor 'sung by all'. However the Vedic hymns were triumphs of religious imagination, and admirably illustrate the mood of *celebration* connected with cosmic phenomena which perhaps comes more naturally to a people free of the 'distancing' function of the scientific mind. That celebration involves ritual may be expected, also that rituals needs specialists, i.e. priests skilled in the carrying out of ritual acts. Religious imagination goes hand in hand with speculation and with sentiment. The *Puruṣasūkta* for example, while it presents the tremendous image of a cosmic being whose parts are envisaged as analogous to the parts of the human being, contains the notion of a primal sacrifice, and a speculative excursus into the notion of macrocosm and microcosm, and these elements must not be edged out by an understanding which sees in these famous lines only evidence of ritualism and the consequent importance of the Brahmanical class whose official functions are engaged thereby. The mythical is not *merely* mythical. Not that it is to be conceived as the matrix of something higher, namely philosophical or conceptual thought, but that it is an independent vehicle of human creativity which, in its very freedom from theology and philosophy, is endowed with a *power* which is denied to the conceptual per se. There are senses in which the passage from myth to doctrine and argument is a retreat, a regressus from celebration to questioning,[2] from acceptance to alienation. For all the ritualism of this early chronic of human experience, mythical awareness was accompanies by a spirit of world-affirmation, a sense of being at home in the universe and a notable lack of other-worldliness.

A turning away from myth seems to have come about in the history of religion under the impetus of one or other of three factors: the rigorous transcendentalism of propheticism, the cultivation of inwardness in mysticism, or the development of a philosophic consciousness. To look at each of these briefly in turn - mythic figures are imperfectly transcedent by reason of their involvement with natural powers and the anthropomorphic character of the stories which tell of their doings. Prophetic religions, in intent at least, are strictly anti-mythological, although we often find that nature-myths are replaced by history-myths. The mystic, on the other hand, finds the mythological dimension redundant, for the mythic will be analogous to the *kośas* to be cast off. The philosopher regards the mythical as a stage to be left behind, believing as he does that the *concept* is intrinsically superior to the *image*. Such a belief can be detected, for example, in Plato's attitude to Homer and Hesiod.

The question then arises which of these is operative in the Upaniṣadic shift away from mythology, or if there are any new factors which need to be taken into account the tenth book of the Ṛgveda anticipates the Upaniṣads (RV, 10.90, 121 and 129). In 10.121 the poet is in quest of a *worthy* object of worship. Prajāpati is still conceived mythically in terms of the golden seed, nut he is also Ruler, Lord, and Father. Hymn 10.129, the creation hymn, speaks of "The One" which "breathed windless by its own power". The Vedas contain both the idea of a personalized entity and an impersonal principle [Prajāpati and Vāc in the Ṛgveda and a close association between Brahman, Ātman and Puruṣa in the Atharvaveda (10.8)]. If the mystical and the philosophical were often at variance in western thought (except for a thinker like Plotinus) and indeed often in Indian thought too, this was not the case in the Upaniṣads. The elucidation of the *Mahāvākya* cannot be done at a mythical level but requires parables - the parable of the bees, the sea, the fig-tree, the blindfolded man from Gāndhāra, sparks and the fire, the spider's web, the sleeper. The *Śvetāsvatara* Upanisad shows Rudra-Śiva transformed beyond his role in the Ṛgveda into the Maheśvara, the Great Lord. Myth is caught up and transmuted into a new religious insight. We find out a subtle use of paradox [cf. "I who am food, eat the eater of food" — T.U., 3.10 (6)]—also present, of course in the Rgveda (10.129)—"He only knows or perhaps he does not know." To move away from myths involves, ipso facto, it would seem, a stretching of language in various ways. Myth appears to be associated with the evolution of personal religion, for the impersonal Absolute presumably cannot accommodate embodiment. Yet, to the extent that an Upaniṣad like the *Śvetāśvatara* oscillates between theism and absolutism, we are not, and perhaps in principle cannot be, free of myhts. Moreover the evolution of the concpet of a Lord which in one sense means a move away from a plurality of deities, at the same time incorporates many elements of the Ṛgvedic deities. There are those who would maintain that the concept of an Absolute is the biggest myth of all. But to say this is to use 'myth' in an extended sense. Upaniṣadic thought does represent a strenuous effort of philosophico-religious thought to get clear of the mythical. As Zaehner puts it: "The Upanishads both start and bring near to completion the process of demythologization."[3]

I earlier characterized Vedic religion by the mood of celebration. The Upaniṣads on the other hand are 'moved' by the spirit of inquiry - by an effort to *formulate*. We would except such a shift to be accompanied by what may be called the 'loss of landscape'. This concept brings us close to much of what is at stake in the debate between mythologizers and demythologizers. The demythologizer substitutes for a landscape on the cosmic scale an inner landscape of the mind. The Tamil 'Akam' poets of course dwell in a single world which encompasses both. The Upaniṣadic attempt is remarkable for all time for its on-all-fronts thrust beyond sensuous symbols to concepts and beyond concepts to what is intrinsically 'unspeakable'.[4]

That the great epic and Puranic literature which followed is mythological with a vengeance will hardly be debated. Devotionalism in Indian religions feeds not on history (as in Judaism and Christianity) but on sacred stories (especially stories about Krishna) whose symbolism proved as potent for literature as for religion. The fusion of the ideas of *moksa* and love unleashed poetic powers in all corners of the subcontinent and covered a period of time which one might roughly date from the fourth century A.D. through to Ramprosad Sen who lived in eighteenth-century Bengal. As in Vedic times, the hymn (this time the devotional hymn rather than the invocatory one) became the leading expression of the new consciousness. 'Identification' is no longer the product of transcendental consciousness (which received its supreme embodiment in the *Mahavākya*) but a projection which is familiar to all who experience human love, that is to say, something for which the word 'union' is more appropriate. Within this mythological framework a variety of impulses could find their voice - a move away from *tyāga* and *vairāgya*, a trust in intuition rather than in inquiry (cf. the Alvārs), a healthy disrespect for caste, an attempt to give body to the personality of the deity (cf. the hymns of Mānikka Vāśagar), the reformism of the Lingāyats (who opposed child-marriage and permitted widow-remarriage), an efflorescence of vernacular literature, the moral insights of a Guru Nanak, the impassioned Mother-Goddess worship of Bengal. The range of religious experience found therein is vast. Common to all, however, is a reaction against ritualism on the one hand, and on the other a reaction against the abstract conception of *mokṣa* given by the philosophers. Myth could cradle reformism no less than it could inspire a passionate type of religiosity.

The relation of mythological systems to changes in society is an intricate matter about which it would be hazardous to generalize. Hindu societies are not unique in finding no difficulty in joint participation in a mythical and a 'real' landscape, a dichotomy which no doubt needs further analysis. Early nineteenth-century Christians of an evangelical persuasion were as familiar with the land of Canaan as they were with the England of the industrial revolution. It would be incorrect to attribute what the Indian reformers of the nineteenth century rightly thought to be 'backwardness' solely to the extravagances of popular religion. The colonial context must not be forgotten. That mercantile activity is compatible with belief in elaborate mythologies can be illustrated no less from nineteenth-century

Christian communities in Britain than from the history of the Jainas. What must concern us next is the nineteenth-century reaction *against* mythology which is found especially in the Brahmo Samaj movement in Bengal.

Reference has already been made to Raja Rammohun Roy in two contexts, that of belief, and that of the universalist hypothesis. There can be no doubt that, along with Max Müller, he was unsympathetic to the mythological dimension in religion, and this because of his lifelong campaign against 'idolatry'. This was a loaded word in the nineteenth century, the main thrust of missionary preaching being against it; and the main thrust of the Hindu reaction to this was a resentment against what they took to be wilful misunderstanding on the part of foreigners of the role of the *eidolon* in Hindu worship. Raja Rammohun Roy's writings present a highly intellectualistic conception of worship. He writes in 1829 that worship applied to the Supreme Being "signifies a contemplation of his attributes".[5] Two considerations, however, make this a problematic matter. The *Trust-Deed of the Brahmo Samaj* (1830) includes the admission that "no human acquirements can ever discover the nature even of the most common and visible things"......[6] If this be so, our ability to contemplate the attributes of God may be presumed to be even less. *The Precepts of Jesus* is as demythologized a version of the New Testament as it would be possible to find. But in the *Second Appeal to the Christian Public* written in defence of this work in 1820 he refers to the doctrines contained in it as "alike founded on reason and revelation" (p. v), opening the way for a not totally rationalist approach to religion. The much earlier work *Tohyfut-ul-Mowahedeen* (1803) includes in the Introduction admission of the fact of disagreement about the 'peculiar attributes' of the Deity. So presumably finite man was scarcely capable of intuiting the Divine nature. The main attribute to be contemplated, and about which there could be no doubt (he thought), was the *unity* of the godhead. That this is what the Raja wanted to stress is evidenced by his constant use of phrases like "the Author and Preserver of the Universe", "One Being who is the source of all that exists and its governor", "One Almighty God", and the like.

There was no question, however, that for the great majority of people (and this applies to men of all faiths) worship takes other forms than contemplation of the attributes of the Deity. The Raja himself came across plentiful example in his own work on the Vedas and resorted to the following explanation of these phenomena:

> The same Vedas represent rites and external worship addressed to the planets and elementary objects, or personified abstract notions: as well as to deified heroes, as intended for persons of mean capacity; but enjoin spiritual devotion, as already described, benevolence, and self-control, as the only means of securing bliss.[7]

The Raja was following a distinction which had been made by most Indologists, between 'popular' and 'higher' religion, and this in turn ran parallel to the philosophers' distinction between lower and higher knowledge. One can recognize without difficulty some of the major characteristics of 'popular' religion which were objected to by him. Although an *eidolon* is not necessary in order to represent a god (a stone, a linga, or a non-figurative emblem will do, Bishop Heber notwithstanding) and although the chose object has to be endowed with symbolic power through a rite, one can easily find in Purānic religion especially, matters of grave offence to one who had been exposed to the Mutazilites, the rationalists of Islam. The very concept of *iṣṭadevatā* is founded on a belief in a plurality of deities among whom an individual choice can be exercised.

Besides the animus against idolatry there lay a more positive purpose behind Rammohun Roy's demythologizing – the desire to humanize belief and the desire to humanize society. Neither could be accomplished, he thought, without a far more *rational* approach to religion, where dogmas, rituals and doctrines would be at a minimum. Moreover if religions grew in response to the needs of society, those who were enlightened as to the needs of society *now* had a duty to stimulate the growth of religion in progressive (I use the word in the strictly etymological sense) channels. The Raja believed that along with idolatry went "injuruios rites" and that these destroy "the texture of society". The inference was that a "purer form of religion" would not only be purged of error, but be beneficial to society, and – not to be forgotten – lead to beatitude. All in all, then, the Raja's work as thinker and reformer tended to the same end – an attempt to pure away the mythological elements from Hinduism and to highlight belief in one God and service of humanity. If he was anti-myth he was no less anti-dogma. It is worth reflecting at this point whether the Raja maintained that belief in one God was what was *left* when the pruning had been done. He certainly took considerable pains in the introductions he wrote to the translations to establish that the pristine form of Vedantic belief was in a Supreme Being. The neo–Vedāntins, year later, were to extract social concern out of the *Mahāvākya*. One might conclude that Rammohun was selective in his approach both to Hinduism and Christianity, and that he gained support from many sources for his conviction that securing "peace and happiness to mankind at lagre" was part and parcel of what a religious man should envisage as his duty. His was a demythologization which was not only a going back to roots, but which owed a lot to cross-fertilization. It should also be noted that if Rammohun was hard on many aspects of his own tradition he was no less critical of much in Christianity, especially, the stumbling-block of the Trinity. In his view this was on a level with the polytheism of the Hindus. And yet he was not insensitive to the factor of *mystery* in religion, and said of Christian and Hindu mysteries, ".....since both these mysteries equally transcend the human understanding, one cannot be preferred to the other".[8] Even so he was unable to accept that to the non-unitarian Christian the Trinity was precisely that – a mystery which transcends the human understanding.

Two other major figures of the Brahmo Samaj movement, Debendranath Tagore and Keshub Chunder Sen, were yet again, each in his own way, very different from Raja Rammohun Roy, Debendranath was a man who had deep religious experiences of his own, who, one might say, did not *need* the prop and imaginative stimulus of a mythology, but yet whose intimations of a spiritual dimension could be said to have mythopoeic overtones. To say this is not perhaps to say much more than that Debendranath's religious life was strongly imbuded with imagination. Personal religion for him expressed itself in an intimate symbolic way, symbolic in the lyric tradition of Bengali folk literature. The 'attributes' of Rammohun's deistic God became transformed into a theist poetic imagery. This was carried much further by his son Rabindranath. The loss of myth cannot be made up for by theology, but the source of mythopoeic activity, from which both myth and poetry spring, can express itself in new creative forms. The devotional temper in men like Guru Nanak (in an earlier era) and Rabindranath Tagore expressed itself with extraordinary richness in a lyric literature which won an immediate response among the literate and the illiterate alike in their own communities. Such a symbolic expression must not be missed as a mode of 'demythologization' (in the sense of a break-away from the mythic world of the saviour-cults of mediaeval India) of no less importance than the rationalist attempts of Rammohun Roy. It was a phenomenon of more lasting import than the eclecticism of Keshub Chunder's New Dispensation, the inspiration of which came from all kinds of incompatible directions. Along with his strong attraction for the Upanisadic way of thinking, Rabindranath brought into lyric poetry a host of symbols that were already there at the folk level – the flying swans, the river, the ferry, the boatman, and so on. It was perhaps natural for a poet to find in the symbol, that fertile territory between myth and concept, the seeds for a rich harvest. Conceptual revision could only appeal to the *bhadralok*, the class which was addressed by the Brahmo leaders. Rabindranath profoundly distrusted this kind of cerebration. His own contribution was, in the last analysis, something which any theologian might well envy - he brought about an extension of awareness, of sensibility, which enabled the man in the street, still more, the peasant in the fields, to read with delight the ciphers around him in the world of nature, to match the infinite spaces of river, sky and sea with the yearnings and aspirations in the heart and mind of man.

Among the demythologizers should also be counted Ishwarchandra Vidyasagar, the remarkable Sanskrit pandit and reformer. A common task which faced all the reformist thinkers of the nineteenth century, whether in Bengal or, in other parts of India, was to rethink the content of *dharma*. Vidyasagar's contribution in this respect is a very massive one, and extraordinary too in view of his firm vantage-point, by reason of his profession, within the tradition. The rethinking of *dharma* was no less important task than the critique of myth and the reinterpretation of symbol. The practical consequences of the former were, in terms of human welfare (especially with regard to the welfare of women), in fact greater. No subsequent reformist thinker who wished to make his appeal broad-based has been able to avoid coming to terms with the concept of *dharma*, for indeed traditionally not only ordinary men but gods and heros too are subject to it.

Demythologizing efforts were still going on while a remythologizing swing of the pendulum came into operation. The two are co-present in an interesting and complicated way in the work of the Bengali prose writer, Bankim Chandra Chatterjee. He fits into the demythologizing programme on three counts: (1) his attempt to maintain Krishna's historicity, (2) his search for the essence of Hinduism, and (3) his belief that myth shrouds that essence. Brajendranath Seal, in commenting on *Dharma Tattva*, has rightly drawn attention to the influence of Comte on Bankim. But whereas Comte advocated that myth should be left behind, we find that Bankim invested the old myths with a new meaning. The way in which, during the nineteenth century, Durgā and Kālī became identified with the motherland had its origins in Bankim's writings, especially in *Kamalakanter Daptar* and *Ananda Math*. Nothing illustrates this more vivdly than *Vande Mātaram* which occurs in the latter novel. Remythologization in the name of nationalism is something which began in the nineteenth century and continued into the twentieth.

The fusion of nationalism and religiosity was expressed in an extreme manner in one of Keshub Chunder Sen's sermons which almost takes the form of a prayer: "Oh India, my motherland, thou art renowned and rich with the bounty of thy ancestors. Give us those accumulated treasures of love and devotion and make our lives glorious......"[9] The early Aurobindo and Swami Vivekananda can also be counted among the nationalist remythologizers. Vivekananda, like Bankim, is a complicated example. His Vedāntic conclusions, arrived at through a critique of Sāṁkhya cosmology, illustrates a rethinking of the essence of Hinduism inspired by the twin vechicles of a scientific outlook and a live social consequences. The idea of "my God the poor" is in effect a powerful new symbol. Trenchant criticism of traditional mythology is implied in the following passage:

> You may invent an image through which to worship God, but a better image already exists, the living man. You may build a temple in which to worship God, and that may be good, but a better one, a much higher one, already exists, the human body.[10]

Nearer our own time we have a clear example of an old myth endowed with new meaning in Mahatma Gandhi's appeal to the idea of Ram Rajya, not as a backward-looking Golden Age concept, but as the idea of a new and just social order for the future. He wrote: "Ram Rajya of my dream ensures rights alike of prince and pauper";[11] and elsewhere spoke of the ideal as "the establishment of the Kingdom of Righteousness on earth".[12] A mythical hero appears in a new form when, referring to Hanuman's love for Rama, Gandhi spoke of his "love for Rama whom I see face to face in the starving millions of India."[13] Gandhi, moreover, was the leading twentieth-century Indian to rethink the concept of *dharma*, a task which in the previous century we associated especially with the name of Vidyasagar. Gandhi's nationalism, however, did not prevent him from thinking beyond frontiers, from advocating an internationalism which was often somewhat puzzling to his fellow-nationalists.

Looking back, we may now see to what extent there has been a pendulum swing between mythologization and demythologization in the history of Indian religion, more particularly in the history of Hinduism. We began with a highly mythological form of religion in early Vedic times, succeeded by a philosophical form of demythologized religion which is at the same time 'high poetry'. With the cults we are back in mythology again. The reformist movements of the nineteenth century (the Arya Samaj was discussed elsewhere[14]) reacted against mythology in the belief that it was tied up with the backwardness of society. As the nationalist movement got under way, a new myth became current—that of the nation. This wave continues into contemporary times as is evidenced in the presence of pictures of national leaders in the puja room .

Against the hypothesis is first and foremost the consideration that even where a new period is entered upon in terms of phases sketched above, the earlier phases are not left behind. There is also a phenomenon which I describe as 'grasping the pendulum' (not letting it swing either this way or that) which can be found in Sikhism and, somewhat differently, in Mahatma Gandhi. Sikhism is unique in that whereas devotionalism in Indian religions feeds not on history (as in Christianity) but on myth and cult, in Sikhism we have a break-away from myth and a new form of devotionalism. Gandhi holds the pendulum in an ethico-religious world-view which utilizes old myths selectively in keeping with a general style of opting for development from conservation. Both Sikhism and Gandhi grasp the pendulum in the interest of a this-worldly devotionalism allied to the concept of *Sevā* . The this-worldliness brought in by nationalism clearly in the conflation of the mother-goddess and motherland ideas expressed by certain writers in Bengal.

The next phase (if the course of events elsewhere is any indication) we would except to be a demythologized one—that of secularism. The verdict of history, however, is that demythologized phases in India's past have been explicitly non-popular ones. This was true of the Upaniṣadic period and it was true of the Brahmo movement as well. It is not surprising, therefore, that a concomitant of centralized attempts to promote secularism has been a proliferation of new cults of various kinds, even among the middle class who might have been supposed to understand what secularism was about. Another phenomenon about the contemporary scene can also be noted. To become self-conscious about the distinction between myth and doctrine is often to regulate participation in myth to the aesthetic level. This is probably a fair description of how the educated Hindu responds to the Rama Lila drama which is performed in the metropolis with a high degree of sophistication and utilizing all the gimmicks of modern stage-cult.

In order to assess the contemporary position in the Indian religious spectrum, we need to look again at the concept of 'spiritual landscape' which was introduced a few pages back. The spiritual landscape of any people at a particular time is not confined to myth, although the mythical landscape is perhaps the most colourful part of it. Cosmogony provides easily identifiable loci in spiritual landscapes. Some cosmogonies include the idea of a hierarchy of worlds. The Vaiṣṇava *brahmāṇḍa* is said to consist of fourteen worlds beyond which are the *āvaranas* and the *kāraṇasamudra*. The highest region is the *siddhaloka* where *nirviśeṣa Brahman* dwells. Nearabouts we have the *avatāras* who are *svāmsās* to God.[15] To accept a framework of planes of consciousness is to be at home in a landscape where ascent and descent are possible.

Religious art is one of the best clues to the spiritual landscapes of a people. The spiritual landscape of ancient Judah contained not only the mythology of Mt. Sinai and the cosmic powers of thunder and wind, but coincide with the actual landscape of time and space. This was incorporated by the Christian world which did not share the actual landscape of the children of Israel. Christian art gradually introduced the actual landscape with which the artist was familiar and so we find, for example, the Holy Family posing against the hills of Tuscany. There was theological warrant for the incorporation of all landscape into sacred landscape in the idea of the redemption of nature through the incarnation. Thanks to the doctrine of creation, nature was never as much of a bar as *prakṛti* was (at least in the eyes of some of the philosophical schools). It was man that sinned and not the rest of nature. So actual landscape became part of spiritual landscape via belief. The office commuter of fundamentalist persuasion can march daily upward to Zion in his journey to Charing Cross.

Now spiritual landscape in a traditional society changes very slowly in its broad features. If technology can make Hanuman's flight more convincing this is accepted with full appreciation by a village audience. But the deliberate transformation of spiritual landscape, by the reformer especially, may not 'catch on', and this perhaps most of all in lands where actual and mythical landscapes fuse. The divinized landscape of Indian bas-reliefs is a peopled landscape where the familiar earth is alive with men, gods, animals, trees and a host of mythical beings who, as it were, 'fill in the gaps' between one order of being and another. It still fairly represents the spiritual landscape of the vast majority of people in India today.

So the pendulum thesis stands in somewhat qualified

manner. But the demythologized phase which we are possibly on the brink of has little or nothing in common with what the word has come to indicate elsewhere. Here we find neither the quest for the historic (in the sense in which Biblical studies have usually been motivated by this quest) nor any widespread attempt to recast religious language in response to scientific and other challenges. The mystique of nationalism, something which affects all peoples in their pre-independence and early post-independence phases, *tends* to be succeeded by the mystique of secularism (unless it is succeeded by the mystique of sub-nationalism[16] or ethnic pluralism). The 'daylight' world of peace and justice which the secularist strives to carve out of the tough-grained timber of actualities is inspired by an eschatological idea. In so-called developed societies the high priests of the new mythology are the technocrats. Because of the far-reaching impact of the new mythology through the media, and the prestige attached to the 'efficient' and the 'successful' and, above all, because of the level of economic prosperity achieved under its inspiration, the secular world-view in such societies provides the dominant style of life. The implication is clear. What started as a demythologized model, a rebound one, itself acquires the characteristics of a myth. The secularist model 'catches on' when it is seen to be visibly at work. But in societies where there are many levels of living, in Dr.B.N.Ganguli's illuminating phrase, secularist thinking will be, and is, confined to upper middle-class circles in towns. The factors which offer resistance to secularist changes in spiritual landscape are, it would seem, economic. The country boat[17] is relied on in the absence of any effective alternative. Not too much importance, then, should be attached to the opinion of some scholars that a world-view which centres on the working-out of individual destinies over many lives will necessarily set its sights on an other-worldly existence. Similarily *māyāvāda* could never have been extensively operative as a concept in the everyday thinking of a mainly agricultural people whose daily existence centred on the stark realities of the land, cattle, seed-time and harvest, pestilence, famine, and invasion. How then do the changes come about? A sense of spiritual crisis comes about when there is a visible conflict between the various contents of the 'life-world', e.g. the clash between urban affluenc and unhappiness in personal life, the profession of democracy and the prevalence of undemocratic practices, the assumption that education provides an open sesame and the fact of educated unemployment, etc. It is also almost a commonplace to say that the chasm between the rich and the poor sends some of the latter straight into the camp of the secular eschatologists. All these factors produce, or at least help to generate, a change in spiritual landscape which may take the form of anomie, a search for 'other gods', or a retreat to the private landscapes of fantasy.

The many-levelled, many-structured character of the Indian spiritual landscape allows for alteration in some sectors accompanied by a sense of time standing still in others. The mode of rationality which sees good sense in the principle of each thing in its proper place (e.g. antibiotic drugs for virus infections and the astrologer's advice before making an important journey) is different from the mode which sees in consistency the only possible form of rational belief and behaviour. The principle of each in its proper place (I am not thinking here of this as a directive principle of social organization, for there is more mobility in Indian society today than it is usually given credit for) can work in various ways. Let me illustrate. It can allow for reform in one sector along with letting things be as they are in other sectors; say, a willingness to go in for family planning but continuing to consult astrologers about one's daughter's wedding. There is also a counterpart to the anomie induced by complete efficiency of the western urban kind, namely the anomie induced by complete *inefficiency*, e.g. "the town has always been infested by mosquitoes as long as I can remember", "the electricity supply constantly goes off", etc. There is also another consideration. Although the Hindu life-world is apparently loose-linked, and 'tinkering' (a la Popper) is possible without disturbiung the whole balance, certain moves to bring about change tend to trigger off the cry that the whole 'system' is in danger. No one who fails to be prepared for such phenomena in the Indian subcontinent will be able to understand why a host of relatively simple matters should sometimes spark off social disturbances of a violent kind.

If the above excursion is anything to go by we can begin to see why at the present moment in Indian history conceptual revision of the kind undertaken these days by theologians in the West is not conspicuously present in the writings and pronouncements of religiously-minded Hindus. Even those who rethink the tradition in order to stress activism, meliorism, etc. do so mostly on the ground that the tradition *already* contains this-worldliness, atheism, rejection of transcedence, and so on. Even in a demythologizing period of history, when the new gods of science and technology are being somewhat hurriedly installed, the symbolism which spoke to earlier generations has not lost its power. The village-level social worker who uses puppetry to carry a message, enlisting epic heroes of ancient times on his side, the psycho-analyst who does not as a matter of routine automatically import Freudian or Jungian approaches but who is sensitive to the symbolism revealed in his patient's case - these are as yet pioneers. Myth and symbols enter not only into the life of worship, but into man's entire creative life, including his aspirations to change his environment. It may be that the craftsman, the artist, and the social worker may yet have as much, if not more, to offer in the on-going 'open' period of history in which we now live, when old symbols are being enlivened and new ones are acquiring power, as the scholar who pores over texts and attempts to wrest the meanings from words whose resonance has been lost in the corridors of times long past.

NOTES

1. Vide Chapter 2, p. 15 ff.
2. In the Persian tradition Ahriman proceeded from one of Ormuzd's doubting thoughts.
3. *Concordant Discord*, p. 117.
4. In the sense in which K. C. Bhattacharyya used this word.
5. *The Universal Religion*. Religious instruction founded on sacred authorities. *World of Raja Rammohun Roy,* Vol. 1, ed. by Jogendra Chandra Ghose, p. 189.
6. Ibid., p. 346.
7. Introduction to translations of several principle books, passages and texts of the Vedas and some controversial

works on Brahmanical Theology, 1832, p. viii.

8. *The English Works of Raja Rammohun Roy*, Allahabad: The Panini Office, 1906, p. 908.
9. *Sebaker Nibedan*, pp. 178-79.
10. *Complete Works*, II, p. 313.
11. *Amrita Bazar Patrika*, 2-8-1934.
12. *Young India*, 4-5-1921.
13. *Young India*, 24-3-1927.
14. Vide Chapter IV.
15. Vide Rupa Gosvamin's *Laghu Bhāgavatāmṛta*.
16. This can, but need not, release forces which work against secularism.
17. A very suggestive analogy used by Professor Nirmal Kumar Bose to demolish the association of the 'tradition' with the 'backward'.

Chapter-6

Cultural Transmission in Indian Civilization

McKIM MARRIOTT

Chapter-6

We see the civilization of India changing before our eyes from a rich old cultural mansion of many levels and varied styles into a more uniform structure comprising a few levels of standard design. One way of understanding this ongoing transformation may be to examine it in relation to changes in channels of cultural transmission[1].

Networks, Centres, Levels, and Specialists

India's indigenous channels of cultural transmission formed very wide and complex networks of many kinds. They connected each small rural community with multiple centres of many types — market towns, seats of different political powers, shrines of diverse deities, educational centers, and so forth. Each indigenous center of Indian civilization was at once distinctive and culturally heterogeneous. The area of influence of each center was also likely to overlap broadly with the hinterlands of other centers. Such an organization of networks and centers interrelated many territorial subscultures (Cohn and Marriot, 1958). Articulating these networks were cultural specialists (Singer, 1955-29-30), serving as "hinge groups" (Redfield, 1956: 43-44) or cultural "brokers" (Wolf, 1956: 1075-76). There were legions of intermediaries in the networks of Indian civilization, and thus was little need for direct communication between cultural levels. Such a tangled web of indirect and specialized contacts seem to have favored an elaborate cultural stratification and to have conserved and promoted cultural variety (Cohn and Marriott, 1958).

The cultural stratification referred to here as characteristics of past Indian civilization may be defined as a series of broadly coincident distinctions between the more authoritative or widespread cultural traditions, or those which cultivated by persons of higher standing, or maintained through literary and especially Sanskrit media, on the one hand; and the popular or local cultural traditions, or those carried on by persons of lower standing, or those existing only in vernacular media, or without literary, on the other hand. Redfield and Singer (1954) have dealt with the extremes of this stratification as a contrast between a "great tradition" and "little traditions". In actually, one may always have confronted a more subtly graduated series of relatively greater or lesser, more or less authoritative, more or less wide spread levels (Srinivas, 1952 : 212-18; Singer, 1955, 1958).

That cultural stratification and variety were permitted and promoted by the old networks of communications is shown by several recent studies of cultural transmission. V. Raghavan (1958) lists a large number of media of "popular religious instruction" which for centuries transmitted the messages of the greater Indian traditions of unlettered audiances. Among these media were recitation of fixed oral texts, story telling, singing, drama, and so forth, each medium having its own specialists, often of several kinds. To Raghavan's list of traditional media, William McCormack (1958) adds the performance of sacraments of the individual's life cycle and the holding of fairs; these media were significant for followers of the Virasaiva or Lingayat religion and undoubtedly have had importance everywhere in Indian civilization. Shah and Shroff (1958) further shown how a caste of genealogists in Gujarat worked to connect their earthly patrons who were not always of the high castes, with ancient, mythical, or even cosmogonic traditions of the prestigious past.

Within a single medium, such as the continuing epic drama, one can see how chains of specialists operated to transmit cultural materials from higher to lower levels. Norvin Hein's description of the Ram Lila (1958) exemplifies the complexity of this process. Following priestly ceremonies, the biography of Ram is cantillated by a specialists, who reads from a famous seventeenth-century poetic text composed in the vernacular of a neighbouring region. This text is itself an adaptation and reworking of an ancient, very widely revered Sanskrit prototype. But even the seventeenth-century text is not easily understood by modern audience, and not all parts are of interest; yet it is sacred, and must be read in its entirety. Actors fill this gap, dramatizing the more popular passages while the cantillation continues, but putting these passages into succint modern speech, accompanied by music and gesture, on the stages provided by loacal houses and temples. Materials of the Hindu great tradition are and were thus conveyed, altered first to religion, then to parochial and nonliterate forms, by a series of intervening specialists. The transmission of cultural materials through such an old-style network, whether downward as in this complex dramatic movement or upward (Marriott, 1955 : 197-99), typically involved several translations and therefore tended to preserve cultural variety at each level.

Villiage Structure as a Nonimitative Order

The old structure of Indian rural society was also in several ways inimical to the transmission of cultural materials: to a surprising degree, the old Indian village's social order was a nominative order. A case in point is the finding, by John Gumperz, of six distinguishable dialects in a single North Indian village of about five thousand persons. Although one of these dialects is identifiable as the "standard, prestige dialect" of the area, five large segments of the village population do not imitate this model. Instead, they preserve nonstandard dialects peculiar to their respective castes, kin and neighbourhood groupings, or conservative outlook. Lack of contact among speakers of these different dialects cannot explain most of the differences, for villagers who speak differently are often engaged in the same tasks and otherwise meet frequently. Yet only friendships among villagers of equal status seem to present effects channels for cultural transmission across dialect boundaries within the village (Gumperz, 1958). Reasons for the conservation of such linguistic diversity must rather be sought in the social structure of the community: occupants of different or lower statuses — members of separate groups or persons standing at the lower end of a ranked relationship, as employee-employer, for example — seem not to regard any higher or more standard dialect as a model appropriate for them to emulate.

One here senses a positive valuation of knowing one's reference group and keeping to it. Martin Oraons, in his recent report on cultural change among the Santals of southern Bihar (1959), notes the reluctance of certain tribesmen overtly to adopt higher Hindu ways. He explains that emulation of Hindu ways would conflict with the demands of tribal solidarity, which dictate a maintenance of distinctive ethnic features. Such social considerations surely also limit cultural transfer among the Hindu castes[2].

Probably of great effect, too, in discouraging imitation were certain aspects of village caste hierarchies. Caste ranking in existing villages of old style seems generally to depend on gestures showing actual ritual dominance or subordination in relation to other local castes. For most castes, rank is not much affected by customary attributes as such. The ancient, four-fold classification of *varna*—the Brahman, Ksatriya, Vaisya, and Sudra ways of life—represents for villagers not so much a classification of caste ranks as a set of alternative interactional strategies emphasizing use of ritual knowledge, pwer, wealth or service, respectively. A caste may rise or fall many steps of rank by use of any one of these four strategies. Generally it has little local incentive to imitate the ideal way of life of any *varna* other than that of its own identification (Marriott, 1959). Thus the majority of the meat-eating, liquor-drinking Kodagus of Coorg can gain recognition as an exalted Ksatriya-like caste merely by employing Brahmans and other castes and by stressing their own landed power; they have no need themselves to emulate Brahman vegetarianism, teetotalism, and so forth (Srinivas, 1952 : 32-34, 227).

Furthermore, even when a higher caste's way of life was emulated or exaggerated by a lower caste, as sometimes happened with the same or related *varnas,* it was usually the way of life of the local high caste which was taken as a model, not the distant classical ideal. Thus a Distiller caste in the remote village studied by F. G. Bailey, wishing to identify itself with a Brahman like standing in the community, does not feel obliged to give up eating mutton, for the local Brahmans themselves eat mutton; the Distillers merely demand their mutton on the hoof and do their own butchering to insure purity (Bailey, 1957 : 188-89). This example recalls once more how cultural variety and an elaborate cultural stratification have been generally favored in Indian civilization by the many intermediaries who have stood astride the tangled web of traditional communication channels.

Changing Communications : Two Phases

The changes which have overtaken Indian civilization during

recent times may be compared in their effects with several centuries of momentous events in the history of European civilization — the Protestant Reformation and the Reniassance, the development of printing, the establishment of parliamentary governments, the rise of nationalism, the beginnings of mass education and the mass media, and so forth. A partly parallel series of events began in India during the last century of the British period, was greatly accelerated during the past generation, and has been moving towards a climax since Independence.

Such changes have had great consequences for India's channels of cultural transmission. A few of the larger centers of civilization have been strengthened in their influence through growth of their own populations, and through the metropolitan concentration of industrial, financial, and political control. Central strength and govenment patronage have diminished the importance of the many small civilizational centers and have introduced the possibility of developing a more authoritative central version of the national civilization. At the same time, the new means of quick and large-scale communication have been setting up more direct contact between civilizational centres and rural masses, obviating an elaborate corps of intermediary specialists and cutting through many previous layers of cultural stratification. Where dozens of readers and actors once played a local version of the epic drama of Ram in each of hundreds of provincial towns, a movie on the same theme now issues straight from Bombay or Madras (cf. McCormack, 1958 : 334-35; Singer, 1958 : 357-59).

These alterations in the channels of communication appear to be having large effects upon the content and organization of Indian civilization. Two phases of change may be distinguished speculatively : the first affects mainly the little traditions, relating them more immediately with greater levels of tradition, often replacing parts of their content with borrowing of a more Sanskritic sort; the second affects both greater and lesser tradition, as the higher levels are themselves subjected to choice and reduction.

The first phase of change is characteristic of the later

nineteenth century, although similar tendencies were to be seen in medieval devotional movements and still continue today. In this phase, indirect, specialist-mediated communication from high to low levels of culture is supplemented by more direct communication on a larger scale. Such communication may have been assisted occasionally in the past by vigorous oral propaganda, but now is facilitated by printing, rapid transportation, and other devices of the new technology. The movement of people and ideas is hastened and intensified both along existing channels in education, pilgrimage, and politics, and along new, shorter, more immediate routes.

This first phase of change in an era of big books, and of increased popular contact with the great books of ancient and medieval Hinduism. This is the juncture at which the oral texts of the vedas were first reduced to writing. It is the time when epic, philosophic, and ritual texts were first fully published in extensive editions. This first phase thus also initiates the decline of the older oral media, including both the techniques of Vedic memorization and the many styles of oral interpretation. Walking libraries begin to be replaced by stationery ones (cf. Ghurye, 1950 : 1-22).

In the second phase, characteristic of the twentieth century and actuely characteristic of the years since 1947, there arises a national demand for authoritative cultural knowledge. The need to possess a common national culture begins to dissolve the old cultural stratification. In this phase there is necessarily a condensation and selection of small parts out of the vast corpus of classical tradition for mass dissemination. Selection for mass participation means that the more esoteric elements tend to be neglected while other more readily intelligible and accessible, if less sacred, elements are brought to the fore as representative of the transformed great tradition of the civilisation. If the first phase is an age of large books, this second phase is an age of pamphlets.

Phase of Change in a Civilizational Center

One can readily perceive the impact of these alterations of cultural channels in one of the great centers of Hindu pilgrimage.

The sacred city of Gaya may serve as an example, through the recent report by L. P. Vidyarthi (1961). For more than a millennium, Gaya in Bihar had been celebrated in Sanskrit myths and manuals as one of the foremost places for observing shraddha, the Brahmanic ritual for the worship and pacification of the spirits of departed ancestors. Even by primitive means of transportation and under conditions of political insecurity, probably close to twenty thousand pilgrims had come annually to Gaya during the closing years of the eighteenth century. For Hindus in the more distant corners of India, a pilgrimage to Gaya in each generation had been a mark of cultural aristoracy.

The advent of the Pax Britannica rapidly raised the annual volume of pilgrims to one hundred thousand persons; later, the establishment of a major railway junction at Gaya helped to raise the number to three hundred thousand person per year by the early twentieth century. Lavish private donations to the hereditary high priests of Gaya had nourished an elaborate local stratification of sacred specialists, shrines, and theology. But since the Gaya pilgrimage had grown to be a prominent national insituation, government patronage and control had become virtual necessities. Priests, pilgrims, and hostels were now licensed and regulated. The claims of formerly subordinate specialists were recognised by courts of law. The wealthy pilgrims' lengthy original tour to fortyfive shrine in holy Gaya was reduced for the masses of impecunious visitors to a peremptory call at a mere three or four architecturally notable points. National monuments, state parks, and the buildings of international associations have now begun to rise over the ruins of the sacred ground, while the volume of pilgrimage has declined sharpy, a victim of secularism and economic leveling. The great-traditional complex at Gaya thus gained at first a new and more direct relationship with a massive clientele, but was itself then radically transformed by forces inherent in its new network of communications.

Change at the Village Level : Caste Cultures and Mobility

Recent field studies focussed on religious changes among certain low Hindu caste may serve to illustrate the distinction between the two phases as observed at the village level. Bernard Cohn (1955, 1958) shows how the Camārs of one village expressed their ambitions during the nineteenth century and until recent times through the Siva Narayani devotional sect, medieval in origin. The sect stresses the direct relation of the worshipper with certain sacred Sanskritic texts and in its rites imitates Brahmanical rituals. Ambitious Camārs were also seeking to make their family customs conform more closely with what they considered to be model features of the high caste Hindu family, ignoring an opposite trend among families of the dominant and high-ranking Thakurs in their own village. A second phase of change has begun to emerge only since independence with the extension of political suffrage : the new religious focus is not on ancient models (texts and rituals) but on the person of a Camar saint, Rai Das, and on legends of his personal virtues and spiritual achievements. Whereas the earlier phase of change was Sanskritic in charatcter and concerned with fuller adoption of the prestigious and esoteric content of high Hinduism, the second phase is popular, exoteric, greatly simplified, and politically oriented to participation in the mass society.

A parallel development may be seen in the changing religion of a group of Sweepers studied in another village by Pauline Mahar (1960). What may be identified as the first or Sanskritic phase was begun for these Sweepers by missionaries of the Arya Samah movement of the later nineteenth century. This movement advocated a direct return to the original Vedic texts and ways of worship, and a rejection by the group of intervening levels of culture and specilization. The second phase, inspired at first by the independence movement and led by urban leaders, reinterprets the earlier cult to favour individual effort, education, thrift, and service to the nation.

Difficulties are sometimes met in trying to distinguish these two phases of change chronologically, for the two may occur toghether. The situation depicted by Chon (1955, 1958) is by no means rare. Here, members of a low caste were occupied with emulating what they perceived as a high-caste model while members of the local high castes were themselves abandoning that model and looking towards a new national culture. Occasionally a single group will show both tendencies simultaneously, or a single institution will seem to show two directions of change (e.g. Mandelbaum, 1948 : 137-39, and 1955 : 244-45;

Gough, 1958 : 476). A distinction between the two phases may nevertheless be made analytically if attention is given to differences of reference and content in the emulatory process. And generally, the first phase has probably precede the second.

The foregoing instances concerning the ambitious of contemporary low-caste groups imply that there are modest regularities in changing types of social mobility. It has been pointed out above that before the occurrence of the changes under discussion caste mobility in villages was achieved more by dominance in ritual interaction than by imitation of higher ways of life; when loftier models of customary behavior were chose, these were usually the actual usages of higher castes in the same village.

Changes in methods of mobility appear to parallel the phases of general civilizational change. Under the condition of the first phase, low castes typically attempt to improve their standings by altering their customs to resemble the ideal ways of life of the caste or theoretically higher *varna* with whom they claim identity. This is that naive, direct, literal approach to upward mobility which M.N. Srinivas has called "Sanskritization" (1952 : 30). While the problem of mobility has undoubtedly been approached in this manner by certain ambitious castes even in earlier times, universal prerequisties of such an approach would seem to include a workable knowledge of the great traditional ideals of the upper castes and a vivid sense of the reality of a wider sphere of social reference than the village (Marriott, 1959). A wide sphere of social reference does come clearly into view for many castes in the later nineteenth century, as suggested by the parallel development of Sankritization and Westernization (Srinivas, 1956). Srinivas points out, however, that Sanskritization as a technique of mobility is older than Westernization and that the social structure conditions of its earlier occurrence are unknown. Earlier instances of Sanskritic emulation thus need to be re-examined: the present analysis leads to the hypotheses that such older instances will prove to involve castes having a broad social or political stance and an unusually close contact with representative of higher cultural levels, owing either to their possession of predominant power over a large area, or to other special circumstances.

Finally, the Sanskritic fashion of attempting upward mobility seems to be superceded, as in the examples cited, by a second, modern phase, in which the criteria of rank and the models of high caste conduct are radically altered. Overt ritual dominance and the ideals of *varna* are both rejected in favour of newly drawn, universal standards of economic and intellectual achievement.

Consequences for Cultural Content

The first shape of change described above may be regarded as a continuation of tendencies already inherent in Indian civilization. At first there need be no alteration in the cultural content of the greater levels of tradition. The basis for a broad cultural consciousness has been in existence for many centuries (Redfield and Singer, 1954: 68-70), but participation in the higher levels of culture was not previously accessible to many. Aided by printing techniques, increased literacy, and better means of transporation, higher levels of Indian culture are brought within easier reach of favoudably placed local groups throughout the society. A broader field of social, as distinguished from cultural, reference comes into existence for more villagers, while the cultural contents of that field are still represented for most persons by great traditional materials, specially the widespread Sanskritic culture borne by Brahman castes and other high castes among the "twice-born" *varnas*. Regional and local variants tend to be bypassed, as do many of the intermediary cultural specialists. But the content of higher cultural levels remain essentially unaltered while they are imported into the village scene more readily.

The second phase of change, when masses of people come to be directly involved, sees the appearance of greater consequences for Indian Civilization; a standard authoritative version, limited in size and scope, must be selected out of the vast and varied range of the ancient whole. School text-books must be rewritten, symbols of national unification created, ways of representing the nation to the outside world established. Milton Singer has called this process "democratization" (1958 : 379). Where on an important ceremonial occasion parts of all four Vedas would once have been recited, the time limits of a large gathering now admit room for fragments of but one one Veda or none. Where many types of marriage and divorce were normally practiced in rural areas, a single narrow code of law now tends to be imposed on all (Karve, n.d.: 211-13). While singers and story tellers used once to travel slowly across the land, bringing high art to each locality in the varied styles of a wide area, many talented performers now look to the radio for an audience and a living, and thereby submit their art to a competitive process of selection, condensation, and standardization. The radio or the mass meeting many communicate cultural material more rapidly to a large audience, but the sum and variety of the material communicated by them are likely to be less.

So also with pilgrimages. The people of each small community once maintained personal, pedestrian ties with a unique series of dozens of regional shrines; now the prestigious grand pilgrimage is accomplished by purchasing a railroad ticket for one of the "standard round tours" encompassing a large part of the whole nation (Central Railway, 1955). The mileage of each pilgrim's travels may be as great as before, but all paths are now narrowed to exlude those hundreds of once-eminent sacred places which are not conveniently close to the main railroad lines. A map of the Indian railroads may thus become a better guide to the sacred geography of the emerging India than any painstaking research into the epic wanderings of Ram and the Pandavas.

Conclusions

Whether one plots railroads and pilgrimages, the dissemination of books, the movement of personnel and ideas through the modern educational system, the organization of government and elections, or the influence of radio broadcasting, one discovers channels of cultural transmission whose radical or pyramidal form contrasts starkly with the tangled networks of medieval Indian civilization.Dominating the new channels are a few metropolitan centres, nearly identical culturally, having clear and separate jurisdictions. Dominating each urban center are a few relatively centralized institutions.

The emergence of such a new pattern of communications brings with it a newly formed Indian civilization. Two phases may be distinguished. In the first, communication is intensified, one way, from higher to lower levels of culture; Sanskritic models are taken for direct emulation, while intermediate levels and specialists are by passed; the contents of lesser traditions are replaced by borrowings from above. In the second and succeeding phase, popular needs begin to work changes in the contents and form of the higher cultural levels themselves, selecting and condensing material suitable for mass dissemination as part of a new democratic national culture.

BIBLIOGRAPHY

Baily, F. G.

1957 Caste and the Economic Frontier, Manchester, University of Manchester Press.

Central Railway

1955 Standard Round Tours for Business, Pleasure and Pilgrimage. Economic Weekly 7 : 330. Bombay.

Chon, Bernard S.

1955 The Changing Status of a Depressed Caste. *In* Village India, ed. McKim Marriott, pp. 78-101. Chicago University of Chicago Press.

1958 Changing Traditions of a Low Caste. *In* Traditional India : Structure and Change, ed. Milton Singer, pp. 413-21. Journal of American Folklore, Vol. 71, No. 281.

Cohn, Bernard S., and McKim Marriott.

19587 Networks and Centres in the Integration of Indian Civilization. Journal of Social Research I : 1-9. Ranchi, Bihar.

Ghurye, K. G.

1950 Preservation of Learned Tradition in India. Bombay, Popular Book Depot.

Gough, E. Kathleen

1958 Cults of the dead among the Nayars. *In* Traditional India : Structure and Change, ed. Milton Singer, pp. 446-78. Journal of American Folklore, Vol. 71, No. 281.

Gumperz, John J.
1958 Dialect Differences and Social Stratification in a North Indian Village. American Anthropologist 60 : 668-82.

Hein, Norvin.
1958 The Ram lila. *In* Traditional India : Structure and Change, ed. Milton Singer, pp. 279-304. Journal of American Folklore, Vol. 71, No. 281.

Karve, Irawati
n.d. Some Studies in the Making of a Culture Pattern. *In* Essays in Anthropology Presented to Rai Bahadur Sarat Chandra Roy, ed. J. P. Mills et al, pp. 206-18. Lucknow, Maxwell Co.

Mahar, Pauline Moller
1960 Changing Religious Practices of an Untouchable Caste. Economic Development and Cultural Change 8 : 279-87. Chicago.

Mandelbaum, David G.
1948 The Family in India. Southwestern Journal of Anthropology 4 : 123-39, Albuquerque.
1955 The World and World-view of the Kota. *In* Village India, ed. McKim Marriott, pp. 1712-22. Chicago University of Chicago Press.

Marriott, Mckim
1955 Little Communities in an Indigenous Civilization. *In* Village India, ed. McKim Marriott, pp. 1712-22. Chicago University of Chicago Press.
1959 Interactional and Attributional Theories of Caste Ranking. Man in India 39 : 92-107. Ranchi, Bihar.

McCormack, William
1958 The Forms of Communication in Virasaiva Religion. In Traditional India : Structure and Change, ed. Milton Singer, pp. 325-55. Journal of American Folklore, Vol. 71, No. 281.

Orans, Martin
1959 A Tribe in Search of a Great Tradition : The Emulation-Solidarity Conflict. Man In India 39 : 108-14. Ranchi, Bihar.

Raghavan, V.
1958 Methods of Popular Instruction in South India. *In* Traditional India : Structure and Change, ed. Milton Singer, pp. 336-44. Journal of American Folklore, Vol. 71, No. 281.

Redfield, Robert
1956 Peasant Society and Culture. Chicago, University of Chicago Press.

Redfield, Robert and Milton Singer
1954 The cultural Role of Cities. Economic Development and Cultural Change 3 : 53-73. Chicago.

Shah, A. M., and R. G. Shroff
1958 The Vahivanca Barots of Gujrat : A Caste of Genealogists and Mythographers. *In* Traditional India : Structure and Change, ed. Milton Singer, pp. 246-76. Journal of American Folklore, Vol. 71, No. 281.

Singer, Milton
1955 The Cultural Pattern of Indian Civilization. Far Eastern Quarterly 15 : 23-46.
1958 The Great Tradition in a Metropolitan Centre : Madras. *In* Traditional India : Structure and Change, ed. Milton Singer, pp. 347-88. Journal of American Folklore, Vol. 71, No. 281.

Srinivas, M. N.
1952 Religion and Society among the Coorgs of South India. Oxford, Clarendon Press.
1956 A Note on Sanskritization and Westernization. Far Eastern Quarterly 15 : 481-96.

Vidyarthi, L. P.
1961 The Sacred Complex in Hindu Gaya. Bombay, Asia Publishing House.

Wolf, Eric R.
1956 Aspects of group Relations in a Complex Society : Mexico. American Anthropologist 58 : 1065-78.

Chapter-7

THINKING ABOUT THE HINDU WAY OF LIFE[1]

A. AIYAPPAN

Chapter-7

Introduction

I am a Hindu and when I talk of Hinduism and Indian faiths allied to Hinduism, it is extremely difficult to avoid getting ethnocentric. I have some advantage over most other Indians in an effort to look objectively at India; this advantage I owe to my training in anthropology and to my familiarity with a wide range of faiths from the simplest to the most complex. Some of you may be curious about my own personal beliefs and convictions, so I had better confess that I have acquired them the hard way, beginning as a rationalist, and then rediscovering for myself, in a lay fashion, the profundity of Hindu religious thought by personal contact with men and women near the sources of religious light. The understanding of one's own religion is difficult for most of us whether we are of the east or of the west, Hindu or Christian or Moslem. The difficulty becomes almost insuperable when you are trying to understand the faiths of other people. Those of you who have tried to translate poetry would know very well how difficult it is to render a set of linguistic symbols correctly and intelligently into another language. To translate the religious thought of the Hindus is a difficult job, due to my own inadequate religious experience, due to the difficulty of the language employed and thirdly to our ethnocentrism, yours going against mine in spite of our best efforts to counteract its influence.

How Misunderstanding Arises

Misunderstanding thrives when there are lacking two essentials of understanding, namely, sympathy and empathy. If this impediment is added to the natural difficulty of understanding the religious experience of people with strange cultural background, the situation becomes intolerable to men of goodwill. India has been lucky in having such great European and American admirers of her religion and culture as Max Muller, Romain Rolland, Bloomfield an Emerson, but a good number of the lesser fry have been quite unable to understand her. The most recent example I have come across is an American diplomat's condemnation of Indians as worshippers of the phallus. This diplomat must have got his information second-hand from missionary writers of the eighteenth or the seventeenth century, for Christian missionaries of the present day known their field better. By mis-interpreting a Hindu religious symbol to his readers all the world over, this person not only misleads them but also does a grievous wrong to millions of Indians. He tries to denigrate Hindus as a set of depraved people who have not outgrown barbarism. If he had taken the trouble to ask any Hindu, he would have got the straight and honest explanation that the stone cylinders or *lingas* installed in the temples of Siva do not have any association with sex in minds of the devout men and women who venerate them as the symbol of the third person of the Hindu Trinity. What these religious representations, images, rituals, etc., mean and do to the people concerned is the subject that interests the unprejudiced observer who, I am sure, will find his task as interesting as a voyage of exploration. I have found it interesting myself.

Try to imagine the pain you would be inflicting on a devout Roman Catholic if you were superciliously to refer to him as a worshipper of blood and wine or of crossed battens of wood.

An American friend of mine, who was Professor of Sociology in the Colombo University, used to offer a coconut to the Hindu god Ganesa in the same manner as his Hindu companions, and the amount of good will this simple act of his produced was, believe it or not, immense.

I would therefore ask for your sympathetic understanding, for in talking about religion, unless one is assured of it, the sharing of religious experience and awe becomes impossible.

India Not Hyper-Religious

In an article of his published a few years ago in the Journal *Visvabharati* of poet Tagore's University in Bengal, Professor J. B. S. Haldane tried to demonstrate that England was a more religious-minded country than India. His argument was that for the practice of such simple virtues as charity, honesty, etc. and for the capacity to stand up and fight for one's principles and convictions, a certain optimum standard of living and security was essential. In the absence of these things, most Indians, according to Haldane, are condemned to a vegetative existence. Though I cannot accept his reasoning, yet the statement serves as a corrective to the common belief that India is a hyper-religious country. In schools and colleges, in political groups and parliaments, in towns and villages of India, it is possible to see as much irreligion as in any other country. The state of disrepair of several of our temples gives clear proof of the decreasing support religious institutions are able to enlist nowadays. For political and other reasons, the Government of India, at present seems to me to be one of the most secular of governments. My knowledge of the religious climate of the United States in very slight, but I get the impression that this country is far more religious than most outsiders suppose it to be. In the small town of Ithaca[2], I was surprised to find a dozen churches most of them well supported and used by the local communities. On Sundays I spend a great deal of my time listening to talks on religion, the fervour of some of which I have found most impressive. This seems to me to be a land of people who seek salvation through hard work — *Karma Yoga*, as Hindus call it.

Experiment in Life of the Spirit in India – Yoga

Life in God is a trait shared by all mankind; India does not have more of it than other nations of the world. Interesting experiments in dealing with the supernatural have been carried out by men all through the centuries, all over the world. The mystic spiritual exercise known under the generic name Yoga with its elaborate intorspective psychology and philosophy is perhaps the most significant contribution which India has made to our common religious heritage. I was not interested, for a long time, even in reading about these esoteric practices, because, as a rationalist, I had prejudged them as meaningless mental and physical acrobatics. But a few years ago something happened which compelled me to change my attitude. In my home town in India I cam across a man who demonstrated to the complete satisfaction of medical men that the autonomous nervous system which, we are taught in physiology classes, cannot be brought under volunatry control, *could* be controlled by the will of the practitioner of yoga. Body control is one of the minor branches of yoga, but it shows the mood and achievements of the ancient Hindu experiemtalists in the field of human physiology. They observed the lowered rate of heart beat, etc., in hibernating animals. If frogs and snails could do it, they thought, it should be possible for man also by practice to regulate the functioning of his heart and lungs. They succeeded in developing a system of exercise which gave them a great deal of control over the body. Psychial exercises based on Yoga which have the advantage that they do not strain the heart are being popularised in India and I am glad that they are getting known in the United States too.

Exercises of a psychological character to amplify the powers of the mind must have been the next step; and the pioneers in this line were probably the practical philosophers and seers of India, who were not satisfied with the adumbration of theories, but felt called upon, like the experimental scientist of the present day, to test the validity of their theories in the laboratory of life and often they became their ownb guinea pigs. The first great work on yogic spiritual exercises is the sage Patanjali's *Yogasutra* of about the second century B.C., considered by the most competent occidental philosophers as one of the clearest and most astounding works of philosophical prose in the world.

What is the nature of the "I", or the "Ego", is the question which Patanjali seeks to answer. And the answer can be experienced not heard or read, only when all the spontaneous activities of the mindstuff have been intentionally stopped.

Mind, according to the science of yoga, is in constant flux, transforming itself into the shape of all the subjects of which it becomes aware. There are five great obstacles to the complete stilling of the mind, which might be summed up as the conscious human personality and the unconscious biological drives that support the personality structure. The human being is afraid of the dissolution of the strands of its individualisation, but the revelation of the true Self can take place only after such a dissolution. In seven stages of self discipline, withdrawal of the senses, contemplation and final trance, the yogi realizes that the true self is the "still witness", which is unattached to the mental processes. The true "I" is thus isolated, a process which is said to give heavenly joy to the fortunate person who effects this dissolution.

Yoga is an attempt to enthrone God in your heart to the complete exclusion of everything else; or, in lay language, it is the answer to the prayer for the capacity to see yourself as objectively as possible. Criticism has been made against yoga that it is a kind of auto-intoxication. But the proof of the pudding is in the eating. I have derived considerable benefit not directly, but indirectly from some of the great yogis of modern India, integrated men shedding light and radiance everywhere. Sri Aurobindo of Pondicherry, Ramana Maharshi or Tiruvannamalai near Madras, and Sri Narayana of Travancore, who were in our midst until recently, Sri Ramakrishna and Sri Vivekananda of Bengal, who flourished in the second half of the nineteenth century, were modern yogis to whom all Indian owe a great deal. They were practical mystics, but also most effective leaders of men.

Yoga in India is very ancient; if the interpretation of the significance of some of the seals and figurines of the Indus Valley civilization is correct, then the practice of yoga has a history of at least 5,000 years. Whatever be its antiquity, yoga of the variety I have described could not have been anything but esoteric and possible of attainment by a very limited number of people. The common people found, in the numerous temples of India, the means for spiritual discipline, solace and security. In some of the shrines of the backward sections of the people, animal sacrifices, and the propitiation of the spirits, personifying disease and pestilence, are in vogue, but the Brahmins and others practising more refined forms of worship seldom troubled themselves about stopping such practices, for Indians have generally been very tolerant. In fact, some Indian sects such as the Jains consider it a sin to try to convert other people to their faith; it is regarded a form of violence.

Temples directed to yogic ends

A temple houses the symbolic or anthropomorphic representation of a god or goddess. Though the representation by itself becomes a sacred object after the series of rites to invest it with "life", there is no confusion in the mind of any worshipper about the image being a mere symbol, so that the expression "image worship" or idolatry applied to the Hindus is incorrect. The object of worship is the deity represented by the symbol. The god worshipped in the temple is a highly humanized god, for abstract concepts are beyond the powers of comprehension of most of us. The grandest temples of India are in Southern India where they are referred to as the "palace" of such and such a god. In fact the rituals of these temples follow the daily and seasonal routines of the court of the Hindus monarchs. Early in the morning the god-king is roused from his sleep by the strains of soft music and the devotional songs of devotees some of whom reach the temple by 3 a.m. The image is bathed and dressed and decorated and various offerings are placed before it, including flowers, incense, lighted lamps, and food. The sweet scent of the incense fills the air, the sound of the bells fills the ear, and the worshippers now view the image through dozens of little flickering lights and offer their worship. Though I am not a temple-goer myself, I cannot deny that the whole atmosphere of the temple at the time of the public worship has an elevating character which in the Christian world people experience at the time of Holy Mass.

Both in the rituals of the temple and in domestic worship, various psychological and mechanical devices to imprint on the mind and even on the body of the worshipper the idea and the presence of the deity are employed. The devotee purifies his body and mind and invokes the presence of the god in the lotus of his heart. Ritual formulae with sound symbols resembling, when reduced to writing, some kind of spiritual algebra, gesture language, geometrical representations of the deity and religious dances are included in the devotional paraphernalia. The object of all these is to bridge the seeming distance between the worshipper and his god, and when this is acomplished the two no longer are separate. The worshipper becomes a liberated man by the grace of his god; he reaches the same goal which the yogi reached by following a more troublesome course.

Religious Universalism of India :

Religion is a matter of insight and intuition, and it is difficult for me to agree with some of my fellow anthropologists who talk about religion evolving. In spite of the seeming outward differences in form and symbols, the quality and flavour of all religions are, at their source, the same. This is the belief which Ramakrishna Paramahansa, Vivekananda and Mahatma Gandhi have been advocating and which most Indians do not have any difficulty in subscribing to Ramakrishna, the priests yogi of a temple in Begal saw visions of Christ and Mohammed just as he saw visions of Krishna and the Great Mother Kali whose priest he was. In the dozens of his most wonderful parables he taught his vast body of disciples that the differences which we see in religious practices are the result of the differences in the cultural background of the people. They are not the result of any qualitative differences in religious insight.

Before coming out to this country, I used to have the impression that domestic life in the United States would be different from ours. I do not know how I got this impression, but that is the stereotype current in India. After some familiarity with the life of the American men and women at Cornell, I find that parental affection, conjugal love, friendship, *etc.*, function with the same primeval charm (shall I say universal charm?) here as in India, and the basic similarity overshadows the differences in secondary details. We see differences more readily than similarities; we have to look for similarities. What is true of domestic life should, I feel, be true of religious life also, if we examine the problem with the attention it deserves.

One of our teachers, Sri Narayana of Travancore, used to compare the dull men, who cannot see the beauty or truth of faiths, other than their own, to the six blind men of Hindustan who tried to describe the elephant. They see reality in bits, but do not see the whole of it. Thanks to the influence of our great teachers, the capacity to see the other man's point of view in religious matter is growing among the men and women of India, which is indeed something most desirable.

India is on the whole a conservative country where changes are difficult to initiate and also to accelerate. For example, Vedic customs, rituals, and the Indo-Aryan tongue used about 4,000 years ago survive unchanged as living fossils. New forces are now at work and the pace of change seems to be unbelievably great there at the present moment. We hope that the good things of the spirit will not be swept away by the silent revolution which India now is witnessing in many spheres of life.

Both Hindus an Buddhists believe in new avatars, or incarnations. Our great philosophers Sri Aurobido believes that men with superconsciousness would evolve and set things right in this confused world. So we are full of hope about the future of mankind and thus hope is rooted in the belief that our universe is God-governed.

Chapter-8

Hindu Sects and Food Patterns in North India

K.N. SHARMA

Chapter-8

I

In recent anthropological literature on India one can find two converging trends of village and caste studies in prominence. An under current of these studies has been the study of food patterns of the people. Rural studies have offered ample opportunities to anthropologists to observe the social system of Indian villages in general and caste system in particular. Food patterns have been studied with a view to analyse inter-caste and intra-caste commensal relations, status evaluation and mobility of caste groups within the caste system from one status level to another.

Thurston found two main divisions of Brahmans in India of which the southern Panch Dravidas are pure vegetarian, whereas the Panch Gaudas need not abstain from meat and fish, though some, who live among Panch Dravidas, do so (1907-9 : 268, Vol. 1). Srinivas says that today the Brahmans are, by and large, vegetarians except the Saraswat, Kashmiri and Begali Brahmans who are non-vegetarians (1956 : 74) and that a low caste is able, in a generation or two, to rise to a higher position in the hierarchy by adopting vegetarianism and teetotalism, by sanskritising its ritual and pantheon (1952 : 30). Stevenson says that of the concomitant beliefs of the population concept some — like those concerning human emissions — are rooted in the Sanskrit scriptures (though they may antedate them), and are therefore current throughout India. Others, for example, those concerning the propriety of eating vension or fish (Hutton 1946 : 67) are subject to local variation. There is also a marked decline in the intensity of beliefs about population from South to North India. These regional variations, however, are of degree rather than of kind, and they do not affect the general framework of the caste status system, which has a considerable morphological uniformity throughout India (1954 : 48). About the prevalence of non-vegetarian food in some areas Stevenson further says : The local ritual status depends not only Indiawide beliefs, but also on variable local beliefs concerning pollution which carry most weight in their locality (Hutton 1946 : 67, 98). For example, the members of a high caste status group, who eat vension, would not thereby lose relative local ritual status (Lacey 1933 : 33) if they lived in juxtaposition with a higher status group of Rajputs who eat the meat of wild boars (Hutton 1946 : 67), or with a group of Brahmans (Ghurye 1932 : 26; Srinivas 1952 : 28) who eat meat.

If these statements are read together, the following line of reasoning emerges :

(*i*) Brahmans are vegetarians and only exceptionally non-vegetarians.

(*ii*) South[2] and North and other regional variations are of degree rather than of kind and they do not affect the general framework of Indian caste status system, through variable local beliefs have relevance in their localities.

(*iii*) The general caste status system is dependent on vegetarianism and other criteria of the Pollution concept; The local variations in it are insignificant. And,

(*iv*) therefore, a low caste is able, in a generation or two, to rise to a higher position in the caste hierarchy by adopting vegetarianism and teetotalism and by sanskritising its rituals and pantheon.

(*v*) This general framework of caste system is found throughout India, because the beliefs are rooted in the Sanskrit scriptures.

These generalisations like all other generalisations about Indian Social sysatems overlook the significant variations. It cannot be safely assumed that the value of vegetarianism is rooted in the Sanskrit scriptures and, therefore, it is prevalent throughout India. Nor can it be said, without reservations, that this value is part of caste system as such and local variations are insignificant. After going through the above statements one is left wondering why and how these local variations are persisting.

In this paper an effort has been made to explain the general prevalence of the value of vegetarianism and 'variable local, value of non-vegetarianism. No effort, however, has been made to examine its influence either on status evaluation or caste mobility. The data offered in support of the statements are from North India and therefore the statements have a direct relevance to North India only, though they may be equally valid for South India. Before the presentation of data and their analysis, it is necessary to give a brief introduction to the four important Hindu sects viz; Vishnuism, Shivism, Shaktism and Smartism, as they have played a significant role in establishing socio-religious values regarding vegetarianism and non-vegetarianism.

II

Vishuism, Shivism, Shaktism and Smartism

In the Rigveda we find reference to Vishnu but as a deity he is of no special eminence. After the Vedic age he becomes the undisputed Lord of the Universe for his worshippers. Today, theworship of Vishnu, especially in North India, is conspicuous by its absence. Two most important incarnations of Vishnu — Ram and Krishna — were born in U.P. and are more popular than Vishnu himself. But Vishnuism flourished exceedingly in the South, where it gave rise to a series of sub-sects. Nearly all of them reject sacrifice and make personal devotion the basis of salvation. All of them stress ceremonial purity of food as well. Even in the category of vegetarian food the Vaishnavas have two categories of prescribed and prohibited food. For example, potatoes, onions, garlic and other roots, chilies etc. are prohobited to a Vaishnava. Such food cannot be offered to deities.

In Northern India the Shaivas are less distinct as a body than in South India. However, in the South the real division is not between the worshippers of Shiva and Vishnu but between Smartas (those who follow the ancient ritual observances) and those who seek for salvation by devotion. Another school of Shivaite philosophy flourished in Kashmir from the Ninth century and Kashmiri Brahmans still follow it. In the Kashmiri school of Shivaite philosophy devotional element in non-existent. In the South, however, this aspect is as prominent in Shivism as it is in

Vishnuism. The Southern devotional Shaivas are vegetarians, while the Kashmiri Shaivas are non-vegetarians.

Shaktism flourished in North-East India with its chief sanctuary at Kamakhya in Assam. It has spread to other parts of North India but its Tantric aspects are no so prominent in North-West India as in the North-East. One of the most important doctrines of Shaktism is Tantric one, that passion can be destroyed and exhausted by passion. Panch Tattva or Five 'Makars' or Five M's are foremost features of Tantrism. These five M's are : wine (*Madya*), meat (*Mansa*), fish (*Matsya*), holy finger gestures (*Mudra*) and copulation (*Maithuna*). The devotional aspect of religion cannot exist along with these doctrines which encourage both eating of certain kinds of non-vegetarian food and wine.

The fourth sampradaya is those of Smartas. Smartas, etymologically, are followers of the behaviour pattern prescribed by Smirits. So far as the worship of deities is concerned they worship all the five important deities, i.e. Brahma, Vishnu, Shiva, Ganesh and Shakti or Mother Goddess. Smartas are without vegetarians. In the South they are in prominence. In the North their number is small and they are, therefore, less distinct.

Thus we see that preservation of life is a cardinal value in Vishnuism. Shivism is silent in this respect. Shaktism, however, encourages animal sacrifice. Eliot says : with the Vishnuism it (non-violence) is an article of faith, nor do the worshippers of Shiva usually propitiate him with animal sacrifice, though these are offered by Shaktas and also by the small class of Brahmans, who still preserve the vedic ritual (1954 : 171 Vol. II).

Each one of these sects emphasizes the worship of a specific type of class of deities. It is necessary as part of the rituals connected with the worship of a particular deity to offer some kind of food. This offering is usually called as 'Bhoga'. After the symbolic 'eating' by the deity the priest and the devout take the food so offered as 'Prasad' (favour of god). To the various incarnations of Vishnu e.g. Krishna and Ram, only vegetarian food can be offered. In the traditional Shaktism of the North-Eastern variety Mother Goddess is always offered non-vegetarian food. There are only three kinds of animals which are offered to her i.e. fish, goat and occasionally buffalo. Even in Kashmir the Shivaites never offer non-vegetarian food to Shiva but they do offer meat to Bhairavas, and lesser Rudras, such as Vatak, associated with Shiva (Madan; T.N.: personal communication). Thus Shiva himself may be treated as a Vegetarian God; his associates are, however, non-vegetarians also in the eyes of some of his devout.

It is to be noted that these sects are non-church type or in other words there is no religious bureaucracy controlling the behaviour of the followers of these sects. This situation maximises the possibilities of religious deviance (Levy, M.J.: 1952 : 373). This deviance can be observed in the behaviour of the followers of these sects. One can observe the Shivaites worshipping Vishnu and Mother Goddess in some form or the other, Vaishnavas worshipping deities of the other two sects and so on. However, there are certain sects of Vishnuism which do not allow the worship of any other deity except Krishna. These deviations have been traced at the group level. On individual level also deviation occurs, because the non-church type religions may emphasise individual religious responsibility; among the Hindus it is so. The result is that even in the same family one member may become a complete Vaishnava, leaving non-vegetarian food altogether, while others may continue to be Shaktists.

One can observe two major types of deviances. First, in which a person remains a Shakta, Vaishnava or Shaiva according to the orientation of his family, but also worships the deities of other sects. This kind of deviance is found in many groups of North India. The Shaktas of North-Eastern India are the best examples of this kind of deviance. Most of them also worship Krishna. The prominent exceptions are the followers of Ramanuja sect. These Vaishnavas worship only the incarnations of Visnhu; they do not worship any other deity. Some unorthodox Vaishnavas and Smartas worship Shakti or Mother Goddess. The difference between the Shaktas worshipping Krishna and Vaishnavas and Smartas worshipping Shakti is that the former are normally non-vegetarians and when they worship Krishna or observe the fasts and festivals associated with Vishnuism they are vegetarians; the latter are always vegetarians. They offer only vegetarian food to the Mother Goddess. This difference can be explained by the fact the offering of vegetarian food to Krishna by the Shaktas is not against Shaktism, while offering of non-vegetarian food to Mother Goddess by Vaishnavas is against the trends of Vishnuism and their behaviours have been pattered by Shaktism and Vishnuism respectively.

Secondly, one may renounce one's own sect altogether by initiation into another sect or by exigencies of natural circumstances renunciation may be persumed. This kind of variation is found among Shaktas. One may be initiated by a Guru (precepter) of a Vaishnava sect into Vishnuism. One of the important symbols of this initiation is a 'Kanthi' (a string of Tulsi beads). After such an initiation one has to renounce non-vegetarian food for all times to come. In the case of woman renunciation of Shaktism is presumed at the time of the death of her husband. A Bengali widow is not allowed to eat the non-vegetarian food at all.

In the light of the above analysis of the four sects, as they affect the behaviour of their followers in relation to the eating of vegetarian and non-vegetarian food and worshipping of deities, we can draw the following categories :—

Sect Catagories	*Major Deities Worshiped*	*Kind of Food*
1. Pure Shaktas	Shakti (Goddess Mother)	Non-vegetarian
2. Unorthodox Shatkas	Mainly Krishna besides Shakti	Normally non-vegetarian, vegetarian when Vaishnava fasts and festivals are observed.
3. Non-Shaktas	Shakti & Krishna	Vegetarian.
4. Converted Vaishnavas	Mainly Krishna	Vegetarian.
5. Pure Vaishnavas	Ram or Krishna or both	Vegetarian.
6. Unorthodox Vaishnavas	Also worship Shiva, Shakti and others	Vegetarian.

7. Shaivas (devotional)	Shiva	Vegetarian.
8. Shaiva-Shaktas	Shiva, Shakti, Krishna, etc.	Normally non-vegetarian, vegetarian when Vaishnava fasts and festivals.
9. Smartas	Brahma, Vishnu, Shiva Shakti and Ganesh	Vegetarian.

III

Broadly speaking Northern India may be divided into three regions from the point of view of the spread of these sects. In the first 4 regions may be included Assam, Bengal, Bihar and Orissa. In this region we find both Shaktism and Vishnuism, but the pre-eminence of Shaktism is apparent. Shivism also prevails, but it has been overshadowed by the other two sects. The evidence in support of the above statement is the importance of 'Durga' (Mother Goddess) in the socio-religious life of the people of this region. 'Durga-Puja' (worship of Mother Goddess which falls in Sep.-October) is the most important festival in this region. To Durga the devouts offer goats and occasionally buffaloes. In the famous temple of Kali in Calcutta the ritual sacrifice is presided over by Brahman priests and the Brahmans are not prohibited from sacrificing the animals themselves. Both the priests and the devouts partake of the sacrifice as 'Prasad' after the symbolic eating by 'Kali' (Mother Goddess). In this region many devouts of Kali are worshippers of Krishna also. On the day of Janmastami (the birthday of Krishna) such Shaktas are completely vegetarians, because Krishna or as a matter of fact both the most important incarnations of Vishnu–Ram and Krishna—are vegetarians. They fall in our first two categories respectively.

Besides Shaktists two other categories of people are also found in this region — converted Vaishnavas and non-Shaktas (for the want of a better term I have used this term). There is an initiation rite of Vaishnavas, known as 'Diksha'. The Vaishnava Gurus perform this initiation rite. When a person has been initiated into Vishnuism, he renounces Shaktism and then non-vegetarian food is tabooed to him. Such Vaishnavas never eat meat or fish. In the categories of non-Shaktas are included the widows. As soon as a married woman becomes widow she loses her rights to take non-vegetarians food. She may be initiated into Vishnuism and thereby she becomes a Vaishnava; even otherwise she does not remain a Shakta in the strict sense of the term. They fall in the third and fourth categories respectively.

In Bihar and Orissa both Vaishnava and Shakta ritual-complexes prevail. At Gaya these two complexes are represented by two famous temples of Narayan Pad and Durga. The priests and worshippers Narayan Pad are completely vegetarians. Moreover, the Marwaris coming from Rajasthan and living in Bihar have made Durga a Vaishnava (vegetarian) deity because they are basically Vaishnavas. They have adopted Durga because they have been influenced by Shaktism prevalent in this region. Their Durga is a 'Vaishnava Durga'. This is evidenced by the fact that the temples of Durga constructed by them in Girdi and other places in Bihar are called as 'Vaishnava Mandas'. In these temples, no sacrifice is offered to her. The effect of these conflicting values has been that sometomes in the same family some persons are Vaishnavas and vegetarians and some person continue to the Shaktas and non-vegetarians. (Sinha D.N., Vidyarthi L.P.: personal communication). Such Vaishnavas are converted Vaishnavas and fall in our fourth category.

The second 5 region consists of U.P. (excluding the Himalayan hills), M.P., Delhi, The Punjab, Rajasthan, Gujrat and Maharastra states. In this region Vishnuism is the most dominant sect, probably due to the factor that Ayodhya and Mathura, the birth places of Ram and Krishna respectively are in U.P. and they are the centres of several sects connected with either Ram or Krishna. The important Brahman castes or Jatis of this region are Saryupari, Kanyakubja, Sanadhya, Gauda, Malviya and Saraswat. Among Saryuparis and Kanyakubjas there are several important groups of families which are traditionally non-vegetarians. Among Saryuparis 'Bheri' and 'Bakarua' ('Bheda' means sheep and 'Bakra' means goat) clans are non-vegetarians and they are in the highest status group of Saryupari Brahmans. Among Kanyakubja Brahmans also there are several Gotragroups which are traditionally non-vegetarians and several of them are members of the highest status group of Kanyakbuja Brahmans *i.e.* twenty Biswas (Sharma, b. 1956 : 18-28). One of the most important gotras is Katyayan (the worshippers of Katyayani Mother Goddess). In this group on the occasion of Mundan (the first hair-cutting ceremony) a goat is offered to Mother Goddess. The relations of the host gathered on this occasion partake of the meat of sacrificed goat. In Gamras village at Kanyakubja Brahman families belong to middle (Panchadar) and the lowest (Dhakar) status groups and a majority of them are non-vegetarians. (Sharma, a.1956 : 181). In both of these caste groups hypergamy is prevalent, with the result that vegetarian groups enjoying lower status offer their daughters in marriage to these non-vegetarian groups which enjoy highest status in the caste, (Sharma, a. 1956 : 18-28). These Shaktist — non-vegetarian families fall in the second category. There are many families which are either pure Vaishnavas (category 5) or unorthodox Vaishnavas, who also worship Shiva *etc.* (category 6). There are some families, specially among Kanyakubja and Saryupari castes, which are Shaivas of non devotional type (category 8). Gauda, Sanadhya, Malviya and Saraswata Brahmans are traditionally vegetarians. There is no group in these caste which is traditionally non-vegetarian. So is the case with the Brahmans of Gujrat and Maharastra. These Brahmansd are either pure Vaishnavas or unorthodox Vaishnavas, worshipping Shiva, Durga *etc.* Thus they fall either in the fifth or sixth category.

In the third region are included jammu and Kashmir and the whole of the Northern hilly area. In the hilly area which falls in U.P., the two most important groups of Brahmans are the Kurmachalis and Garhwalis. They worship both Shiva and Shakti. Both of these groups are traditionally non-vegetarians. In these groups also the Brahmans eat only vegetarian food on the occasions like Janmastami, Purnima (full moon day) and Ekadashi (the eleventh day in each fortnight of every month). They fall in the eighth category. The Kashmiri Pandits on Shiva Ratri worship Vatak, a child of Shiva's wrath against Yoginis, who stole Pravati. On this day the Kashmiri Brahmans eat meat and fish. The most important goddess of Kashmiri is Sharika, who is regarded as the patron-goddess and she is also offered meat. This caste-group is also a Shiva-Shakta group in the sense that in their rituals Shiva and Mother Goddess are most important. They do worship Krishna and observes fasts and festivals prescribed by Vaishnava Dharma but Vishnuism as such has not been able to influence their behaviour appreciably. Their behaviour still continues in the traditional Shiava-Shakti style, because normally they are non-vegetarians. They also fall in the eighth category.

Similarly, on food habits of other clean castes also the influence of sects can be traced. A majority of Kshatriyas (popularly known as Thakurs) of U.P. are basically Shaktas. The Thakurs of the village Bachhna in the District of Kanpur say that about four hundred years ago some families of Kshatriyas belonging to Somvanshi clan came to this part of the district from across the Ganges. After walking for the whole day they stopped at a place for passing the night. They were carrying the statue of Durga (Mother Goddess) with them. They set the statue of Durga at one place and divided themselves into six groups. Each group moved in a different direction. One of these groups, while passing through a dense forest, noticed a temple of Durga and close to it they saw a cow feeding her calf. They decided to inhabit this auspicious place. They named it as 'Bachhra' (calf) which is now known as Bachhna. This mythological history of the village suggests the importance of Durga in their lives. The Thakurs of this village like other Thakurs are mostly non-vegetarians. However, those Thakurs who have been to Gaya, in Bihar have left non-vegetarian food altogether (Singh, J.N. : personal communication). Tej Bahadur Singh who is an elderly Thakur of Kanpur says that this is generally true of all Thakurs of U.P. and Rajasthan.

The 'Istadevatas' (main gods) of Khatris are 'Devis' or goddess and thus they are also Shaktas. Many Khatris of Northern India, however, are followers of Radhaswami sub-sects which prohibits non-vegetarian food. Other sub-sects of Vishnuism are also popular among them. The result is that among Khatris one can find both non-vegetarian and vegetarian families depending on their affiliation with Shakta and Vaishnava sects respectively. Among both, Thakurs and Khatris, there are converted Vaishnavas who fall in the fourth category. For Vaishyas the most important goddess is Lakshmi, the spouse of Vishnu. Therefore, she is also vegetarian. The result is that traditional religious families of Vaishyas are pure vegetarians. Nobody in their families ever eats non-vegetarian food.

The Bhakti (adoration or worship) movement of the Medieval period of Indian History has rendered singular service to the spread of the behaviour pattern set by Vishnuism. The greatest advantage with the saints of Vishnuism and Shivism was that they spoke in the language of the people. The most important of these saints in the South were called as the Alvars, Nayammars and Adiyars, who belonged to various castes and classes. Ramanuj (1016-1137), Madhwa (13th century), Ramanand (last quarter of fourteenth and first half of the fifteenth century), Tulsidas (1532-1624), Chaitanya (1485-) and Namdeva and Tukaram spread the Vaishnava values throughout India. They emphasized the superiority of the path of devotion over ritualistic sacrifice and mere book knowledge and wisdom (Rao 1958 : 201). Many saints of this Medieval period like Raidas belonged to lower castes. They were heard and followed by low caste people with respect. Besides devotion the other important value emphasised by these Vaishnava and Shaiva saints was abstenance from meat and wine. Thus these Vaishnava values spread in all castes and, the values of Vaishnava Dharma, which have contributed to the Pollution concept in great measure, have been brought to the illiterate masses by the saints of Medieval period, because they adopted the language of the people for communicating their ideas.

This fact explains the vegetarianism of women belonging to the families of non-vegetarians. The women of India have adopted the path of devotion and abstenance from non-vegetarian food and wine without much exception. In these cases adoption of vegetarian food is to entitle oneself for salvation and not for the membership of a higher status group. When a person belonging to any lower caste or untouchable caste adopts Vaishnava way of life he is called a 'Vaishnava' or 'Bhagat' (devotee) by his friends and neighbours. In such a situation an upper caste Vaishnava would feel close to him because both belong to the same sect-group. This in-group feeling is at the sect-level.

Vegetarianism is a Vaishnava value and not a value of the whole of Hindu religion or of caste system as such. This is further evidenced by the fact that throughout Northern India vegetarian food is equated with Vaishnava food. One can observe it in the cities where vegetarian restaurants are known as 'Vaishnava Bhojnalayas' and not 'Shakahari' (vegetarian) Bhojnalays'. On the occasion of feasts among many castes of U.P. every guest is asked whether he is a Vaishnava or not for ascertaining the number of persons who are vegetarians and non-vegetarians respectively.

Thus we see that non-vegetarian and vegetarian foods are associated with the rituals-complexes of Shaktism and Vishnuism respectively. Other sects are not so important in this respect. These ritual-complexes and other tenets prescribing or prohibiting certain kinds of behaviour are the most important variables in analysing the way of life of religious Hindus even today. For studying the food patterns of non-religious or secularised Hindus one has to take into consideration the contending values of Westernization and Gandhian Ethics of non-violence. Among the Westernised Hindus a vegetarian and teetotalar is an 'Outcaste'. In the Westernised group of people the scientifically-proved superiority of non-vegetarian food for nourishment of body is a defence which cannot be challenged on rational grounds.

In certain areas (Mayer 1960 : 45) the emergence of popular governments dominated by vegetarian castes is also influencing the food of the people. Prediction for the future is risky. Nevertheless, it is true that increasing secularisation and westernisation will preclude the Hindu sects from influencing the food of Hindus. In a secularised milieu much will depend on the success of competing values of non-vegetarian food of westernised group and of vegetarian food of the group which is emphasising the ethical consideration. In the political and economic systems, it seems, the westernised group is gaining status, and therefore, they are likely to influence the food patterns of the Hindus considerably.

Conclusion

1. The 'Pollution concept' of Hindus, as developed by Stevenson, is not universally accepted by all sections of

Hindus. It includes values prescribed by Smritis for the different castes and also the values prescribed by sects for their followers.

2. The different castes can be grouped under these sects according to their dominant influence on a majority of person belonging to a caste.
3. Vegetarianism is specially a value of Vishnuism so is teetotalism. They are bot values of Brahmans as such.
4. Broadly speaking the whole of India can be divided into four regions from the point of view of the spread of these sects. Assam, Bengal, Bihar and Orissa can be grouped into the first region in which Shaktism is dominant, but Vishnuism is also found. In the second region we may include U.P., Punjab, Rajasthan, M.P., Gujrat and Maharastra. In this region Vishnuism is dominant, but Shivism and Shaktism are also found in certain castes groups. In the third region may be included all the hilly regions of the Northern India in the Himalayas, right from Kashmir to Assam. In this region Shivism, aligned with Shaktism, is prevalent. A mild undercurrent of Vishnuism is also found. The whole of the peninsular India may be included in the fourth region in which Shivism associted with Vishnuism in the devotional form is prevalent.
5. The individual variations and taking of vegetarian food by non-vegetarians on certain occasions like Janmastami, Purnima and Ekadashi and vegetarinism of women among the non-vegetarian families can be explained only through the influence of Vishnuism.
6. The saints of Medieval period succeeded in spreading the values of Vishnuism among the masses belonging to all castes, upper or lower or even untouchables because they spoke in the language of the people.
7. Many lower castes and untouchanble castes like the upper castes found a way out to achieve salvation through the adoption of Vaishnava way of life. Thus the adoption of vegetarian food and teetotalism, in a majority of cases, has been to equip and entitle oneself for salvation and not necessarily to raise one's caste status.

8. In the group of secularised Hindus, Westernised persons holding high social status are disseminating the scientifically — superior value of non-vegetarian food. With increasing secularisation, non-vegetarian food and wine are likely to be adopted by more and more Hindus.

REFERENCES

1. Bailey, F.G.
1957 *Caste and Economic Frontier*, Manchester University Press.
2. Chaturvedi, P: *Vaishnava Dharma* (Hindi)
1953 Allahabad, U.P.
3. Eliot, C
1954 *Hinduism and Buddhism* (three vols.), Routledge and Kegan Paul Ltd, London.
4. Ghurye, G. S.
1950 *Caste and Class in India*, Popular Book Depot, Bombay.
5. Gauda, Ramdas
1939 *Hindutwa* (Hindi) Banaras,
6. Goswami, R. N.
1961 *Guru-Shishya Relationship in Madhwa-Gaudiya Sampradoya*, unpublished M.A. dissertation,
7. Hutton, J. H.
1946 *Caste in India*, Cambridge University Press London,
8. Hussain, Yusuf
1957 *Glimpses of Medieval India Culture* Asia Publishing House, Bombay,
9. Kapoor, S. N.
1959 *Marriage customs of Khatris*, unpublished M.A. dissertation,
10. Levy, M. J.
1952 *The Structure of Society*, The Princeton University Press, Princeton.
11. Lacey
1931 *Bihar and Orissa*, Part I, Census of India.
12. Mayer, A. C.
1960 *Caste and Kinship in Central India*, Routledge

and Kegan Paul Ltd, London.

13. Misra, Jwala Pd.
1926 *Jati Bhaskar* (Hindi), Venkateswar Steam Press, Bombay.

14. Rao, S. H.
1958 The Bhakti and Reformist Movement in '*An Outline of the cultural History of India,*' The Institute of Indo-Middle East cultural Studies, Hyderabad, India.

15 Srinivas, M.N.
1952 Religion and Society among the Coorg of South India, Oxford University Press.

16. " "
1956 'Sanskritisation & Westernisation' in *Society in India*, Ed. Aiyappan, S S.A. Publication, Madras.

17. Stevenson, H.N.C.
1954 '*Status Evaluation in the Hindu Caste System J. Rai* pp. 45-65, Vol. 84.

18. Sharma, K. N.
1956 *Urban Contacts and Cultural Change in a Little Community* (unpublished Ph. D. dissertation), Lucknow University .

19. " " b.
1956 'Hypergamy in Theory and Practice', *Journal of Research*, Vol. 3, No. 1, D. A. V. College, Kanpur.

20. Thurston, E
1907–9 *Castes and Tribes of Southern India,* Vol. 1.

21. Weber, Max
1958 *The Religion of India,* Tr. Gerth and Martindale, The Free Press, Glencoe, Illinois.

Chapter-9

PATTERSNS OF RELIGIOUS OBSERVANCE IN THREE VILLAGES OF RAJASTHAN

G. M. CARSTAIRS

Chapter-9

In India, religion is omnipresent, and manifests itself in such a multitude of seemingly unrelated, often contradictory, forms, that the Western observer commonly despairs of ever confining it within an ordered descriptive scheme. This is especially true of popular Hinduism, the religion of the poor and uneducated which shows an inexhaustible variety of local expressions of belief and practice.

It is no doubt for this very reason that European scholars concentrated for so long on the study of the Sanskrit texts, and the writings of the classical philosophers: voluminous though these texts were, they did at least the re-assurance that there was a physical limit to the data which they must comprehend. In recent years, however, the development of modern field studies by social anthropologists has confronted us with the need of grapple with this vast conglomeration of popular beliefs, and to find some clues by which it may be better understood, some consistencies in its different manifestations which will enable us to classify and marshall the phenomena, and which (if they are soundly based) will make it easier for future field-workers to recognise similar patterns in the religious life of villages in different parts of India, as yet untouched by field research.

The first major classification is between orthodox Hinduism (also described as Brahmanical, Vedic or Sanskritic Hinduism) and primitive animism. This distinction has been recognised for many centuries by Hindu religious teachers: they know from their study of the Vedas that the Aryan precursors of modern high-caste Hindus found a savage, short-statured, dark-skinned race of peoples living in jungles, and that these people's worship was all of demons and local godlings. The concept of the elect and the barbarians has been incorporated into the caste structure of Hinduism, and every high-caste Hindu considers it quite natural that the Sudras should have primitive and unelightened cults of their own. Critical reading of the earliest of the Hindu scriptures, the Rig-Veda, combined with the findings of modern

Indian archaeology, have however thrown a new light upon this old concept. It now appears that the orthodox Hinduism of today is vastly different from the religion of the first Aryan conquerors (in contrast to the ascetic, non-violent, world-renouncing ideals of contemporary Brahmans, they were a robust, carnal warrior-people, taking pleasure in feasting and drinking, and apt for love); and it has also been shown that when the Aryans came, they found not only jungle tribesmen in India, but also the highly developed, centuries-old civilisation which had built great cities like Harappa and Mohenjo-daro. The Aryans defeated the city-civilisation in war, but it seems probable that many of that culture's values and beliefs lived on, to become part of Hindu orthodoxy. As yet, too little is definitely known about the character of religion in those old cities to amplify these suggestions: but at least it seems established that the worship of Lord Shiva, and his symbolic representation by a phallic stone, comes from that source. It remains for the archaeologist and the prehistorian to piece together the evidences which will no doubt come to light, to show in what other respects the religious beliefs of the old culture modified those of the new.

The social antropologist has a different contribution to make. By studying and describing the complex of existing popular religious beliefs, he can show how they fall into a number of different categories. Eventually, these in turn may be related to their historical precursors; but in the meantime they can be shown to illustrate different concepts of the relationship between man and the universe of his experience, and to provide alternative means of appeasing men's emotional needs. With this aim in mind, the writer proposes to review the different manifestations of religious life which he saw while living in three villages of Rajasthan, in 1950, 1951 and 1952. All three were in the western half of the Udaipur Division (formerely the State of Mewar) which is here traversed by the low ranges of the Aravli hills. He stayed in the first village (Sujarupa) from January, 1950 to June 1950, being accompanied for 2½ months of that time by an Indian Christian youth, who acted as interpreter; thereafter he relied on his own command to Hindustani. He stayed in the next village (Delwara) from January 1951 to November 1951, and in the Bhil hamlet of Khajuria from December 1951 to February 1952. In the first and third of these villages the normal dialect of the people differed considerably from Hindustani, but this was spoken by most adult males; in Delwara, everyone spoke Hindustani, although village dialects were also used in speaking with peasants coming in from the surrounding countryside.

I. SUJARUPA

This village, lying on an uneven plateau near the main ridge of the Aravlis in the north-west corner of Udaipur Division, was really only a *baria,* or hamlet. It consisted of a huddle of cottages with mud-plastered stone walls, and roofs covered loosely with homemade earthenware ties. All round its periphery there stood man high-fences of thorn branches, enclosing the cattle-yard of each household. There was one main entrance to the hamlet, a heavy door and behind it a lane which traversed a long room, with a raised floor on either side of the lane. This room was the village *paul*, a meeting-place and guestchamber for the whole village.

There were 25 households in Sujarupa, of which 24 were farmers, of the *Rawat* community, and one (whose house was built apart from the rest) a leather-worker or *Regar*. All the Rawat families were descended from a common great-grandfather, Suja Singh, who had moved out from his natal village of Lakhagudha two miles to the west, in order to break new fields for himself and his six sons to cultivate. At the same time his brother also built himself a house in the un-reclaimed jungle, where there is now the closely related hamlet of Hematon-ki-guar. They cleared the jungle, dug wells, and levelled out new fields which are still the mainstay of both these villages.

The Rawat people have an interesting history, claiming to the descendants of children begotten by Rajputs with women of the Mina tribe, which is found in many parts of Rajasthan. They remember their Rajput ancestry, invariably claiming to be of the line of the hero Prithviraj Chohan, who ruled in Ajmer at the beginning of the twelft century, but they are never willing to admit their Mina strain. Indeed, the most important feature of their social life is the insistence with which they assert their full Rajput status. During his stay in Sujarupa, the writer twice accompanied wedding parties which went for the marriage ceremony to villages in the hills some fifteen and twenty-four miles away respectively. At every stage of the proceedings from the preliminay betrothal visits, to the rites performed after the bridegroom has brought his young wife to her future home, the familiy *Dholi* or *Bhat* plays an important role. He is the historian, herald, and ministrel of those Rawat lineages to which his family is hereditarily connected. When he meets any member of that lineage for the first time after an absence, he greets him with an invocation of his ancestry, thus : "Moti Hama ka, Hama Teja ka,. Teja Suja ka, Suja Rupa ka, Rupa Devi ka — Bara Salam!"

It is he who sees that the formal etiquette appropriate to each stage of the ceremonies is observed, and he who precedes the wedding-party on their way, singing resonant, if unintelligible, ballads of the prowess of the bridegroom's ancestors. He represents in fact the corporate memory, as well as the claim to social esteem, of the lineage: time and again the old men of the village, when asked about events of one or two generations ago, would say : "Ask the *dholi*, he knows all those things better than we do".

On the other hand, it is these same old men who take the most evident delight in exchanging formal courtesies of address and deportment which imply a high-born status for their community. When visiting another village, they liked to dress in what might be their only respectable suit of white *dhoti*, coarse village shirt, and massive turban, with a shawl of white hand-woven cloth over one shoulder, and the family sword in one hand. Thus attired, they did indeed look very like one of the proud but penniless Rajput Thakurs, squires of a few acres, on whom they model themselves.

All over Rajasthan, one finds similar instances of low-caste groups who are trying to raise themselves in the social scale by adopting the dress, customs and titles of the Rajputs. In Delwara village, for example, there is a caste called Yadow, which was formerly engaged in leather-work, and so ranked very low indeed: but for the past three generations they have turned to farming and stone-masonry as their sole occupations, have adopted the suffix *Singh* to their names, and now claim to be Rajputs. They are not the only ones. On one occasion the writer stopped before a country cottage, near Delawara, and after talking with its owner for some minutes, asked him his caste. "Rajput", he said.

Then, on being asked to which clan of Rajputs he belonged, he became confused and said: "Kumhar Rajput" (that is, "a potter-Rajput")

Such claims are contemptuously rejected by the real Rajputs; but they represent a means of social mobility which has perhaps always existed to some degree, but which is ripe for rapid expansion under the new socially progressive Congress Governments. They are made with the greatest conviction by those groups which can actually assert that they possess some Rajput blood in their ancestry. In Delwara this is true of the Daroga caste, one-time personal slaves of the Rajput rulers, and still their servants. The Darogas constitute a sort of below-stairs aristocracy, patterning their lineages on those of the princely families with whose service they have been associated: and they also add the suffix Singh to their names. In the Bhil country there exists a similar sub-division, the Garasias, being the descendants of Bhil women who have had children by Rajputs. In this case, however, the Garasias have not evolved appreciably different customs from their Bhil Kinsmen. They regard themselves as superior, and will not marry or sit to eat with Bhils, but in their dress, their names and speech and religious beliefs they are indistinguishable.

The Rawats' affectation of nobility is a precarious one, and collapses at the first test. The Rajput prides himself on the fact that Rajputs widows never re-marry: indeed they still sometimes commit *sati*, voluntarily submitting to being burned to death on their husband's funeral pyre, which is considered a mark of extreme piety and brings great honour on the husband's family. Nothing of the kind exists among the Rawats. Instead, widows are often taken in a less formal but still recognised type of marriage called *nata*. Traces of their Mina origin also survive in fragments of old custom. For example, on the third day after a death, Rawats prepare a dish of rice and milk and sugar, called *sirauni*, and leave it at the burning place, calling out the name of the dead person as they do so. This is common Hindu practice:

but only the Minas and the Rawats, in this part of the country, have the additional custom that the bearer of the *sirauni* should be followed to the burning-ghat and back by another man who carries a toy bow and arrow "at the ready" as if to ward off a supernatural threat. Again, the Rawat men-folk have given up dancing, at which Minas excel: but at Holi they perform a traditional stick-dance, called *gher*, which is found also among the Mina and the Bhil tribespeople. It will not be surprising, therefore, if the religious practices of the Rawats reflect the ambiguity of their social pretrensions.

Satsang and Bhakti—Marg

The writer's first introduction to the religious life of Sujarupa was on the evening of 18th January, 1950, just two days after he had pitched his tents outside the village. In the course of the day he had happened to ask one of the younger men whether they sometimes sang *bhajans* in these parts, and in reply he promised to come to the tent that evening with some friends for a hymn-singing. They came, and with them several small boys and older men, until over a score were seated close-packed in the tent, and sang for a couple of hours to the music of a five-stringed guitar, and to the rhythmical chiming of small brass cymbals, called *majera*. Some of the hymns which they sang were of recent composition, but the majority were traditional, many of them by Kabir, some by Mirabai: all of them were in broad "*Magra*" dialect, and had to be explained to the writer in Hindustani.

But this was only a foretaste of what was to come two nights later. Then, guests arrived on foot from distant villages, summoned to attend a special *satsang*, a night devoted to hymnsinging. They were entertained to large platefuls of a sweet pudding, called *churma*, a portion of which was also delivered to the tent, and at about nine p.m. the writer made his way to the *paul*, which had been re-plastered with mud and cowdung for the occasion. The floor was covered with white cloths, and mid-way along one wall a folded quilt had been set for the most important guest, a dignified, authoritative midlde-aged holy man, dressed in saffron-coloured robes, who sat cross-legged and stiff-backed, as if in contemplation. This was the Saddhu Bhur Nath, a hermit from the other side of Goram hill. He amiably invited the writer to sit at his elbow, and throughout the evening leaned across from time to time to explain in clear Hindustani what was going on. In front of the Saddhu was set a brass tray covered with a red cloth, and on it two brass bowls filled with flowers, and another in which were set one or two burning incense sticks. Opposite the Saddhu, a white cloth had been hung against the wall, and on it hung a framed colour-print depicting Krishna as a young man.

As each new arrival entered the *paul*, he discarded his shoes in the lane, climbed up to the floor level and greeted the whole company with clasped hands, saying : "Jai Guru Maharaj". To this, all those present made the same reply. The new arrivals then came forward and clasped the Saddhu's ankles as a token of deference, then gave a formal hand-clasp to their friends in the audience before themselves sitting down on the floor. A young man of Sujarupa, Devi Singh, eventually came in carrying his *bina* (the five-stringed guitar) and several pairs of *majeras*, one of which was taken by the Saddhu. Devi Singh struck up a slow musical chant, an invocation to Ganesh; and after it, another hymn with many references to the God Ram-Devji. The Saddhu beat time gently with his *majeras*. At the end of this hymn there was a cry of : "Sath Guru, Dev ki jai!" — but not many people took it up. There was still a feeling that they were at the preliminary stages.

Seeing the writer taking notes, the Saddhu explained to him that "Sath Guru" meant Parmeshwar, the supreme God, and "Jai Guru Maharaj" is a greeting which is exchanged by all who are earnestly seeking the truth. Much later, one learned that it is the greeting especially favoured by members of all religious sects known as the Kabir Panth. Already this evening it was noticed, as one *bhajan* followed another, that many were by Kabir: their last stanza containing an envoy in the form: "Thus saith Kabir....." As the hymn-singing got properly under way, the audience's enthusiasm increased. After each hymn, someone would call out: Bolie Satjh Guru!", and everyone would reply: "Sath Guru Dev Ki Jai!" At times, some would exclaim : "Kabir, Kabir!", as people cry out "Hallelujah!" at a revival meeting in the west.

In the intervals between hymns,; the Saddhu would call upon the singer to expound the meaning of the verses he had sung, and this frequently gave rise to an open discussioin, ended at times by an authoritative exposition on the part of the Saddhu, at other times by a call : "Sunao bhai, bhajan bolo!" — "Strike up brother — another hymn!"

The *bina* was passed from hand to hand, being played by the one who sang the verse most (*bhajans* had a refrain in which many singers joined). Late in the evening, the Saddhu called out : "Give it to the *harijans*, let's hear them." At this, the writer became aware that three sweepers from Lakhagudha village were sitting in the dust of the lane, in the middle of the *paul* but at a lower level than the rest. They sang three hymns, the refrain of one being : "Why do you avoid my touch: am I really so unclean?" and the others emphasising the equality of all who devoutly seek truth.

The climax of all the evening came after midnight, when a cowdung fire was brought in upon a tile, and the Saddhu made offerings of coconut and melted butter upon it. A new hymn with a very lively rhythm was now played and sung, everyone standing up and joining in it with fervour. Three members of the audience were so carried away that they began to perform a dance in the middle of the crowed room: it consisted of a few shuffling steps, turning to one side and back, while the trunk and arms swayed in gestures expressive of slef-abandonment in sort of ecstasy. Meanwhile a five-wicklamp was set on brass tray, and this was carried all round the audience by three worshippers in turn. Before each person, they waved the lamp three times, and he held his hands as if warming them at the flame, then saluted it. Each worshipper thereafter went all round the audience, clasping everyone's ankles in a gesture of humility, and being slauted in return. The ceremony concluded with the scattering of flowers and then red powder over everyone: some crystalline sweets, called *misri* were then offered to the fire, and the remainder distributed among the audience.

After this ceremony the company sat down again, and gossiped and handed round pipes. There was a feeling of cheerfulness and relaxed tension. In a few minutes' time another *bhajan* was struck up, and one succeeded another, with intervals of discussion, until dawn.

This *stasang* has been described at some length for two reasons. Firstly, the singing of *bhajans*, either for a few hours or all nights long was the commonest form of religious activity in Sujarupa. This was done especially on the second, eleventh, or fifteenth day of each half of the lunar month, but it might take place at any time when there was a quorum of five or more participants. Secondly, this particular *satsang* was a special occasion, being held in honour of the *Guru* of Hira Singh, one of the senior members of the village and a devotee of this type of worship. In October 1950 this Guru, by name Maharam, who lived in a village near the town of Beawar, some 40 miles from Sujarupa, announced that he was about to take *samadhi*. This meant that he had advanced to such a point in his religious life that he was ready at a given moment voluntarily to take leave of his body whole his soul passed straight into that of Parmatma, the all-encompassing divine soul, and so became released from the bondage of re-birth. Some hundreds of his followers gathered together for the occasion, singing hymns day and night, and at the appointed hour they lowered him, sitting cross-legged in a state of contemplation, into the ready grave, and buried him alive. The writer was later shown the white marble shrine which was built over the spot. Twelve days after this event, a great *satsang* was held at that place, in which over seven thousand worshippers took part — the local Government authorities gave them a free issue of grain rations for the event — and this satsang in Sujarupa was one of many organised by that Guru's disciples to celebrate his *samadhi*.

Later, the writer was to learn that the *satsangs* are an expression of bhakti-marg (the way of devotion) which is one of the great divisions of Hindu worship. Followers of this way attach themselves to one, or sometimes more than one, of a number of sects. The total number of such sects is very large, but in any given area only one or two will be represented. Their teachings also vary, some emphasising the worship of Vishnu or Shiva, or one of the lesser Gods of the Hindu pantheon, some (like the Kabir-panth) teaching a refined monotheism and the brotherhood of man. It is noteworthy that the Kabir-panth is the most widely prevalent in this district, because the most celebrated of local Gods is Ram-Devji, or Rama-Pir: and tradition has it that he, like the poet Kabir, sought to unite Mohammedans and Hindus in one form of worship.

The name of Ram-Devji is also associated with the worship of *sakti*, or female-energy, as personified by the Goddess, Devi. This form of worship is akin to the other *panths*, but with the difference that the supreme object of their devotion is not represented by light or fire, but by the act of sexual intercourse, and by semen, which is believed to issue from both male and female in that act. To the genuine adherent, these sects represent a more profound and compelling religious experience than do the others; but to the sceptical outsider they are the object of ridicule and disgust. This ambivalent attitude is expressed even in the verbal traditions of the Ram-Devji cult, which describe how, when he wished to be accepted as a member of the Mahadharam (one of these sexual *panths*) his wife was revolted by their rituals and refused to accompany him. New members are admitted only in pairs, so it was not until his adoptive sister (*dharm-bahin*) Dali accompanied him that he was accepted as a member of the Mahadharam. Incidentally, this shows how completely the ritual act of sex was divorced from the idea of promiscuous intercourse. Because to have sexual relations with a *dharma-bahin* is considered no less sacreligious than to commit incest with one's true sister.

Great secrecy attaches to these sexual panths, which are condemned by high-caste Hindus; but the writer was able to learn that one variety, known as the *Kanchli-panth* (so called because at their meetings the women members discarded their *kanchlis*, or bodices, and put them in a large vessel, and during the course of the hymn-singing the presiding Guru called out the men one by one, giving each a *kanchli* chose at random: this couple then retired behind a curtain to perform the ritual act of sex) was extensively practised among the Rawats living some twenty miles to the North, while one householder of Sujarupa and his wife were not only members of the Mahadharm, but also Guru of that sect, with their own disciples.

The Bhopa.

Within a few days of the great *satsang*, the villagers of Sujarupa invited the writer to leave his tent and make his home in the *paul*; and this, though lacking in privacy, made an excellent vantage point from which to keep in touch with all the goings — on of the vilalhe. On the night of 24th January, 1950, several persons went out of their way to remind him that there was to be an all-night ceremony at the shrine on top of a little hillock near Hamaton-ki-guar. It was the bi-annual festival of the god Devji. The oldest inhabitant of Sujarupa, white-bearded Pitha Singh explained that this shire is maintained by the potters of Hamaton-ki-guar. It is they who are in priests and they and their women-folk will sing long songs appropriate to this night — songs about strife between Gods and men. Devji himself was "a Rajput, someone near the Rajah: he wore a ring on his right fourth finger"; and that is all he can remember about him.

At nine p.m. it is dark and cold. Some thirty or forty men sit round a large log fire close by the shrine on the hill-top. In the outer darkness a crowd of women and girls is gathering. When some more people have arrived, one of the attendants of the shrine goes round giving each one a pinch of chopped *bel*-leaves. The writer is told that when the Gods are worshipped at a festival such as this, those taking part will fast until the worship is over. By eating these leaves, which have been offered to the Gods in the shrine, they are united in a worshipful mood, and in the morning they will all break their fast together.

The three potters who are the priests, or *bhopas*, of this shrine are called Kesa, Dola and Anjari Kumhar. It is Kesa who begins the formal proceedings by chanting a series of stanzas in a high-pitched voice. Dola, the oldest of the three, sings a short refrain, in which many voices join. At times Kesa pauses to explain the substance of his song in conversational tones, and others in the audience also put in a word now and again. Meanwhile the women, sitting now beside another fire a few yeards off, sing songs of their own. When this has been going on for over an hour, a young man sitting near the front of the main group gives a sudden cry, and goes into a sort of fit. He shakes convulsively, where he squats, so that his turban falls off, and his arms wave impulsively about his face, while his breath comes in loud gaps. As suddenly, after about five minutes the fit leaves him: he sits breathing heavily, then gropes for his turban and ties it on again. This was Anjari, who was not excepted to become possessed at this time.

The men's singing is now continuous and charged with emotion. In the shrine, two young men blow long notes on conch-shell horns, and another beats a gong. Suddenly Dola, who has been sitting as if waiting for something, takes a loud indrawn breath, and then he also goes into a shaking fit, rocking back and forward on his heels where he sits. For many minutes he quivers and shakes and gasps, as if he is in the grip of some physical orgasm which will not reach its climax. At last he gives a strangled cry and gets to his feet, his whole body still jerking convulsively. Then he runs into the shrine, picks up a handful of chains and belabours his own back, panting and grunting as he does so. After this he issues from inside the shrine and shouts a few phrases over the heads of the audience, then goes in once more. This happens fifteen times, and then everyone turns back to face the fire, but he remains crouching and quivering, squatting upon a low platform on the floor before the row of images.

The writer is told that he has been uttering prophecies to the effect that the rains would be good this year, the crops would be plentiful, the cattle spared from disease. He did not prophesy anything bad. Afterwards, as he sat in the shrine, people came to him singly, pouring out their offerings of a few handfuls of corn on to the floor before him, and asking what would be the outcome of a sickness in their family, or a proposed marriage, or the loss of one of their cattle. Still shaking and panting, he would look towards the images of the gods, and then gasp out a brief reply.

Next day, the youngest *bhopa*, Anjari, showed the writer the whole array of gods, whose images were cast in relief on heavy earthenware plaques. Two are standing male figures representing Kala and Gora Bhaironji; another is Ganesh. There are four plaques representing Devji-Maharaj, whose shrine this is, and these all show the forms of a black snake. Next to these again are two well-designed cobra-shapes, described as Kagal-Dev. Anjari says that this is where people come if they are bitten by a snake, to be cured. Asked if it is he who cures them, he says : "No, it is their work," pointing to the snake-gods. By standers explain that when this happens the *bhopa* appeals to Kagal-dev, and his spirit comes to them, causing them to "play" (*khelna* is the expression used to describe the quivering state of trance-possession) "Unko dev ka bhav ata hai" — the breath of God enters them).

For a time, one was at a loss to know whether this Devji were himself a snake-god, or a human being who had assumed that for. A later informant, describing the Devji songs, said that he was one of the Bagh-Rawats (a division of the Rawats supposedly descended from a lion-headed youth); but it was left to a Sujarupa villager called Mol Singh to clinch the matter. He described how one night he was coming back from Lakhagudha, and he was pursued by a ghost. First it cried with the voice of a sheep, and then it whimpered like a child, saying : "Wait for me!", and : "Carry me!" But he knew that this was a favourite device of ghosts and so he hurried on; and then, out of the corner of his eye he saw it coming after him, like a flickering flame. Just as he reached the turn of the road near the shrine, he saw Devji Maharaj himself appear, a shining figure on a white horse, and the ghost turned tail : but for this it would have surely killed him.

Nearly everyone in Sujarupa went to this festival, and listened to the prophecies that were given; but no-one seemed to go there for advice on their personal troubles. Instead, the writer herd constant references to the great gifts of another *bhopa*, who "played' each Sunday night at a shrine some six miles off. His god was, strictly speaking, a demon, called Danaji. In former times he had lived in that little valley, which he still haunted in spirit. The *bhopa* there is a Rawat named Goma Singh, and he was "called " to do this work by a visitation of the Dana in a dream. At first he refused to become a *bhopa*, saying that he wasn't cut out for that sort of work: then he felt sick, and again saw the Danaji in a dream, and this time he consented to do what he was told.

The writer attended one of his Sunday-night sessions, watching him tremble in his tance-like state for over two hours, while a succession of patients and supplicants crouched before him in turn. He diagnosed some as being struck by ghosts, some by witches: often he left the diagnosis unspoken, and simply called out his instructions. Some had to bring offerings of nuts and lemons, some were to tie twelve knots in a coloured thread — "Five in the name of Rama-Pir, five in the name of Danaji, one for Ishwar and one for Mahadev" — and wear this round their neck. The parents of children were frequently told to carry their sick child thrice round the little shrine. One man, thin and wasted, complained of a chronic cough. He was very probably consumptive, there being a great deal of tuberculosis in this region. The Bhopa declared that this was a simple illness, not a case of witch or demon. He made the patient sit near, then leaning over him sucked noisily at the nape of his neck, like a dog worrying a rabbit. He gasped for air once or twice, then announced that he had sucked out the poison: now the man would get well.

It was noticeable that the villagers approached him respectfully but quite without awe. Sometimes they would fail to catch his instructions, and ask him to repeat them; sometimes they would grumble and complain that a promised improvement had not come about, and sometimes the *bhopa* would crack a joke in between his statacco commands. Always, however, they would make a deep obeisance to him at the end of their interview, addressing him as Maharaj, or Andata. At the end of the long session, the *bhopa* gave a loud cry: "Listen! Two things I tell you. Come here regularly to pay homage to Danaji: and worship God." He gave one more frenzied shout, pointing his right hand in the air, then slowly it was lowered, and he became a man again. His first action was to bow down towards the shrine, pressing his head on the ground, and then he went round all the men who sat waiting in the firelight, clasping their legs and slauting them with folded hands, and then he sat down to smoke a pipe. He now greeted the writer as if seeing him for the first time, and reminded him that they had met before, when he had been sick with double pneumonia in the government hospital of a nearby small town. "You felt my pulse and examined me, and said: 'You will get better'. I have not forgotten that."

"You and I do the same work, we try to help sick people."

To this he replied by pointing upwards with one finger : "It is God's work. We can only do it when it is His will: By ourselves what can we do?"

There were many other *bhopas* practising in the vicinity, but not other commanded such confidence of this of Danaji. For one thing, it was said that the virtue of a shrine would only be at its full strength for one *jug*, here defined as a span of twelve years; and for another, it was known that sometimes *bhopas* were dishonest and simulated possession by a God although in fact the spirit did not come. In one such case, some young men of the village playd a trick on the *bhopa* to show him up. They secretly heated his chains until they were nearly red-hot, and then when the bhav supposedly came to him, he reached for the chains to belabour himself — and then danced with rage, pouring out a stream of oaths as he nursed his burned fingers. The elders of that village pronounced that this was no true *bhopa*: were he really possessed, he would not have been aware of any pain.

Village Gods.

At the roadside in front of Sujarupa there are two conspicuous objects. One is a square pillar, shoulder-high, faced with white plaster, and with a crenellated top, and other a low stone platform, with a dark stone set upright above it. This stone is daubed with red paint and above it there hangs a red pennant at the end of a bamboo pole. The former was described as a *pathwari*, or as *Ganga-Mata*, and latter as Hanuman. Later, two other wayside *chaukis*, or sacred sites, were pointed out, one an inconspicuous stone on a mound near the *pathwari*; this was a *Bhaironji*. The other was a tumbled-down stone platform, built round the base of a young tree, consecrated to Sitala-Mata, the Goddess who controls small-pox.

These shrines were generally quite neglected, except for special occasions. Thus, on the seventh day of Cheth month, which is here regarded as the day especial to that Goddess, the women of the village tidied up the Sitala-Mata platform and left offerings of flowers upon it. It was not, however, until a few days before the marriage of one of the Sujarupa youths that the writer became aware of the full number of the shrines associated with this hamlet. On the night before the bridegroom set off to the bride's village, attended by most of the men and grown up boys, he was conducted by the *dholi* round all the village gods, in order to make a token offering of coconut and melted butter to each, and to pay homage *DHOK DENA* at each shrine. He was followed by a procession of his women relatives, singing appropriate songs. The possession visited first a small hill-top on the north side of the village, where there was a chain of stones, on top of which lay a weather-beaten earthenware plaque with the representation of a seated figure. This was Goramji, the God of the mountain peak, six miles off, which is the chief feature of the local landscape. Nearby there is a platform at the base of a young tree, similar to for Sitala-Mata, but this is for Piplaj-Mata, the special Goddess of the Rawat people. Near that again, a stone had to be marked with red *sindur* and paid respect. This was the Bhaironji of Piplaj-Mata.

Next, the procession made a wide circle round the back of the village, in the fringe of the dry jungle, stopping to worship at four more Bhaironjis, which were simply stones, indistinguishable from many others unless one looked closely, to find faint stains of former offerings of dye and melted butter. While he squatted barefoot before each of these, a youngh unmarried girl cousin laid her hand on his head and cried out: "Be thou blessed with many grandchildren"! As she was a mischievous and irreverent girl, she spoiled the solemnity of the event by adding an obscenity, in an audible aside, after each invocation. A sixth Bhaironji stone was found, with some difficulty, buried under the dust of the path leading to the door of the *paul*. It was cleared, and washed with water, and then worshipped. The next pause was at the big square stone sitting place, or *hathai*, outside the *paul*. Here again an inconspicuous stone, which had clearly been disregarded for months if not years, was identified and honoured. This was called *Ajipaul*.

The final act of worship that evening was called *dori napna*. The *dori* was the local dialect name for the heap of dry animal manure, a separate one for each household, which was laboriously gathered throughout the year, and on whose abundance would depend the richness of the yield from their fields. Here the groom squatted before the dung-heap, symbolically "measured" it with a cubit's length of rope, and then groped underneath the dry manure to retrieve an iron key which had been hidden there; and finally saluted and made offerings to the *dori*.

When he returned to the village four days later with his new bride, a similar procession took place, both of them paying homage side by side to these various shrines. This time, however, the *dori* was omitted, and they went to the door of the paul, where they were ceremonially greeted and given the sacred forehead-mark (tilak) by the bridegroom's mother. They then went first not to his own house, but to that one which had been built first of all by Suja Singh, the founder of the hamlet. There, they worshipped a small image of Ganga-Mata, which had been Sujali's, and next gave their respect to a small first-floor room, or *meri* (the only one of its kind here) in which was kept a stone image representing Chaut-Mata. Lastly, they went into the bridegroom's house, where a gaudily coloured lithograph of Ganesh was plastered to one wall, and worshipped him.

Two things were particularly striking to the writer in studying these ceremonies. First, the completeness with which the hamlet was protected, as if by divine sentries, at every approach and second the vagueness attaching to these same protectors. Literally no one in Sujarupa could tell him clearly who they all were. About Bhaironji, for example, who is worshipped in many parts of India as the terrible, the wrathful aspect of Shiva, all they knew was that he was a God, but not a great God; he was rather the lieutenant of the others, and especially of the Goddess. He was known to have two forms, Black and White. They differed in that the former liked blood sacrifices, the latter only sweet things. One old man said that many years ago Black Bhaironji lived in these parts. He was a tall, powerful black man, like a negro; and he was notorious for making free with men's wives. That is why people wear his image on their breasts, he said, in order that this misfortune should not come to them. Everyone did however associate this god with anger. Thus, when a furious, screaming quarrel broke out in one household, one of a group of men talking with the writer remarked : "There, Bhaironji is "playing" ! and everyone laughed.

As to the others, they said: "It is just a God", or, of Chauth-Mata: "She is a Goddess, you know, just like the others: they have so many names, but they are all one."

Usually, they referred one to the *dholi* once again: he was the man who knew these things. But he was able to add very little, except on the score of Piplaj-Mata, the *Kul-Devi* or special Goddess of the Rawats. Her chief temple was in glen not many miles away and there, many years ago, the Rawats used to appease her with the sacrifice of a first-born son. According to the legend, it was just eleven generations ago that a youth of fifteen years had been promised to the Goddess as a sacrifice. He was a handsome boy, and excelled in playing the drum, of which he was very fond. When he was taken to the temple, he asked only that he be permitted to play in honour of the Mataji, before he was decapitated and his head offered up in the customary way. He played to such effect that the Goddess spoke through her *bhopa* and renounced her taste for human sacrifice. Ever since, she has been offered a male water-buffalo instead. In the years before the pacification of these hills, when the Rawats lived chiefly by fighting and looting the settled villagers of the plains of adjacent Mewar and Marwar, they used to rely on the supernatural aid of Piplaj-Mata on their marauding expeditions, and when they returned successfully, they would sacrifice many buffaloes to her, and then have great feasts — because in those days they did not have any scruples about eating buffalo meat, or even beef in a lean year. "Things are different now," said the Dholi : "They are all becoming Brahmans now. That *bhopa* of Piplaj-Mata even goes about saying that they should not take life, they should offer her only sweet-meats. But still, when they want her help in an important matter, they go secretly to that temple and kill a young buffalo or a black he-goat in her name."

Veneration of Ancestors

In Sujarupa, the highest regard is paid to the memory of its founder, Suja Singh. Stories about him are already acquiring a legendary character, but it is clear that he enjoyed a wealth and renown greater than that of any of the present-day Rawat villagers for many miles around. Thus, when he gave a great feast after performing the pilgrimage to the Ganges, to scatter his father's ashes on its waters, his guests were numbered in hundreds, and even included the Rao of Deograrh, one of the senior nobles of Mewar, and two lesser Rajput Thakurs, each of whom was housed for the occasion in a special marquee. It was he who built the first house, and the *meri* in which the goddess-image stands, and also the *dhuni* or altar, which stands in the centre of the hemlet: and it is here that he is remembered with worship. Every morning Hira Singh, who lives in the cottage which was Sujaji's, throws out a handful of grain in the direction of the *dhuni*, for the pigeons to eat, and he "remembers the name of Sujaji" as he does so. On special occasions, such as on embarking on the negotiations for a betrothal, or a purchase of land, or a lawsuit, and householder of the village may come and light a fire on the *dhuni* offering Hom (usually an oblation of melted butter, and chips of coconut) and asking Sujaji to let his errand prosper.

No other of the parents and grandparents of the present generation reveives similar veneration: the writer made repeated inquiries on this point. There does however exist a vestigial custom which indicates that the practice of ancestor-worship may once have been more general. This is the wearing of a small silver medallion on a string round the neck, by both men and women, but more commonly the latter. The medallion represents a warlike figure, an is described as a *devta*, a godling. Originally these were bought and worn in memory of some member of the family, usually father or mother, and they are still bought from the goldsmiths of the larger villages for this purpose: sometimes they commemorate the death of a son. "*Deva* vegia", they say : "He became a goldling," which is one way of saying that he died. These medallions are handed down from mother to daughter, until the occasions of their origin is forgotten. The writer was not present in Sujarupa in the month of Bhadwe (August-September) to observe whether Sujarupa families observed orthodox Hindu custom of giving *Shraddha* feasts in honour of the dead; certainly none of them mentioned this practice when he asked them about the worship of one's ancestors.

Other Gods

The names of many of the principles gods of the Hindu

pantheon were known to these villagers, especially to those of them who had been out in the world, serving in the army, or working in the mills at country towns like Beawar and Pali, or the distant city of Ahmedabad. In practice, however there were only three outlying temples which concerned them in their everyday living. These were the temple on top of the Goram peak, behind which the sun set all the year round; the Ram-Devji temple in Miala village, four miles to the west across the jungle; and the temple of Mahadev in the hamlet of Dadalia, some seven miles to the north-west. The last of these had acquired a recent fame, although there were legends to link the natural spring there with a miracle performed by Lord Shiva. In accordance with this legend, it was believed that the waters which issued from this spring were those of the Ganges itself; but it was only in the life-time of the holy man now living there that the place had acquired a more than local reputation. He had spent some 40,000 rupees, contributed by his followers, in building rest houses, gardens, and cemented bathing pools where males and females pilgrims might bathe in the sacred waters in decent privacy, and now people came from many miles around, especially at the time of the two annual Shivratris, the festivals peculiar to Shiva.

Although everyone mentioned Dadalia with pride, as a showplace of this country side, by no means all the adults in the village had ever been to see it. The same was true of the temples on top of Goram hill, which could be clearly seen. Often, first thing in the morning, after slauting the sun and pronouncing one of the names of God, men would turn towards that temple, now glowing in the level rays of dawn, and raise their hands in salute also to it; and on sacred occasions among the other cheers that were put up, would be included "Goram Nathji ki Jai!". But whereas everyone knew that the objects of worship in Dadalia were the holy Ganges, and Mahadev (splendid but rather remote God of the high Hindus), even this much was not known about Goram-Nath. Some said he was a holy man who had been buried alive in the heart of that hill; and when the railway engineers had tunnelled through it, they had seen him there, with their spyglasses, as he sat in contemplation. Others said it was a demon, others some kind of God: but all were agreed that he watched over the twelve villages, and their hamlets, which lay in the valley on this side of the hill. In fact, the writer found on visiting it, it was a small temple of Mahadev, tended by a priests who lived on the other, or Marwar side of the range.

This was not the case with Ram Devji. Fragments of his story were known even to the children, and the women and girls all learned the songs which described his miraculous career. The annual *mela* at his temple in Miala is attended by tens of thousands of pilgrims drawn from many other groups besides the Rawats — but chiefly from the lower castes. He appeals to the Rawats because he was himself born into a Rajput family, a family of small farmers like themselves, and every incident of his life takes place in a familiar setting. Accordingly, in time of trouble there are many who turn to him instead of to the Danaji for help. The priests at the Ram-Devji temple do not become possessed, as do *bhopas*, but they have other methods of diagnosing the effects of attack by witch, or friend, and they have magical remedies, which are effective because of the power of their God. It is profoundly re-assuring for an anxious parent, or a sick man, to have Ram-Devji's assurance that all will be well.

Supernatural Beliefs

There were many comparatively trivial superstitious current in Sujarupa, whose observance was not strictly observed. These seemed to be most current among those who had travelled abroad in India: they used to retail them to the others in the evenings how it was inauspicious to shave on Tuesday, or travel on a Wednesday (but few people in the village kept count of the days of the week any way), and how it was unlucky to meet a widow-woman in your path, or a women carrying an empty water-pot: but to meet a married woman carrying water brought good luck. These and others like them, were learned from contact with Hindus of other castes.

More serious attention was paid to another class of omens, derived from the wind life of the jungle. When a man set out on an errand, if he heard partidges call on his left, he was re-assured, but if one called on his right, and the call was heard three times, he would be so surely convinced of ill omen that he would come home and renounce his business for that day. There were several other such signs, relating to other birds, and to snakes. At night, if a jackal was heard to call three times from the burning-ghat, it meant that there would be a death soon in the village. There were however three types of superstitious fear which particularly concern them. These are the fear of evil spirits, of witches, and of devlish charms which can be used to kill one's enemies.

Evil spirits are of several kinds, the two commonest and most dreaded being the ghosts of men who have died violently, or by a sudden accident, "before their time" (called *bhut*), and the female ghost, with a hideous face, eyes in her breast and feet which point backwards at the ankle (called *churail*). The latter are the ghosts of women who have died in childbirth. *Bhuts* are encountered most commonly at the burning-ghat, or else at the spot where they were killed: their haunting is most intense for a span of twelve years, and then continues with less severity for another span. Many illnesses are due to the anger of such ghosts, and they must be appeased before the victim can recover.

When women or especially small children are sick (and there is a high death rate among children in these villages; in recent generations in Sujarupa, forty per cent of children have died before the age of five) the cause is very commonly ascribe to the action of a *dakan* or witch. There is believed to be one such witch in every village, and sometimes more than one. No woman ever willingly submits to the allegation; indeed, "witch" and "whore" are the two most insulting epithets, to be úse in the height of a very angry quarrel (and invariably so used). In spite of this, the belief is so strong that a whole delusionary system has been built around it — about how one witch seduces another woman into going the same way; how they can take the form of a cat at will; how they go out on Saturday night to consort with other witches, stripping naked and ridding on hyenas backs while they shriek in the dark; and how destructive is they baleful glance.

The psychological motives which give rise to such powerful projections of hostility and aggression are an interesting study in themselves. The whole question is attended with great secrecy, out of fear of the power of the witch. It was with difficulty that the writer found out that his nearest neighbout in the hamlet, an old woman called Dhapu, was a supposed witch, blamed for numerous sicknesses, and for the death of several children. After he had left, in December 1950, another young woman fell sick, and becoming "possessed" in a form of hysterical dissociation, announced that the possessing agent was this old witch, who was determined to consume her liver. At this the relatives of this girl set upon Dhapu, intending to beat her until she admitted her guilt and promised to leave the girl alone: but they beat her two hard, and the old woman died. This gave rise to a bitter quarrel between their family and that of Dhapu, who called in the police; but no one denied the propriety of their action. It was only regretted that she had, most inconveniently, died of it.

Death-dealing magic is different again. It works by means of charms, which have to be made effective by enlisting supernatural aid. This may be done by sitting all night at the burning-ghat (which few would dare to do) or by sitting in the dark near the Hanuman shrine, repeating the charm over and over (the writer once surprised a villager called Nathu Singh in this act). The secret of these charms can be bought, at a high price; but more usually people pay their owners to direct them against someone whom they specify. There are certain celebrated "knowing men" (*janne wale*) who are known to possess the antidote to such charms; and no doubt they can also exercise them, but they never boat of this, as it would make them most unpopular. Whereas in the case of witch craft, it is always one particular witch who is suspected, and either bought off (for example, by killing a black goat and exposing its head and entrails in a broken pot, at night, at a spot where three paths meet) or threatened with death if she will not desist, in this matter of charms the hostile agent is usually left unspecified, and the victim concerns himself only with undoing the effect of this particular charm.

II. DELWARA.

The village of Delwara lies in a valley 18 miles north of the city Udaipur, the former capital of the State of that name. Twelve miles further down this valley lies the town of Nathdwara, a pilgrimage centre celebrated for its possession of the image of

Sri Nathji, a tall, dramatic figure executed in black stone. This image was once in a temple in Mathura, but it was sent to Udaipur in the sixteenth century for fear that it should be vandalised by the Moghul armies. It is housed in a vast Vaishnavi temple (Sri Nathji being one of the forms of Vishnu) whose high priest is also the ruler and landlord of the rich little town. Four miles to the south of Delwara there is another pilgrimage centre, in the village of Eklingji. Here, in a temple built in the fifteenth century, is a famous *lingam*, a black phallic stone representing Shiva, which has been worshipped by the Hindus of Udaipur since the 12th century, if not before.

The tradition is still maintained that the rulers of Udaipur (Rajputs of the Sheshodia clan, who trace their succession in an unbroken line of the ninth century) are really only the viziers of the God Shiva, who, as represented by his black *lingam*, is the real Rana of Udaipur. The high priest of this temple is chosen from among a small number of ascetics who have renounced their caste and all their worldly possession in order to serve there. He is not wealthy, as is the priest of Sri Nathji, but he has the honour of being the Maharana's personal Guru, and of being the only man in the land who is entitled by right to sit at a higher level than he.

Delwara is a larger village than most, having a population (in February 1951) of 2,424 persons, in 597 households. A total of 39 different castes are represented, but of these only twelve are numerically important. These are as follows :–

Banias (merchants) ...	578
Moselems (servants & artisans) ...	228
Yadows (stonemasons) ...	205
Daroga formerely servants of the Ruler, (now finding work as tailors, shop-keepers) ...	183
Bhil (labourers) ...	157
Balai (leather-workers) ...	154
Bhoi (market gardeners) ...	111
Khatik (butchers, labourers) ...	106
Brahmans (priests) ...	85
Nai (barbers, servants) ...	79
Kumbar (potters) ...	78
Rajputs (landlords) ...	63

Unlike Sujarupa, this village has been established for centuries. One of its temples bears an inscription dated Samwat 411 (1355 A.D.). There is a tradition that in very early times there existed a series Jain temples all the way from the ruined village of Nagda, on the other side of Eklingji, to Delwara. In the middle ages, the authority of the nominal ruler of Udaipur over his nobles was a precarious one. For several generations, the fortress-palace of Delwara, and the surrounding country was held by a Rathor Rajput family from the rival state of Jodhpur: to this day there exists near the village burning-ghat a memorial to the last Rathor ruler, dated Samwat 1642 (1585 A.D.). Since that date the village and the surrounding estate which includes sixty other villages have been ruled by a family of Jhala Rajputs, adherents of the Maharana of Udaipur.

The size and importance of the village derive from its being the seat of government of this Tikhana, or earldom. The village is dominated physically by a towering whitewashed palace, built on a high rock, and surrounded by battlements. Here lives the Raj Rana of Delwara, and here until 1949 was the judicial and administrative centre of the whole region. The Ruler had a personal staff of over 200 retainers, and there were courts, and a prison, and the offices of the revenue collectors within its walls. The police were under his authority, and he could command scores of Rajput warriors to attend him in case of need. The Ruler dominated the social and economic life of the village as well: the merchants sought his approval before opening a new shop or building a house, and their sons went formally to pay him their respects and to ask for his patronage. Indeed there was scarcely a single family which did not hold some minor office or contract from the Raj Rana. The prosperity of the little bazaar, and the preponderance in numbers of the merchant caste were due to the constant coming and going of tenants and litigants.

All this has abruptly changed since, soon India became independent, the central government took over the civil administration from the former quasi-feudal Rajput rulers. In order to emphasise the change, they removed the magistrate's court and the administrative offices to a town some twenty miles distant. Now, the palace stands empty and deserted. Most of the retainers have been discharged. The Ruler sits at a high window looking over the village, playing chess with his few remaining attendants and speculating over the next turn of the wheel. In the village itself, people have not yet got used to the sudden reversal. The older men regret it, and take every opportunity of grumbling about the injustices and corruption of the new regime, but the young men feel liberated and hopeful of finding new openings for their personal elsewhere. Many have already left home to take up work in government service — which is the ambition every boy who matriculates in the village school. As yet, however, the village community has not crystallized its rank order, to take the place of the clearly cut hierarchy of posts of authority under the Raj Rana, which have dominated social life for so many generations. Encouraged by the Congress government, the village council has assumed certain responsibilities, in dealing with disputes and brawls, and matters concerning communal welfare; but so far it has not acquired much prestige, so that little respect is paid to its members or to its decisions. In this trasition period, two alingnments are emerging, and competing for the ascendancy in village affairs. These may be described as a party relying on its wealth, against another party relying on its political influence, each trying as get on top.

The writer and his wife came to stay in Delwara at the end of January 1951, and remained there with brief interruptions until November of that year. They were given accommodation in an outlying part of the Ruler's palace, and the writer secured a room in the centre of the bazaar, where he conducted a medical clinic, and talked with his informants daily. He found that in this more sophisticated setting it was a much slower business than in Sujarupa to break through the cloud of distrust and suspicion with which the villagers surrounded him. Gradually, however, they decided that there was nothing to fear from him, and became generous in inviting him to take part in their festivals and in all the ceremonies of their daily life.

In a community containing so many distinct sub-groups there was a marked diversity of patterns of religious observation; and these in turn were found to be graded in social prestige, just as Church preceedes Chapel, and both are counted superior to the Missioner's marquee.

Temple Worship

Delwara was rich in temples. There were three particularly spacious Jain temples, subsidised by the merchants (all but three families of whom belonged to that sect) containing numerous marble images of the Tirthankars, the deified Jain saints. There was also one small Jain temple peculiar to their Digambar subdivision (whose images are represented in the nude, and whose ascetics discard all clothing). Each of these temples had a paid caretaker, whose duty it was to bathe the idols, wash out the temple, and offer worship there morning and evening. They were frequented more by women than by men, and there were few families who visited them with any regularity.

There were 35 temples to various Hindu Gods, each with its regular attendant. Many of these were reserved for one or another caste, having been built by subscription by members of that caste — the goldsmiths had a Vishnu temple, the potters of Thakurji, the Audich Brahmins a Charbhujaji temple. There were others also, endowed as a public benefaction, which anyone except the untouchable castes' the sweepers and leather-workers and butchers might attend. There were however there such temples which were more frequented than all the rest, namely, the Charbhuja temple in the main bazaar, the Laxmi Narain temple near the village bathing-well, and a Hanuman temple in the gardens belonging to the palace. All of these had been endowed by previous Rulers of Delwara.

It was noticeable that each of these three temples had certain devotees who were especially assiduous in promoting evenings of hymn-singing, and mid-night worship (often attended with a clamour of ringing bells, and drums and exploding fire-crackers). One of the most ardent at the Hanuman temples was a Jain merchant who had risen from penury to own a very flourishing shop, and who believed his success was due to Hanuman's divine intervention. Most, however, were members of the poorest castes — washerman, darogas, barbers or artisans of one trade or another. One obscure little temple near the cross-roads of the bazaar was celebrated because it was kept up by a prosperous sweetmaker seller. On the last day of each month, he would decorate the interior of this temple with flowers and offerings of fruit and sweets, and summon a harmonium player to lead the singing of hymns for some hours. Everyone who attented was given a share of the offerings to the God, so this was a popular occasion, especially among the children.

At the Charbhuja temple, from time to time a Brahmin was employed, by the gift of one of the more prosperous citizens, to sit and read *Kattha,* that is, passages from a Hindi translation of one of the Sanskrit scriptures, such as the Ramayana or the Mahabharata. The reading and expounding of these texts was still, here in Delwara, the chief means by which ordinary villagers learned the basic mythology of Hinduism: elsewhere in India, this function has largely been taken over by the popular cinema.

There were temples also in the palace, one in the secluded women's quarters, one where the Ruler attended daily for prayers (to Ranchorji, a Vishnu incarnation) and one in the outer courtyard (to Chalak-Raiji, again a form of Vishnu). The dowager Rani, grandmother of the prsent Raj Rana lived in a special house on the other side of the village, and she has had built an ornate little temple to Baikunt Laxmi Nath (Vaishnavi) at which any but the lowest castes might worship. Each of these temples had a Brahman priest who performed the officers, made *arti* (the offering of flame) and repeated Sanskrit verses before the God each morning and evening.

Goddess Worship

The Mother-Goddess, Mataji, or Devi, who appears in so many forms, and with so many different names, is revered by every caste in delwara, in differing degree. She is worshipped most ardently by the Rajputs and by those other castes which are beginning to assume that title, and by the farmers. Each Rajput clan has one form of the Goddess who is their *kul-devi.* In the case of the Jhalas, this is Ad-Mataji, of whom there is a fine image in a temple high up in the palace. There are three other Mataji temples in the village; a very modest one, to Piplaj-Mata, where low-caste labourers, washermen and Bhils attend, another a small white-washed shrine on top of a hill, with an image of Sitala-Mata. All the women of the village dress in their best clothes on the festival of Sitala-Mata and go in procession to worship at this temple. They do the same sometimes later in the year, particularly if there is an out-break of smallpox, or if (as happened in 1951) there comes a succession of particularly hot days. The name Sitala means "the Cool One", and is a euphemism for the fierce heat of her influence, which is reflected in the high fever of small-pox : and the object of worshipping her is to cool her wrath with sweet offerings, while the image is bathed with cold water.

There is an interesting contrast between the Ad-Mata and Sitala-Mata temples on the one hand, and those of Piplaj and Vijayshan Mata on the other. The former are attended by Brahmin priests, and their offerings are of flowers and sweets: although during the nine nights of the annual Navratri festival, goats or sometimes a buffalo, will be sacrificed to Ad-Mata, in the courtyard outside her temple. Both of these Goddesses are worshipped by members of all castes. It is different matter with Vijayshan and Piplaj Matas. They are attended by *bhopas* (in both cases, the *bhopas* are Bhils, who rank just above the untouchables in the social scale) who become possessed by the spirit of the Goddess, and speak oracles and effect cures by virtue of her power. Both delight in offerings of goats and of *daru*, the strong countrymade liquor. When a worshipper presents these offerings, the *bhopa* emerges from the little shrine and stands, still quivering with the possession, on the level platform before it. A young Rajput called Prithvi Singh draws his sword, and cuts off the head of the goat with one clean stroke. As the headless animal stands for one moment, before it falls, the blood which spurts from its served carotid arteries is caught in brass cup, held by an attendent of the *bhopa*, who adds some of the *daru* and then carries it up to him, and he drinks the warm mixture in the person of the Goddess. Later, when he has emerged from his trance, he and the other worshippers will sit round a log fire and finish off the rest of the liquor, with scraps of roasted goat's liver for an appetiser. In all three villages, the writer found, when people sit to drink *daru* together, whether on a sacred or a secular occasion, the first taste is taken with the invocation: "Jai Mahaji !", and sometimes a few drops are spilled on the ground as a libation.

Bhaironji Worship

The Mata shrines occupy an intermediate position between the High Gods of orthodox Hinduism and the lesser Gods, which are felt to be easier of access, and more intimately related to the everyday concerns of the poor people. In Delwara, the generic term which covers all these little gods is Bhaironji, or Bheruji. They are thus identified with the Hindu concept of the destructive aspect of Shiva (Bhairava): but the ordinary village worshipper knows nothing of this. To him, each such God is an individual, often known by a special name, like Reglia-Bheruji, or Kotcheta Bheru; or he is identified with the caste-group which he serves, and among whose houses his stone is set, as the Yadows' Bheru, the Khatiks' Bheru, and so on. Officially, the three tops castes have no Bheruji; but this rule has its exceptions. There is one, whose sacred stone is among the ruins of what was said to have been an ancient Jain temple, and he has a Jain shop-keeper as his *bhopa*. The possession, and the answering of people's personal problems is the same, but this Bhaironji does not accpet blood sacrifices.

Bhaironjis occur in two forms, either alone or in association with a Goddess or with an image of one of the forms of Vishnu. If the latter is the case, blood sacrifices will not be offered; if the former, they will. Where Bhaironji occurs alone, he usually prefers such sacrifices.

All of these Bhaironjis have their regular *bhopa*, sometimes more than one. There is no formality about the selection of those who will become *bhopas* : the spirit moves them, and that is all. Sometimes an interval will elapse after the death of a *bhopa* before his successor becomes possessed, either at the same shrine or it may be at another one, and announces that such-and-such a Bhaironji has come to him. The *bhopas* are not, however, the only one to become possessed: not uncommonly a man may consult the Bhaironji to help him over an illness or other trouble believed to be due to magical causes, and himself become possessed in the process. When this happens, and is followed by his recovery, he may elect to adopt that Bhaironji as his special protector. In order to do this, he provides a generous offering of sweetmeats, and may hire musicians to play before the shrine during a late-night session of worship, in the course of which the *bhopa* gives him ring consisting of three turns of flattened copper wire. This is called *gor*, is worn on the fourth finger of the right hand, and is a sign that the wearer is committed to the service of his protector. His service is a nominal one, but it remains an obligation for the rest of his life.

Radaji

In every part of India it is usual to find a god which protects the fields and the crops. Here in Delwara, every family holding (or several adjacent plots, which once belonged to a single family) has such a god. He is represented by an inconspicious stone, daubed with red paste and referred to as Radaji. These gods are believed to dwell in and watch over that particular patch of land. One, more imposing than the rest, consists of a stone raised up on a platform, with a cement-finished canopy over it: this is Radaji which guards with approaches to the village itself, and this is the only local one to possess a *bhopa*; but he seldom has occasion to become possessed.

People had no very clear notion of what the Radaji was like but thought of him as being in appearance rugged and uncouth, a peasant like themselves. One young farmer described a dream in which he was going through the jungle at night to some distant fields, and was set upon by a dark, half-naked man: they wrestled and belaboured each other for a while, then the other desisted, and let him go on his way. He rather thought this must have been a Radaji which thought his spirit was trespassing, and this belief was confirmed next day when he learned that a neighbour of his had been bitten by a snake during the night, near the place of his dream. "You see", he said: "I wrestled with the Radaji, but it is he who has got hurt."

In so saying, he conformed with the very general belief that this god can take the form of snake most commonly a cobra and will bite any who come to the fields to steal. When this is believed to have happened, the victim turns to a man who knows the appropriate charms. The exorcist will have the patient bound hand and foot, and then will speak his charm, which has the effect of causing the god to come and possess the victim, speaking through his mouth. The god's first impulse is to attack and kill the exorcist, and hence the precaution of tying him up; after a parley, he is persuaded to leave him alone or sometimes he is not so persuaded, and the patient dies.

Ancestor Worship

The spirits of a family's ancestors are remembered in most Delwara homes, and in all those of the upper castes. During the first half-month of Bhadwe month, *shraddha* feasts were held in every wealthy house, on the day of corresonding to the death of a father, grandfather or great-grandfather, and many guests were invited to take part. In the proper homes, a ceremony, offering incense, flowers and sweet food in the name of the dead was customary: if a silver-medallion devta were possessed, it would be put in a special place and worshipped at this time. All this was accepted Brahmanical Practice, but the same could not be said of another phenomenon, which was found in several households, both of the merchants and of lower castes, though never among Brahmans or Rajputs: this was the presence of a *purbaj*, or ghost of a recently deceased head of the family, who manifested himself by "possessing" a surviving member, commonly his own widow, and so having a continuing authoritative say in the conduct of family affairs. Usually the *purbaj* was believed to hount the houses, in the form of a cobra. Accordingly, if there were a *purbaj* in a family, they would never kill a snake, because this *purbaj* was believed to protect the household in the same way as the Radaji did his fields.

The family of the Ruler made a practice of building monuments to perpetuate the memory of their predecessors. This was always done at an interval after the death of the Raj Rana who was to be thus honoured, because it was customary for this memorial to be built during the rule of the grandson, and not that of the son — reflection of the rivalry and tension underlying the strict parental discipline of the Rajput family. Memorials were also built to celebrate the performance of sati. There were three such in the village burning-ghat, the best preserved being one of the late 18th century. This was, unusually, an instance occurring in the Bania caste: a girl of the Bokriya lineage had been betrothed to a Mandawat boy, who died before their marriage took place. Although still a virgin, and unmarried, she elected to burn with him, and hence the sacrifice was held doubly honourable. To this day, young people of both these lineages come to this memorial to offer worship, before and after their wedding ceremonies.

Demoniacal Possession

One of the commonest explanations of sickness in Delwara is that the sufferer has been "struck", by a witch, a ghost, or some form of demon. It is unusual for a patient who is sickening — it may be for typhoid, or for a bout of malaria — to shake convulsively and pass for some minutes into a state of dissociation, similar to that of the *bhopa*, or of the person who is visited by a *purbaj*. While in this state they may speak, voicing their own fear, that they have offended one or other of these supernatural agencies : or they may simply quiver and grunt, and their relatives will form their own conclusions, or call in a "knowing man", or a *bhopa* to establish the diagnosis. Here again it is usually women who are affected by witches (though by no means always: one man described how a woman of the village met him in a lonely place and urged him to have sex with her; after he had refusaed, and abused her, he went home and later experienced an attack of dysentery — he was sure that she must have been a witch and this was the result of her anger), and ghosts usually attack men. Such sicknesses are regarded as dangerous only if one had aroused the especial hatred of the supernatural agent. Ordinarily, they can be qu ite easily apeased with a gift. The gift would generally take the form of an offering of food, which would be nominally given to the spirit, but actually shared by the diviner and the family concerned. Sometimes, in the case of witchcraft, it might take the form of fine clothes, to be passed over the head of the patient, symbolically offered to the witch and then aside. The patient could except to inherit these same clothes soon after her recovery; and this obvious "seconday gain" as it is termed in psychiatry, may well have persuaded some young wives to be readily prone to such attacks. It was the case that two of the most respected witch-diviners in the village used at times to conclude that there was in fact no witch at work: and then would slap the girl smartly on the cheeks. This seldom failed to bring them promptly out of their trainee.

Death-dealing magics were also mentioned, though infrequently. Much more common was reference to the extraordinary, and destructive, magical powers of the primitive tribesmen, the "wild" Bhils who lived in the hill jungles to the South-west of Delwara, and especially to their *sikotri*, which were variously described as very potent witches, and as a sort of familiar which went abroad to do their will. It was regarded as a dangerous undertaking to attempt to cure anyone suspected of being a victim of this magic, for fear that it should overpower and destroy the exorcist as well: but in fact, though everyone talked of it, few had ever known as actual case, other than those which had ended in the victim's death and had afterwards been ascribed to the action of a *sikotri*. The Bhils were credited with other magics beside the killing one. Through the agency of their familiars they were supposed to be able to know of events happening at a great distance, and to be able to blight a tree as if by a shaft of lightening, and to cause an enemy's house to rattle and shake as if in an earthquake. It was these tales, as well as his glimpses of the boisterous exuberance of Bhil popular ceremonies, such as their dances, and their folk-opera, which stimulated the writer to move into their country in order to learn more about their peculiar way of life.

Travelling Holy Men

In Sujarupa, the only holy men who commanded the villagers' reverence and attention were those, often of their own caste, who had risen to become Gurus in their respective devotional *panths*; and most of these were at the same time farmers or artisans in their ordinary daily life. In Delwara, however, it was different. Most of the Bania families (the most numerous as well as the richest group) belonged to that section of Jainism which attaches special importance to reverencing their wandering holy men, ascetics who have renounced home and family and all possessions, who live entirely on charity. The Banias maintained three spacious *noheras*, or courtyards with rooms in which these ascetics might stay. They order enjoins that for eight months of each year they must keep travelling, pausing in any one village for a few days only. In the four months of the rainy season, on the other hand, they are expected to remain in one place. Wherever they stop, they preach their religion, and lead the Jain community in prayer and worship. In Delwara, there were nearly always one or two women "saints" of this order in temporary residence, and less commonly men.

These ascetics are treated with an extreme degree of reverence. They are in fact regarded as if they were already partaking of divinity. It is believed that by their complete renunciation of the world and devotion to spiritual concerns they earn the reward of being released from the necessity of re-incarnation. Accordingly, when one of the saints dies (as happened during the writer's stay in Delwara) the occasion is considered as one for rejoicing. The corpse is placed in sitting position in a gaily decorated palanquin and carried at the head of a procession, everyone wearing their brightest clothes, singing cheerful songs, and with bands playing. At the burning-ghat the corpse's lap is filled with coconuts, incense and other offerings before the funeral pyre is lit, to the singing of triumphant hymns.

The Brahmin caste also has a guests-house for holy men, called a *dharamshala,* and there are two other *dharamshalas* in the village, one provided by the gift of the dowager Rani, another, called Ramdwara (God's dwelling) a small hut built by low-caste villagers themselves. All of these were visited periodically by passing holy men, of a great variety of different Hindu sects, and these would be entertained with gifts of food by some of the village families. Some of these had been before, like one Govindguru, a strange ecstatic character who passed the greater part of his day in a trance-like state of contemplation waking up at dawn and dusk to worship effusively before a framed lithograph of Sri Krishna as a cow-herd. He already had many followers in the village, who vied with each other in attending to him: Others were newcomers, who might never pass this way again, and they were generally treated with purely formal expressions of respect. The villagers were well aware that there are many fraudulent *saddhus* on the roads, and tended to suspend judgement as to the merits of these strangers though their bias was always in favour of believing them not only genuine, but possessed of supernatural gifts by virtue of their holiness. These Hindu *saddhus* rarely imparted any instruction. They might bestow a blessing, or promote an evening's worship to the God of their especial devotion: but generally both they and their hosts felt that a sufficient reward was given in the merit which accrued to anyone whose hospitality they accepted.

In this category of respected teachers should also be included two remaining Brahmin heads of households (Mohan Lal, a school teacher, and Bhuri Lal, an astrologer) who still maintained the reputation for profound learning in the Vedas, and who still commanded the worshipful respect of their fellow-villagers, that once did all elder Brahmins. It was noticable that their own religious life, as also that of other pious Brahmins who did not command such general authority was conducted almost entirely in private and alone.

Forbidden Sects

In Delwara, much more than in Sujarupa, the writer found it easy to obtain copious information (much of which was of doubtful validity) on the subject of the forms of *bhakti* which had the act of sexual intercourse as their central act of worship. The reason for this was that these sects were explicitly denounced as being obscene, indecent, and wholly opposed to the practice of true religion. In the past, the Rulers of Delwara had visited their practitioners with severe punishments, and had rewarded anyone who gave information of their *mandlis*. It was indeed noticeable that the members of the three highest castes took a certain delight in describing the full horrors of these cults, and especially of the two forms which were best known in this vicinity, the *kanchli-panth* and the *kunda-panth*. In the latter sect, not only were its meetings marked by ritual intercourse, but also and this one's high-caste informants found even more repellent — they were the occasion for a communal meal, in which members of all castes sat together and partook of food which for many was expressely prohibited by their caste rule: it was rumoured that they even ate beef on such occasions.

Apart from these hearsay accounts, the writer slowly learned some more precise details of the existence of these sects, which were most popular among the low-caste farming communities of the outlying villages: but which numbered also some of the rustic

Rajput landlords among their adherents. In the whole of Delwara, only three persons were known to have been active members of such sects: but two others had secretly looked on at one of their gatherings. It was one of the latter, a young Rajput, who was the only Delwara informant to concede that the participants themselves regarded this as a form of religion. This attitude of understanding was however quite explicitly met within one nearby village, where the writer, talking with two or three of the elders before going to sleep in the open air, broached the subject of these *panths*. At once, the atmosphere became alert, tense and guarded. When they realised, however, that he did not proceed at once to abuse these practices, they relaxed and spoke of them in sympathetic terms, as the religion of some of the country folk. Still, none claimed any personal experience of the sects; but next morning one of them, in showing the writer over the village Goddess-shrine indicated the flat platform before it and said : "This is where we had one of those *mandlis* last month — you know, that we were talking about last night."

III KHAJURIA.

The Bhil village of Khajuria was selected by the writer after two preliminary journeys through that part of Udaipur which is predominantly inhabited by tribespeople. This is the Western, mountainous part, known as Bhomat. It is divided by one particularly high range into two regions, the more northerly being known as Kotra Bhomat, the other as Kherwara Bhomat, after the two military posts where detachments of the Mewar Bhil Corps have been stationed for a hundred years, to help in keeping order in this unruly and inaccessible tract. The former, which is the more remote, is distinctly less "civilised." The Bhils there preserve more of their old customs and independence of the Hindu world, whereas those of Kherwara Bhomat have copied a number of Hindu prejudices, even to being ashamed of their own tribal designation (they like to refer to themselves as Minas, believing that that tribe has a higher social standing), and they are more law-abiding. These considerations prompted the writer to select a village in the Kotra area for his study.

Bhil villages, unlike those of the Hindus, are not a mass of close-packed huts. On the contrary, each house stands at some distance from the next, sometimes as far as some two hundred yards off. The huts in this area are flimsily constructed, with walls of bamboo covered with the broad leaves of the indigenous stunted teak tree. They are situated strategically, on the top of a knoll, or on a slope with the jungle close behind. Bhils like to have a clear view over the approaches to their home.

These hill valleys have an avergae rainfall of 40 inches, nearly twice that of the plains of Udaipur, and the soil is rich. The Bhils are accustomed to raise a crop of maize during the rainy season, which is sufficient for their needs for the whole year. Some of them will also raise a hot weather crop of wheat, irrigating their fields by diverting water from the streams. Traditionally, the mainstay of their economy was the grazing of cattle in their grassy hillsides, with hunting (and occasional banditry) as an additional source of income. During the last 15 years, communications with the railway line in the plain of Sirohi, 40 miles to the West, have been slowly developing: business men from the outside world realised that there was a profitable market in the produce in which these jungles were potentially rich — bamboo, wax, and charcoal. Using at first camel-trains, and in very recent years ex-army trucks as well, they have penetrated into Kotra Bhomat, with such effect that charcoal-cutters have already depleted many of the most readily accessible forests, and game has become scarcer than before.

It seems evident that this process will continue. The present rudimentary track from the plains, which is partly obliterated after every heavy rainfall, will be replaced by a firm road: commerce and intercourse with the sophisticated world will increase, and the old Bhil customs will no doubt gradually alter as a result. As yet, however, although this area has been under the rule of its military governor for a century, and before that was nominally ruled by the small Rajas whose fortresses are scattered throughout the territory — the Rajas incidentally are themselves of the Garasia community, although they too aspire to be regarded as full-blooded Rajput — yet the Bhils have retained to a remarkable degree their old tribal customs and regulations.

The Bhils are found over a long streatch of country, whose northernmost point is Kotra Bhomat, the most southerly part being over 500 miles to the south-east, in Bombay Province; but they themselves are quite unawere of this, and have no sense of communal solidarity with all their fellow-Bhils. Their corporate sense is limited to the horizons of their own, and the adjacent valleys. Their most important social unit is the village, which may consist of from a dozen to a score of huts, straggling over the whole of a side-valley. Each such village has a *mukhi* or head-man, who represents the village in all its dealings with external authorities, and also in disputes with other villages. The latter is their more important function, because disputes, leading to mortal feuds, are a common occurrence in Bhil life. They occur over the theft of property or of cattle, and over adultery and elopement, which are not infrequent events. The injured party is recognised to have the right to defend his rights, with the bow and arrow which he usually carries, or with his sword or muzzle loading gun. Indeed, so long as his grievance has not been settled, by the *mukhi* of his village meeting the representatives of the offending person and coming to times for compensation, he is liable to make a murderous attack on his opponent whenever they meet. The *mukhi* of every village has always got on his hands one or two such feuds which are still *ubo*, or "outstanding". He is also expected to be present at every corporate activity of the village community. In their weddings, for example, there is no religious ceremony, but the *mukhi* has to witness the event, and all the village neighbours expect to be invited to take part in the drinking and singing and dancing which accompany the event.

One or two things especially strike the attention of the visitor on first coming to live among the Bhils. Their bearing and manners are noticeably more confident and carefree than those of the poor peasant of the plains. It is obvious that they regard themselves as their own masters: and they are always ready to give proof of this by defending themselves in an emergency with the weapons which seldom leave their hands. They are an exuberant people, unburdened with care for the future, ready to enjoy mean, or a carousal or a dance whenever the occasion offers. It is characteristic of them that every man carries a bamboo flute as well as a weapon at his side. When one walks through their jungles on can often hear the sound of a flute being idly played by a herdsman some where out of sight, or a woman's voice singing a song which may have been composed at a previous festival to commemorate a Bhil dacoit and his evasion of the soldiery, or may be one that she herself makes up, or describe how she was wooed and how she ran away with her young man.

Local Deities

The outsider will encounter his first experience of their religious life in the course of his walking through the jungles, because it is beside the forest paths, near a strikingly large tree, or a rock or waterfall that he will find some of their oldest shrines. These consist simply of a painted stone, set up on end, and sometimes honoured with a flimsy roof of sticks and leaves: they represent the Goddess of that little glen or slope of hill, and she must be worshipped if the hunting is to prosper. The traditional offering for these wayside Goddess take the form of an earthenware figure of a horse, of bizarre and simplified design, which is made for them by the Hindu potters of the villages in the Sirohi plains. The shrine presents a mysterious appearance when one comes upon it suddenly, with a circle of twenty or thirty of these red baked-clay horses all standing, facing the central stone: it as if one had burst in upon some secret gathering.

These Goddess-shrines are of great antiquity. They have no formal ritual, no festival, are worshipped only in order to ensure the success of hunting or other work in that part of the jungle with which they are associated. Sometimes one or other acquires a more widespread fame: there is one, for example, near the village of Sandmaria which is believed to be especially benevolent towards robbers. She is still worshipped by raiding parties before they set out on a cattle-lifting expedition, and again if they return successfully.

The other conspicuous type of shrine is found near the village itself, usually on top of a small hillock. This consist of a low wall, forming three sides of room. Exceptionally it may also be roofed over with leaves or tiles. At the back of the room is a low platform, on which are set a row of massive earthenware plaques, of a characteristics design, bearing the figures in relief of certain Hindu Gods and Goddess. These plaques are made by the potters of one particular village called Molera, which lies on the fringe of the mountanious area, not far from the town of Nathdwara. The Bhils have to travel for three days, carrying these plaques on their backs, in order to bring them from their place of origin. This shrine is called a *devra*, a Hindi word, whereas the ordinary speech of the Bhils is a mixture of Marwari and Gujerati. Not only the word, but also the gods, and the worship associated with them, are borrowed from the Hindi-speaking plains: indeed, the Bhils themselves refer to them as "the Gods from Mewar".

The Devalo

After living among the Bhils for some time, one comes to appreciate that just as the *mukhi* is the significant person in the community for all the most important social interactions, so is another individual, known as the *devalo*, of equal importance in their dealings with the supernatural world. The *devalo* is their physician, and it is he who diagnoses the cause of any trouble in the house, whether an illness, a theft, or a loss. He does this by speaking his charms over a handful of maize, and then laying out the grains in a series of patterns — the first in pairs, then in threes, fours, fives and so on up to nine. By the number of grains left over at each dealing-out he tells the nature and the source of the danger, which in most cases is ascribed to the magical wrath of a witch, a Goddess, a demon or in a few cases, to a deadly charm which an enemy has persuaded another *devalo* to launch against the patient.

The *devalo* is respected, if he acquires a good reputation for healing the sick, and he may be feared on account of his dangerous charms: but he is certainly not held in awe. On the contrary, when a Bhil has no need of his services, he tends rather to make fun of his *devalo*, saying that he has chosen the lazy life, just sitting over his grains, and mumbling charms and then collecting his reward; and others repeat the old taunt that when a *devalo* becomes strong in magic, he loses his phallic potency. This is very generally believed, in spite of their denial. When the writer remarked that certains devalos of his acquaintance had young children, his informants only grinned and said : "Yes but who knows may have helped him out !"

The art of the devalo has to be learned from another practitoner. In some cases it may be handed down from father to son, but more often the father refuses to instruct his own children, as there is room for only one active *devalo* in a village. Having learned the charms, and the techniques of divining, the pupil must then accompany his instructor to th village burning ghat on the last night of the month of Kartik (about October). On this night, ghosts are believed to return to earth. The *devalo* sits inside a *kar* or magic circle marked upon the ground, and converses with the ghosts. They may ask him for meat, or wine, or bread, and he comes prepared for this throwing his gifts on to the ground well clear of the *kar*, where he is inviolable. Finally an apparition more terrible than all the rest appears. This is the King of the Dead, called Babrio Joting-walo: and it is by virtue of his unearthy powers that the *devalo's* charms acquire their potency. An apprentice cannot begin to practice with any hope of success until he has paid an experienced *devalo* a handsome sum in order to be initiated in this way. He dare not go alone, because without the protection of a potent charm, he would be destroyed by the ghosts.

An indication of the commoner magical scourges of the Bhil community can be gained from the following list of customary charges made by devalos for diagnosing a variety of afflictions:—

1. For ascertaining that there is no magical cause at work: one and a quarter *paili* (about a half-pint) of maize.
2. A God of the village *devra*: 2 annas. (about two pence).
3. A ghost : 4 annas.
4. A lesser *Vir* (a house-protecting spirit) : 8 annas.
5. A Goddess : 20 annas (one and a quarter rupees).
6. A witch from the same village : Rs. 2/8.
7. A witch from another village : Rs. 4/- or more.
8. A powerful *Vir* : Rs. 5/-.

This does not exhaust the range of their diagnosis. An important omission is the case of afflicition by *Kamria-pat*, a Bhil household Gold: this was said to be one of the most dangerous, and consequently most extensive diagnosis to make. The *devalo*, unlike the *bhopas* did not hesitate in some cases to announce the patient's certain death: if a particular combination of grains emerged, nothing could save him. For this prognosis, however, he made no charge.

It will be appreciated that the *devalo*, although the possessor of certain magical skills, is not himself a religious figure, but simply an intermediary in cases where supernatural influences have complicated a man's life. It will be apparent also that the scale of his charges gives an indication of the relative importance of the various gods and demons in the Bhils' estimation.

Dakan and Sikotra

In Delwara, the writer had been told two things about Bhil witchcraft: that their witches went by the name of *sikotri*, and that it had reached the point where a household did not feel safe unless they also possessed a witch to compete with all the others. Thus, it was said that when the emissaries from a Bhil girl's home went to the house of her future husband in order to arrange for the marriage, one of their questions would be : "Is there a watcher in the house?" Only if this were answered in the affirmative would the betrothal be confirmed.

This proved to be only a little removed from the true facts. The Bhils, like the Rawats, considered the majority of illnesses afflicting women and children to be due to the action of a *dakan*, or witch: but they believed that every single woman, soon after she was married, was initiated into the arts of witchcraft. Consequently, they were ready to tolerate minor exhibitions of this nature without undue concern. Sometimes, however, the witch seemed to be of a stubborn and implacable nature, and the illness she brought about would not be curable. When an unfortunate woman got the reputation of being a really dangerous dakan, the devalo might consult her spirit, in her absence, to ask : "Is it your wish to be swung ?"

If the grains showed the answer to be in the affirmative, the woman was seized forcibly, and swung by the feet from a very high tree, while red peppers were bound as a poultice over her eyes. The swinging would go on for hours, or even in an extreme case day and night, until the woman confessed and promised to cease her witch's work. Such a dangerous witch was generally turned out by her husband, to return to her parents' home unless she found another man hardy enough to risk taking her as his wife. In one instance in the summer of 1950 a woman was accused by the *devalo* of being responsible for her husband's severe and prolonged illness. She was furious, and withstood "swinging" for three nights and two days on end before she confessed, but by this time the man had died, and her eldest son, in a rage at her supposed murder of his father, drew his sword and cut off her head.

It was not true that they were known as *sikotri*, except by non Bhils. The *sikotra* was a very powerful magic, kept in many households, which defended that house against theft and all kinds of attack. It consisted of a Goddess, called *Melri* and her lieutenant, a male spirit called *Vir*. These were represented by two stones, often set into the wall which formed the base of the back of a hut. It was to these agencies taht the betrothal emmissaries referred, when they asked : "Is there a Watcher? (*rakhwali karne wali*)". The confusion was the more easily made because witches are believed to owe much of their power to the possession of charms which enable them also to send the *Vir* on their magical errands.

When a household possessed a guardian *sikotra*, there was usually one member, either male or female, to whom the spirit of the Melri goddess would come, either on special occasions, or at any rate on the occasion of her annual tribute of all-night singing and worship. The writer was told of several occasions when the goddess had appeared to others, in their dreams, in order to rouse them from their sleep because the house was in danger of attack by thieves: indeed if she failed to do so, and they were robbed, it was an indication that she as displeased with them. On one occasion during the writer's stay, a young Bhil was anxious lest some of his crop should be stolen, so he slept in the field outside his house: but the Melri came and slapped his face, saying : "Don't you know that I'm here, watching over this field ?" So he got up and went indoors again.

The Melri is usually handed down from father to son, and

there is an obligation to keep her glad with regular attentions. It happened recently in one household in Khajuria that the Melri fell out so determinedly with the present generation of her keepers that they suffered one hardship after another. This was diagnosed at last by a very shrewd *devalo*, who undertook to offer her a more congenial home in another village. She agreed to go if she were accompanied by two cows, and so the *devalo* left, carrying the dangerous stones, and driving his cows before him, and the household was glad to be relieved of her presence.

Household Gods

Beside the *sikotra*, there were two forms of household god of a purely male character. The first of these was called *Dhula-na-pat*; the other, *Kamria-pat*. In each case the place of worship was in an inner room of the hut, and consisted of a low platform, about ten inches high, a foot wide and a few inches in depth, the whole being neatly smeared with mud and cowdung plaster. The platforms were referred to as the *pat*, (one of whose meanings of "throne"). The former of these two might co-exist in the same house as a *sikotra*, but never the latter. The former was at once milder, and less to be relied upon as a defender of the home. Its worshippers were quite unable to describe its attributes, except to say that it was of God, using the term *Bhagwan*, which they use when they refer to a remote, aloof deity who is behind all reality, but with whom ordinary mortals have no dealings.

Kamaria-pat is quite different. The writer was at first surprised to be told, on asking about his nature : "He is a brass horse." In fact, he is a fierce, jealous and very present God, who is worshipped in the form of a small brass horse. In the majority of instances, the families whoch worship Kamaria-pat do not possess such a horse, but only the empty *pat*. Those which do possess the horse are obliged to spend one month of every year in travelling from house to house of others who harbour the pat, passing their nights in singing and dancing before it. The songs, and the dance rhythms, which are accompanied by three traditional instruments (a type of drum called *sang*, a one-stringed fiddle, and flutes) are of characteristic and very compelling character. *Kamaria-pat* is by far the most dreaded of all the form of protector, but also the most exacting, requiring his worshippers to keep up their singing and dancing hour after hour, for many nights of the year: at the end of the evening his spirit would come to one, or to several of the performers, and they would thrash upon the floor in violent paroxysms of possession. These were not regarded as *bhopas*; it was merely an expression of his benevolent interest in the family. Sometimes one person became singled out for especially frequent and profound fits of possessions, and if this were the case, he or she would be tested by pouring some drops of very hot oil on to the back of their hand. If they did not wince, and if no blister came, then they were regarded as receiving an especially strong visitation of the God, and anything they said during their possession was treated as oracular.

The only two contexts in which the writer found the Bhils really strongly moved in relation to their religious beliefs were, first in describing the menace to the community of a really stubborn witch (if "swinging" did not satisfy her, there was nothing to be done but kill her, in order to protect the children that she might destroy) and in referring to Kamriapat. In all other contexts, the supernatural seemed to lie easily upon them. For example one informant, after describing how Melri must be offered a goat at Navratri, and how her *bhopa* will drink the goat's blood, mixed with *daru* and with milk, goes on to say : "If a Melri fails to protect your house from theft, you sometimes have to reproach her, give her abuse and knock her down, — leave her lying for some days with her face in the mud. Then she'll go and strike the thief, and then you will treat her well again. But Kamria is not like that. If a man ever breaks into a house and sees that brass horse, he'll not dare to steal from there, or try to have sex with a married woman of that family. If he is foolish enough to do so, he will surely die."

The Gods from Mewar

Not every Bhil village a *devra* with its row of earthenware figures, and those that do own one treat it with complete disregard for the greater part of the year are there *jagarans*, or all-night performances of hymn-singing and bhopa-possession, like that at the shrine of Devji in Sujarupa. The writer attented three such *jagarans*, and found certain points of interest. At the earlier stages of the ceremony, a group of the more enthusiastic worshippers gathered inside the shrine, and sang *bhajans* to a guitar-like instrument, and these *bhajans* were not in the brood Bhili dialect, but in Gujerati, showing that they had come from the sophisticated Hindu plains to the south, in Gujerat. This was however only the start of the evening. After the *bhopa* had made offerings to the gods, and been possessed for a time, and had handed out *prashad* (a share of coconut chips and sugar given in offering) the proceedings were resumed outside the shrine, Bhil youths and girls forming two lines, each in Indian file, one close behind the other. These dancers move in concentric circles, to the beat of a large drum: and as they dance they sing songs in quite another idiom to that of the hymn previously hard. These songs have a characteristics rhythm, with a rising and falling note. One man says apart from the rest and sings the verse, which is taken up before has finished each couplet and repeated by the rest, like a cannon. Some of the songs are traditional, some are invented by the singer of the moments. One, with many spontaneous variations, is in honour of the Goddess of a nearby mountain, famous for its abundance of panther and other game; this one is called "*Kali* Dungri Wali — She of the Black Mountain."

It is evident that the occasion has ceased to be one of worship for the little-known and not very seriously regarded Hindu Gods, and has reverted to the pattern of a Bhil festival — but with this difference, that on this occasion they do not get drunk, and young men and girls do not slip away from the dance to meet in the darkness outseide and make love. These two concessions are made to the repressive prejudices which attend the worship of Brahmanical deities. In a typical *devra*, the following gods were observed: (i) Eight plaques representing Dharm-Rajah, a Vaisnavite God; (ii) a black-snake-god, here called Wasingh; (iii) five more versions of Dharm-rajah; (iv) an old black severn-headed Wasingh; (v) three upright plain stones, said to be the original deities of the shrine, described as goddess-images; (vi) a stone to represent Ganesh; (vii) three paired standing male figures, Dard and Light Bhainonji; (viii) three Goddesses, mounted on tigers, called Chaumunda-Mata. Outside, there are two stones set on a little platform, called *pauliys* (a Hindi word, meaning Door-keepers). These are described as "servant-gods — they guard the door."

The *devra* presents a striking contrast between the glitter of bright paint on the newest of these gods, which must have been brought from Molera during the last year, and the dull colourless dilapidated state of the rest, which have been lying out neglected in all weathers since they were brought some years before. It is noticeable too that the *bhopa* commands much less authority here than he does in Sujarupa or Delwara. On the two nights of the jagarans, he is acknowledged to be the central figure, but at other times he is seldom consulted, and he only rarely visits the shrine himself.

Besides the *bhopa* (or *bhopas*) of the shrine, however, there are certain other individuals who are associated with the worship of the Hindu Gods. These are men who have been influenced by the *bhakti* movement, usually through contact with someone who brought its practices back after living for some time in the plains, or sometimes as a result of the teaching of a wandering holy man who taugth this sort of worship. Such holy men are known as *bhagats*, and with their aura of sanctity and of superior knowldge of the sophisticated world beyond the jungles they are treated with very profound respect, indeed are worshipped by the Bhils as if they were already Gods themselves. The pupils of these *bhagats* take pains to learn some of their devotional hymns and like to sing them to the *bina* and *majeras*, which are regarded as their appropriate accompaniment: and such neophytes are called *Sadh*. The *Sadh*, however, has no social function in the Bhil community. His religious instruction encourages him to concentrate in advancing his own spiritual condition with repeated exercises of praise and devotion, and to give up eating meat and drinking *daru*: and the rest of his community regard this as a strictly personal aberration, which they tolerate, without wishing to emulate it. Sometimes a *Sadh* may acquire a widespread reputation among his fellow-Sadhs in surrounding villages, and they will come to his house to join in his hymn-singing evenings. When this happens, his fellow-villagers begin to concede that he must be an exceptional man, in his own way; and he will now be confirmed in his title as a *pakka* (genunie) *Sadh*. This carried with it the distinction of special treatment after death. Ordinary mortals are cremated, at the village burning-place which is usually near the bank of a river. *Devalos, Bhopas* and *Sadhs*, however, are buried instead. If a *Sadh* has acquired a considerable fame, he will be buried by the side of a main road or frequented path, and a small memorial built for him, with a stone set upon it. For one decade or two he may be worshipped by those of the village who remember him, and thereafter the memorial falls to pieces.

It is significant of the different functions of these three roles that the Sadh's funeral is the occasion for all-night hymn-singing by others of his persuasion (out of over 400 individuals living in the immediate vicinity of Khajuria there were only two recognised as Sadhs, and three or four young men beginning to take an interest in learning from them), the *bhopa* is burned near the burning-ghat by his kinsmen and fellow-villagers: but the burial of a *devalo* is a very special and dangerous occasion. The corpse of the devalo can only be carried by other devalos, and only they remain by the prepared grave when the moment of interment comes — all the rest of the villagers retreat to a safe distance, the locality being so dangerously charged with devilish presences.

Ancestor Worship

In the Bhil country, besides the way-side memorial described above in the case of a celebrated Sadh, a similar rough platform, with a smooth stone set on top of it, may be contructed in memory of any Bhil who was outstanding in wealth or personality. Nearly always, such a one will have been the *mukhi* of his village. In a few instances, as occurs in Sandmaria village, the memorial may even have a canopy built over it, and the descendants of the dead may worship there for some generations. Usually these memorials called *sura*, are very crude and impermanent. A commoner form of *sura*, indistinguishable in form from the above, is that built at the spot where a Bhil met with a violent or accidental death. There were five such memorials of recent construction near Khajuria, one to a youth who was killed by a fall from a tree, another to a man shot by an arrow while robbing a neighbour's cornfield, the others a reminder of fights with sword and dagger. After a sudden death such as these, it is necessary for a goat to be killed, and its blood splashed over the newely-erected memorial: otherwise the ghost of the dead man will cause mischief.

The Bhils did not observe *shraddha* rites, but they did "remember the dead" on the occasion of their own most enjoyable festivals, at Holi and Navratri, leaving some food and a few drops of liquor at the *sura* so that the ghost could also partake.

Another vestigial custom concerning the spirit of the dead was the *sakandhol*, a ceremony performed on the occasion of the *lokai* or funeral feast, which took place at an irregular interval (usually about a month) after a death. Inside the dead person's house a puppet of straw was attached to a taut string, and relatives sat round singing songs of morning, telling about the life of the one who died. At the climax of this singing they would gaze at the puppet, and never failed to see it quiver, or stir in the wind, which they took as a sign that the spirit of the dead had momentarily entered it. This was the signal for à fresh outbreak of lamentation, and crying of his name. Then a portion of the feast was thrown outside the house, for the spirit and the rest divided among the guests. As so often the contrast between this ceremony and its corresponding ceremony in orthodox Hinduism is the greater stress on the personal feeling, which is unashamedly expressed.

Early Observations on Religious life of these areas

In spite of the period of a century and a quarter in which the regions in which these three villages lie were under direct or indirect British rule, very few observations have been published on the social life of their people. Significantly, the best were those written many years ago, before improved communications brought the Men-sahibs to India, and gave rise to the creation of the isolated life of the European Clubs. The early administrators, whether or not they took wives in the country, could not fail to a closer appreciation of way of life of the rural population. The writings of Colonel Tod, whose Annals of Rajasthan appeared in 1829, are a mine of information not only about the Rajputs, whom he championed with such vigour, but also about many of the other communities (such as the Garasias of Bhomat) whom he met in the course of his laborious travels. Another classic of the early days of British influence in Rajputana is Colonel Dixon's account (published in 1848) of his thirteen years' work as

Superintendent of Mairwara. He says of the Rawat peoples: "Although they consider themselves Hindoos, their observances of that religion are extremely loose; nor would anyone brought up in the tenets of that faith consider them as associates. They are perfectly regardless of all the forms enjoyed as to ablution, the preparation of their food, and other set ceremonies. Nor do they pay religious reverence to the idols worshipped by orthodox believers of that persuasion. They pay devotion to Devi, Devji, Ullajee, Seetlamata, Ramdevji, and Bhueeroonjee, and celebrate the rites of Holes and Dewalee. They partake freely of sheep, goats, cows and buffaloes, where such food is available. No interdiction exists as to the use of spirituous liquors." He then goes on to describe their very prevalent belief in witchcraft, which he held up to derision with all the authority of his position : "Ridicule had its full force, as was desired, and little is now heard of this superstition."

The Bhils of Bhomat have never been adequately studied, but one interesting article is to be found in the Journal of the Royal Asiatic Society of Bengal, dated 1875. This was written by a Dr. T. H. Hendley, who had served for two years as Surgeon to the Mewar Bhil Corps, in Kherwara. He also dwells on the Bhils' dread of the power of *dakans*, and mentions the practice of witch-swinging — "even now cases are often reported". He makes no mention of their household gods (about which they are still relucant to talk, especially with strangers) but remarks on the numerous Goddess-shrines, with their offerings of horse-figures; but he believes that these horses are themselves worshipped. This may be a confusion with the brass horse of the Kamria pat. His observation : "The women are very chaste and rarely have intrigues with strangers" ready strangely to day, and may have been influenced by an euphemistic informant; but it is of interest to note that in his medical examination of Bhil recruits for the Corps he found veneral disease to be extremely rare. To-day, it is extremely common, at any rate in Kotra Bhomat. He mentions the presence of visiting Hindu holy men, called babas, in the Kherwara area, and says that the Bhils there treat them with great reverence.

Dr. Hendley also quotes an imformant who told him that in former times the local Goddesses (referred to usually as

Chamunda or *Samuda*) were worshipped with human sacrifices. At the time of his article, buffaloes and goates were killed in their name on special occasions.

Classification of Religious practices

Having thus described, in summary form, the chief forms of religious observance in these three communitis, it is proposed to consider what different elements can be distinguished in their midst, and in what degree these elements are stressed in each of these three villages. In order to do this, the subject will first be considered objectively, to show what consistencies of behaviour attend different forms of worship. Next, the whole range will be considered from the standpoint of the informed orthodox Hindu of this region, taking the two best-educated Brahmans of Delwara as representative of this point of view. Finally, it will be shown how each community selects a small segment from the whole spectrum of religious behaviour, as the idiom of its own religious life.

One criterion of analysis is to contrast solitary with corporate worship. In sophisticated Hinduism, the highest levels of holiness are always reached alone, as the result of pursuing a way of approach to the divine; and this leads to experiences which are incommunicable. The ultimate reward of this sort of worship is liberation from the doom of re-birth, into a union with the divine essence. Expressed in simpler terms, a holy man is very near God: and consequently he is frequently worshipped by ordinary sinful martals as if he were already divine, and legends soon spring up to emphasise supper-human powers. For example, when Delwara was visited by the ecstatic Govind Guru, the writer was told several times that he was so holy that when rain fell, no drops touched the holy man or the cloth on which he sat: but the writer's own observation did not bear out this pious assertion.

Ascetics and holy beggars are necessarily an exceptional case, but the principle of solitary worship was observed also by those members of the Brahman Rajput castes who concerned themselves seriously with their spiritual advancement. These were in the minority, except among Brahmans of the older generation. Their essential act of worship was to sit in a place apart, especially in the early morning after bathing but before breaking their fast, and to repeat one of the names of God in such a way as to withdraw their whole mental attention for a time from the outside world, and focus it on this concentration upon the divine essence. This form of solitary concentration and mental reaching-out towards God had also an observe side, in the vigil beside the potent shrine or at the burning-ghat of the man who repeated over and over some magical charm, compelling the god or demon of that spot to invest it with his power. In Sujarupa and Khajuria the latter practice was well-known, but the formmer was found only in a rudimentary form. The *Sadhs* in the Bhil country did not practice it at all, while the *bhagats* of Sujarupa performed it in a mentary manner when they remembered — with the sole exception of one Nathu Singh who claimed that he took the name of God for an hour both night and morning. But Nathu Singh was an untrustworthy informant, and never more so than when praising his own virtues.

Corporate worship was by far the more common. It existed in families, in the village, in persons united by their common adherence to a sect, and in the sense of being a participant in the whole wide range of Hindu observances. *Family* worship consisted not only of the act of remembrance and of homage to the ancestors, which was intense and short-lived among the Bhils, formalised and prolonged in the upper castes of Delwara, and which in Sujarupa seemed concentrated upon their not distant founder; it also entered into everyday behaviour, because to the Hindu, there are religious sanctions governing all the acts of daily life, especially the rules as to ritual cleanliness, the cooking and eating the food, the cleanliness of the home, and the conduct of family members one towards another. On all these points there was a gult between accepted practice in Delwara and that of the Bhils, with Sujarupa occupying a midway position : one thing however all these communities had in common, and that was the expression of family solidarity at certain critical points, such as a marriage, or the period of mouring after a death, or the subsequent funeral feast which had to be performed as an obligation towards the dead. In one respect, the Bhils excelled the rest in family solidarity, namely in the support which they gave each other in the carrying on of a feud. In the other more "advanced" villages, litigation had taken the place of open violence, and prolonged lawsuits were commonly an expression of internal disputes within a lineage. The wider extension of family obligations concerned the caste as a whole, whose authority governed the censure of acts of impiety as well as infringements of purely secular rules (where indeed the two could be divided). Caste meetings were however infrequent. Among the Bhils they were unknown : when large numbers of Bhils met together, it was for political and not for religious reasons. In Delwara, a general complaint was made that the caste-councils had lost their old prestige. Nowadays young men could violate the most important caste rules with impunity, so long as they did not infringe the secular law of the courts as embodied in the Indian Penal Code.

Village religious observances had this quality, that there was no compulsion to show assiduity in worshipping the shrines which served all village community: but that any act of disrespect, or of open repudiation of these shrines whould excite immediate reprisals from the offender's village neighbours. A conspicuous example of this occurred during the writer's stay in Delwara, when a foolish youth accepted a bet of fifty rupees that he would not dare to swallow as much as a pin-head of human faces. The enormity of his offence was so great that not only was he outcastes by his fellow Darogas, but the whole village turned against him and made it plain that he had better go and live elsewhere. On the positive side, the villagers united in common at certain of the big seasonal ceremonies, such as the woman's worship of Seetla-Mata (strictly observed in Delwara, less so in Sujarupa and not at all in Khajuria, in direct ratio to the incidence of smallpox in these localities), and the cheerful feasts of Holi, Divali and Gangor (only the first of which was generally observed in Sujarupa and Khajuria).

Membership of sects was a minority activity, and was seen with its most formal organisation in the rural villages round about Sujarupa, although *bhakti* sects existed, both in their respectable and in their abhorred forms also in the vicinity of Delwara. In the latter village there were a number of enthusiasts who were frequent attenders at hymn-singing sessions at certain of the temples, but these sessions were open to all and sundry and were conducted without formality. Those who were serious adepts of the *bhakti-marg*, like young Nahar Singh, used to travel round the surrounding country to attend *satsangs* at the homes of fellow-members of their sects. In Khajuria, the *bhakti-marg* existed in embryo in the persons of the few *Sadhs,* but was not organised. On the other hand, there was something of this group — identification in the worship of the household gods, *Sikotra, Dhulanapat* and *Kamria-pat*. These had something of the character of family worship, as they bestowed protection on the household which harboured and payed homage to them, but they could also be worshipped and have favours asked of them by others as well. The corporate element in their worship was most apparent in the case of *Kamria-pat*, because every family which worshipped the Brass Horse was linked with every other one, through knowing the same hymns, and dance and song, and through the common experience of being possessed by his spirit. There was another factor which tended to cause a feeling of solidarity to develop among these worshippers, and this was the families which did not subscribe to this cult were reluctant to enter into marriage ties with those that did: they felt that the responsibilities involved in worshipping the Horse were even more onerous than his protection justified, and preferred to keep clear of it altogether.

Finally, there was the sense of belonging to a vast and all-embracing community, whose external symmbols were present in every village temple, and wayside shrine. The people of Sujarupa and Delwara took great pleasure, in their infrequent excursions into the surrounding country, in visiting strange temples, more especially those which had acquired a more than local fame, as was the case with Miala, Dadalia, Eklingji and Nathdwara. This was enhanced by the prevailing belief that one receives a spiritual enhancement from experiencing a *darshan* (literally, a vision), whether of a saintly man or of a celebrated idol of God, The feeling of participation in the Hindu community depends however on one's acceptance of one's own position in the hierarchical order; and for this reason the Rawats of Sujarupa professed a strong dislike for the outside world, where their pretention of Rajput status was ignored or derided. Even those who earned good money in the mills of Ahmedabad always kept the ambition of returning to the Marga to cultivate a plot of land beside their fellow Rawat Rajputs. This was still more the case with the Bhils, who found themselves treated by the Hindus as members of the lowest caste. They are excluded from some temples, and admitted to some others only on certain festival days. Still, there are one or two Hindu temples in large villages on the fringe of the Bhomat which have a fame among them, and where they took like to go, to have a *darshan* of a God about whom they may know nothing but his name.

Another way of considering these forms of worship is to assess them in terms of the universality of their recognition. The narrowest range must then be ascribed to the worship of the family ancestor; and the next, to the purely local god, the protector of some glen or pathway. Yet this is often confused by the borrowing of a name from a wider context, as the Bhils do in calling their local deities Chamunda, or the Rawats with their profusion of little Bhaironjis: it is shown to be a genuine distinction when one finds purly local names, like Radhaji, or Bhumiaji for the protectors of a field, and Kali Dungri Wali for the Goddess of the Black Mountain. Beyond this can be reckoned those especial Gods or Goddesses which are linked with one particular caste, or section within a caste, as in the case of the Rawats' *Piplaj-Mata*, the Jhala Rajputs' *Ad-Mataji*, and the Bhils' *Kamria-pat*. Then there are Gods which are recognised over a wide region, but which are unknown in the rest of India. A good example of this is Ram-Devji, whose name is honoured in Rajasthan (although for the most part among the Sudra castes) and known in parts of Gujerat but not elsewhere, or Devji and Tejaji who are worshipped only in the Rawats' territory. Beyond this again are those Gods and Goddesses which are representatives of the Hindu pantheon, but which are specially reverenced in certain regions because there exists of famous image of them there. This often finds expression in the customary greetings of that part, as in Mewar one says: "Jai Sri Nathji", and further north, "Jai Char-Bhujaji", while elsewhere "Jai Sri Krishna" may be the usual exchange. In this connection it is noteworthy that the Bhil's invariably greet each other with the commonest name of God : "Ram, Ram"; and the Rawats do the same, or else say: "Jai Ramji ki"

With this extension we have exhausted the ordinary villager's knowledge of the Hindu Gods. If he lives in a large centre, such as Delwara, he may learn more, by listening to *bhajans* and to the reading of sacred *katha*, but he is always aware that there are more and more that he has never heard of. For practical purposes he is concerned only with those which he sees represented in the temples and shrines in the vicinity of his home.

Another distinction is between those forms of worship which are associated with possession by a spirit, and those to whom this occurrence is alien. In the former class come all those shrines (most of them small and unpretentious) where there is a *bhopa* to act as intermediary for the God — the Bhaironjis and Radhajis and Matajis — but also the Bhils' household gods, and those instances of *purbaj*-possession in Delwara. This last is closely akin to the similar possession in Delwara. This last is closely akin to the similar possession which marks affliction by a mischievous ghosts, or by the disembodied spirit of a witch.

Finally, the various forms of worship can be classified in terms of the type of offerings which are acceptable to the Gods concerned; and here the great division is between those which accept blood and wine; and those to whom bloodshed and the very smell of alcohol is abhorrent. The latter have a great variety of forms of "cool" offerings: fruit, flowers, coconuts, incense and the flame of a wick burning sweet oil or melted butter being the commonest. The association, as in the Bhil country, of a special form of offering (the clay horse) with a particular deity is most uncommon.

Rank in prestige of various practices

In this consideration of rank-order of the practices which have been described above, it is proposed to take the outlook of Delwara Brahmans as the point of reference. They would no hesitation in considering the highest expression of the religious life to be the most intellectual one, namely the practice of abstinence, asceticism and regular spiritual exercises carried out in solitude with the aim if attaining a direct intuition of the nature of God. This is the Hindu ideal, which justifies the reverence with which holy wandering beggars are regarded, and which also underlies the respect which should be paid to the Brahman, because not only is he by birth set far on the way towards divinity, but his caste obligations of religious study and prayer ensure that he will continue to advance in godliness.

The Brahman respects all acts of piety performed towards the two great Gods of Hinduism, Shiva and Vishnu; and also he is disposed in favour of all those who do what is right, as it is laid down in their Sanskrit scriptures. This includes not only the invocation of the other major Gods at the important moments in one's family life, and their proper worship at their annual festivals, but also the leading of a life in all respects in accordance with the instructions laid down in his texts for the regulation of the proper conduct of every one of the four Estates-Rulers, Priests, Merchants, Labourers. They are naturally very conservative, resenting any departure from the traditional ways of doing things. There is a place in his texts for a disciplined and pious remembring of one's ancestors in the *shraddha* rites, and he considers it right that the Goddess, whether in the form of Seetla-Mata, or Gangaur, or Gangaji should be hoboured with flowers and sweet offerings; but the Brahman disapproves of the taking of life, and so regards the customary blood-sacrifices to the Goddess as a sign of ignorance and error. He is still more condemnatory of all those small Gods which have also have *bhopa*-possession as a feature of their worship, whether or not they also have blood-sacrifices. All these, he says, are so much studpidity: they are not Gods at all — just ghosts and demons, if anything at all.

The writer was for some time confused as to the Brahmans' attitude towards ghosts, witchcraft and malicious magic: they would dismiss all that as "lies, nonsense"; and yet at other times they would say : "Of course there *are* ghosts and witches in this country side, as there are everyday, — but they cannot harm a man who worships God with an undivided mind." (Of medieval European faith in the power of the Lord's Prayer to repell witches and demons.) One Brahman described how he was able to repell ghosts which threatened him in the dusk by repeating holy Sanskrit verses; but one day he was beset by a particularly virulent ghost, that of a Brahman who had died a violent death before his time; and every time he repeated a *Slok*, the ghost was able to cap it with another. As a result of this encounter he became seriously ill, and felt himself lucky to have escaped with his life. Everything pertaining to the "ripening" of magical charms by the aid of ghosts or wayside godlings is deplored by the Brahman as unclean, impious behaviour: impious because it represents an attempt to compell supernatural forces in one's favour, instead of accepting one's fate as it has been ordained[8].

The Brahmans are aware that the tribal peoples have other forms of worship. They do not know exactly what these are, but have no hesitation in dismissing them as low, superstitious practices. The tribal peoples are particularly repugnant to them because of their neglect of the rules as to eating, drinking, and especially as to ritual cleanliness, which are, in the Brahmans' opinion, absolutely essential adjuncts of holiness.

In Delwara, the Brahmans were not observed to take an active part in the public hymn-singing, although they frequently paused to look on for as few minutes. Their attitude was, that the way of devotion was right and proper for the uneducated, lower-caste people of good intention, but not fitting for scholarly men like themselves. They were vehemently opposed to the practices of the orgiastic sects, which they denounced as being in the last degree unclean and sacrilegious.

Degree of Observance of Defferent Practices

The range of different forms of religious observance in these three communities has already been presented. It remains now to indicate where the chief emphasis lay.

The Bhils gave the impression of being a people on whom religion lay lightly: something to be remembered when a favour was to be asked, or a misfortune averted. In their ordinary living, it was this *devalo*, the house-protecting *sikotra* and the threat from other *sikotras* and *dakans* which concerned them most frequently; but here again it was only when sickness or disaster of some sort came, that they would attend to these matters. For the rest, they treated their household gods and their devalo with familiar disregard. The only exception to this was in those families which harboured Kamria-pat, and which had to pay in more strenuous attentions for the greater security which his protection was believed to give. The Gods from Mewar, with their *bhopa* received scanty attention, and the aspiring *Sadhs* even less from the bulk of the Bhil villagers.

In Sujarupa, manifestations of the *bhakti*-marg were the commonest form of religious behaviour: but this had clearly not been the case for many years, to judge from the aloof attitude of the older men, and their occasional grumbling comments to the writer: "What do they mean by this, learning all these Brahman tricks in Ahmedabad — giving up meat and liquor and singing hymns all night ! Don't they know that we Rajputs are entitled to eat and drink that if we like ?" Complete unanimity was shown in their enthusiasm, for the annual worship of Ram-Devji; and a large measure of agreement in their confidence in the *bhopas* of Danaji and Devji (here Nathu Singh was the only one to denounce them as delusory). Little was known of the higher flights of Hinduism, but these Rawats indetified themselves wholeheartedly with the world of orthodox Hinduism, even though the reverse might not be the case.

In Delwara, the whole of the above range of behaviour was exhibited, except for the Bhils' house-gods: even these may have been present, because on numerous occasions the writer heard a strange music and chanting coming from houses in the Bhils' quarter of the village, and months later he was able to recognise a similar refrain in the worship of Kamria-pat; but this was not verified in Delwara. Apart from a very few educated Brahmins and Rajputs intent on their solitary spiritual exercises, and one or two individual adherents of the *bhakti-panths* the greater part of the village religious observance was centred round the many shrines were *bhopas* "played" and spoke their oracles on a given night each week. These ceremonies were attended for the most part by people of the lower castes, who were in the majority in the village; but it was noteworthy that Banias, Rajputs and even occasionally some of the uneducated Brahmans were also to be seen in their audiences. Other regularly patronised, but less numerous groups were those which met to hear *katha* and sing hymns at the three most active high-Hindu temples. The Banias, though nominally a sect apart, were to the fore in both of these popular forms of worship. In their own observances, they were assiduous in offering hospitality to holy men, whether Hain or Hindu, and in listening to what they had to say, with many flattering interjections: but not one of them, to the writer's observation, put his religious interests on a par with the ruling passion of their lives, which was to make money. It is no exaggeration to say that the ceremony which they carried out with the most fervour was the ritual worship of their shop ledgers, and writing equipment, and pieces of money, which took place at Divali — and this was strictly speaking a Hindu observance, which the Brahmans had to conduct for them; it had no sanction in orthodox Jainism at all.

Comparison with mediaeval Britain

To anyone who has read Dr. Margaret Mureay's work: "The Horned God," on the subject of the prolonged underground survival in Britain of the pagan beliefs and rituals which had preceded Christianity, this account of the different orders of popular worship in India must present a close analogy. In fourteenth-century Britain there still existed many of the early inhabitants of these islands, as yet unassimilated either ethnologically or in their religion. It is these, the "little people," who were referred to as the "fairies," and to whom all kinds of magical and terrible powers were attributed. Not everyone will agree with the whole of Dr. Murray's argument, in which she goes on to equate the witches, with their covens and their alliance with the "powers of evil" with the deliberate maintenance of the old pagan beliefs: but to the writer the analogy is very striking between the Christian clerics' denunciation of the witches and the Brahmans' references to all forms of *bhopa*-cult as being the work of devils. Similar too is the attitude of the "elect" Hindu villager towards the Bhils, the "little people" of the hills and forests, to whom, they are quick to ascribe all kinds of magical powers.

It does seem that just as Christianity became the religion of the dominant people in Britain, and slowly over the centuries succeeded in obliterating the last of the stubborn survivals of the old beliefs, so it may well be in the Bhomat. Already in the Rawats we see a community which has discarded most of the practices which once it had in common with its tribal neighbours, and with each generation it seems to enchance its new Hindu respectability. Among the Bhils, this process has only begun, but with the improvement of comunications and the consequent increase of intercourse with the Hindu society of their rulers, it appears likely that the Bhils of Kotra Bhomat will soon apply themselves to adopting Hindu beliefs and Hindu values, as their kinsmen in the more accessible Kherwara Bhomat have already been doing for some generations.

Chapter-10

THE MEANING OF HINDUISM IN RURAL MALWA

K. S. MATHUR

Chapter-10

I

Hinduism is commonly understood as 'the religion of the Hindus'. The diversity of beliefs, philosophies, creeds, dogmas, rites and ceremonies, and social prevalent among the people of this great country, however, preclude any precise definition of Hinduism. "It is possible to find within its range philosophic mystics who disclaim beliefs in a personal Deity, fervent monotheists who direct their devotions towards a single personal God, of Whom and to Whom they speak in terms resemmbling those used by many Christians; and at the other extreme, crude animists whose main concern is with some local godling, generally a female tutelary divinity of the village, and polytheists of a type familiar to readers of Greek and Roman literature, closely resembling the scrupulously superstitious character outlined by Theophrastus". (Bouquet, 1948, p. 11).

The variation is both regional and sect-linked. At different times in the history of our country, different religious sects arose and sought to gain influence among the masses. These sects belong to five broad categories. These categories are : Vaishnava, Shava, Shakta, Smarta, and Tantrik. In each category, there are a number of sects. Each sect has its own characteristics religious beliefs and practices prescribed for its members.

Not all of these religious sects are spread — in their membership and belief — all over India. Some of the sect movements were strictly local and most had their influence only over a part of the country.

The territorial variation in Hinduism is also important for purposes of social analysis. Srinivas had classified Hinduism in three categories from the point of view of its spread, viz., All-India Hinduism, North Indian Hinduism and Peninsular Hinduism, and regional Hinduism (1952, p. 213). Social anthropologists and sociologists who have worked in Indian villages have constantly referred to such regional variations in the religious life of the people. Writes Dube: "Village Hinduism is not easy to describe. It is extremely elastic religion, and within its all-India framework admits of a considerable degree of religional and local variation". (1955, p. 94).

II

The object of this paper is to give a portrait of Hinduism as it appears to the rural Hindu population of Central Malwa and to analyse what they mean by '*Hindu dharma*'. The data on which this is based was collected during a research project in Central Malwa in 1956 while the author was working as a Research Scholar of the Australian National University. This was sought to be done by two techniques, viz., observation and questionnaire. In the first instance, the religious life of the people was observed. This was done in detail in one village and includes data collected on temple and domestic worship, fasts, festivals and solemnizations. Secondly, a questionnaire was prepared and given to about fifty subjects seeking information on their ideas about deities, Hindu religious concepts like *dharma, karma* and *punarjanma,* and their views about what constitutes Hinduism. The subjects were selected from ten prominent castes of the villages in this sub-region, viz., Malwi Brahmin, Rajput, Khati, An jana, Vairagi Vaishnava, Malwi Lohar, Nai, Darzi, Malwi Balai and Malwi Chamar. Fortyone of the subjects were men and nine women. The subjects were of ages varying between thirty and sixty; the men were only slightly educated — none beyond the secondary standard, the women were all illiterate. The questionnaire was taken to the subjects personally by the author and answers were taken down by their consent. On most occasions, such interviews were private at which only the informant and the author were present, but in few cases, other people of the village participated and influenced the views of the informant.

III

In the village which was intensively studied — which we shall here call Patal — there are four temples and seven shrines, dedicated to Hindu deities. On the north-western fringe of the village is an old temple in black stone dedicated to Shiva. In the middle of the village habitation are three temples—mud structures with galvanised iron sheet roofs. Two of these are dedicated to Lord Rama and one to Lord Krishna. These temples house stone images of the deities to whom they are dedicated. In the Shiva temple is the traditional symbol of Lord Shiva — the *lingam*. These temples are served by priests belonging to the Brahmin and other priestly 'clean' castes, like Gosain and Vairagi Vaishnava: the priests at the Shiva temple is a Goasin, one of the Rama temples is served by a Brahmin, and the other Rama temple and the Krishna temple are served by men belonging to the Vairagi Vaishnava caste.

Six of the seven shrines are located in wards predominently inhabited by 'shudra' and 'untouchable' castes. Most of the deities honoured at these shrines are also associated with particular castes; a member of the caste serves as priest at the shrine of his caste deity, and the caste group observes a ritual cult of the deity. The shrine to Shitala (smallpox goddess), for instance, is located in the Balai ward by the village pond, a Balai serves as priests and oracle to the goddess, and every year in the month of *Kuar*, the Balai observe a nine day festival in honour to Shitala. The shrine of Ram Deo Ji, a deity of the Bhambi caste, is situated in the Bhambi ward, and a man of the Bhambi caste serves as priests and minstrel at this shrine. The Desha Chamar have the shrine of their caste deity, Bhawani Mata, in a small hut situated in their ward; the deity is served by a Desha Chamar, who observed a seven-day festival of the goddess in the month of Chait. Kalka Mata's shrine stands on the westernmost end in the village habitation, just opposite the Balai Chamar ward. A Nath Jogi serves here as priest, and a Gujerati Chamar as oracle to the goddess. Mari Mata is regarded as the caste deity of the Malwi Chamar, and her small shrine is built under a tree immediate behind the Malwi Chamar row of houses outside the village. Another small shrine dedicated to the caste deity of the Bagri caste is situated in the cluster of Bagri houses, and a woman of the caste offers occasional oblations at the shrine; once a year, in the month of *Kuar*, the Bagri sacrifice a goat at the shrine, and believe that the caste deity looks after the welfare of the caste.

The only prominent shrine in Patal village which is not located in an 'unclean' or 'unctouchable' caste ward is the 'shrine of the village deities'. This shrine stands on the southern side of the village, across the stream which runs by the habitation area. Its priest belongs to the Mali caste. Once every year, during the festival of Dasehra (in the month of *Kuar*), a goat is sacrificed to the village deities, and once every ten or twelve years a big fair is held at the site, attended by all the people of Patal and many neighbouring villages.

Most of the Hindu villagers of Patal, with the exception of Brahmin and a few others, have no fixed time for daily worship. The exceptios are: males belonging to the two Brahmin families and the single Palliwal Bania family, one Rajput who is a very old man, men belonging to the Vairagi Vaishnava and Gosain castes who are temple priests, two Khati old men, and one old man belonging the Gujerati Lohar caste. For men of the Brahmin, Vairagi, Gosain, and Palliwal Bania caste, daily worship is an imperative, enjoined upon them by their *jati dharma*. They are required to go through the *upanayana* (*janoi*) ceremony at the age of ten to twelve, and wear the sacred thread thereafter.

The early morning daily routine of these men is like this: they get up early in the morning before sunrise, go out to the fields to defecate (in Sanskrit this is called *saucha kriya*, i.e., 'the process of cleansing'), clean the mouth with a *nim* twig, take a bath and don clean garments; then they wipe and clean the place of worship and perform *pooja* in the traditional style; they conclude the morning *pooja* by offering libations of water to the rising sun and chanting the sacred *gayatri mantra*.

The other four men (one Rajput, two Khati, and one Gujerati Lohar) who perform some kind of morning *pooja* every day are old men. They sat that they spent, like others, their youth in wordly preasures, and it is that in their old age, they must remember the creator and try to improve their *Karma*.

Similarly, the number of persons who visit a temple every day is very small. I checked the daily temple attendance in Patal over a month (December 1955). Analysis of these attendance lists revealed that the number of devotees regularly visiting any one of the four temples in Patal village was in no case more than ten. Most of these regular temple visitors belong to the 'clean' castes.

We find that out of a total of 1,037 Hindus in Patal, 37 spend some time every day in the pursuit religion, either performing *pooja* in their own houses or visiting one of the village temples. This analysis reveals two remarkable facts; they are : (i) no woman from any caste was found who performed *pooja* or visited a temple every day; and (ii) with the exception of the Nath Jogi (who are a sectarian caste), no persons belonging to the 'sudra' or 'untouchable' castes were found performing the daily *pooja* or visiting a temple every day.

The scriptural position in this respect is that women and *sudra* are considered to be incapable of the pursuit of divine knowledge and religion, and therefore, debarred from these. The people of Patal do not seem to be aware of such prohibitions, however. They say there are practical difficulties in the way of a woman or a member of one of the '*sudra*' or 'untouchable' castes performing the traditional *pooja* or visiting a temple every day. Some reasons given to me by some elderly women of Patal why women cannot be regular worshippers are : (i) for most of their life, they remain unclean for a few days every month when they have their periods; (ii) they do not get sufficient time from looking after children and domestic business; and (iii) their primary duty is to serve their husbands and children.

About the *sudras*, the general opinion among 'clean' *dwija* castes is that there is no real barrier for a sudra performing daily worship and visiting a temple regularly, and that they (i.e., the *sudras*) are themselves responsible for their 'irreligious' behaviour. The *sudras* have other explanations: some say that they have to work hard to earn their living and thus they do not get sufficient time, money or energy for what they call 'the luxury of worship and religion'. Others say that there is no real necessity for everyday worship and devotion; to them religious worship is like medicine which is to be resorted to only in times of calamity. "When we are in trouble", I was told by an elderly Balai man, "we make vows and promises to the deity, and when the trouble is over, we fulfil those promises by ceremonially worshipping the deity. The deity is usually our own caste deity, but in urgent cases, we may appeal to the great deities of Hinduism, like

Hanuman". Such a view about the use of religious worship is shared by most of the young and able bodied men of all castes. A few educated young men belonging to the *sudra* caste asserted that they would like to go to the Hindu temples and worship there if they were allowed to worship in the same way as 'clean' caste Hindus were. This, however, was disallowed by the 'clean' caste Hindus.

The Hindus of Patal say they worship all the major gods and goddesses of the Hindu pantheon. Such an assertion is made by members of all castes, 'clean', 'unclean' and 'untouchable'. I collected lists of deities they worshipped from a sample of informants drawn from all the castes in the village. Names of deities which are present in all the lists are : Rama, Krishna, Siva or Mahadeva, Surya, Hanuman, Ganesha, Satya Narain, Nag, Sitala, Bheru, and Sati. In the lists given by informants from the 'unclean' and 'untouchable' castes were mentioned some names of deities which were absent from the lists drawn up by 'clean' caste informants. They are Ram Deoji, Bhawani, Kalka, Mari, Bari, Phoolmati, and Lal Begi. There are shrines dedicated to all these deities in Patal.

The Brahmin informant mentioned the names of Ganga, Indra, Parasurama, and Agni also. The Rajputs said they worshipped Ajaypal Maharaj who was represented by a slab of stone (*palya*) on the south-eastern fringe of the village habitation. The Lohar informant included in his list of deities the name of Vishwakarma (literally meaning, 'He who made the universe') also; and the Kumhar said they worshipped Prajapati (literally meaning, 'The Lord of peoples') every time they fired their earthen pots; the Palliwal Bania said Lakshmi (the goddess of wealth) was the special deity worshipped by his caste. The Vairagi Vaishnava said that in addition to the Vaishnava deities (Rama, Krishna and Hanuman), they worshipped Baba Haridas who, they say, was the preceptor of all Vairagi Vaishnava. Similarly, the Nath Jogi said they worshipped their first *guru*, Gorakhnath.

It appears to be only a principle that all Hindus, 'clean', 'unclean', and 'untouchable' — profess to worship all or most of the deities of classical Hinduism as also the local godlings. In practice, however, each caste sticks to a few deities. They are more frequently worshipped by members of that caste and less frequently by other castes. Thus Vaishnava deities — Rama and Krishna — are worshipped more often by the Brahmin and other vegetarian 'clean' castes, like Palliwal Bania, Khati, Darji and Gujerati Lohar, and less other by those castes who in principle partake of meat and alcoholic drinks. It is significant to point out here that all other Malwa and Western India particularly, vegetarian food is spoken of as *vaishnava* food, and non-vegetarian food is referred to as *Rajputi* food.

The Rajput and other castes of the Rajput block worship Shiva more often. These castes are also referred to as the Shiva castes.

In 'unclean' and 'untouchable' castes, the limits are further narrowed down. Here, almnost each caste has its own deity, who is sometimes referred to by the people as their *jati deota* or caste deity. Sitala is the caste deity of the Malwi and Gujerati Balai; Ram Deo Ji, of the Bhambi; Bhawani, of the Desha Chamar; Kalka, of the Gujherati Chamar; Mari, of the Malwi Chamar; Bari, of the Bagri; Phoolmati, of the Bargunda; and Lalbegi, of the Bhangi.

The Hindu conception of deity is that it is a form — one of the numerous forms — of the Supreme Force. Each caste (having a caste deity) regards its caste deity as the most important and prominent form of the Supreme Force, even though, it recognizes that other deities are also forms of the same Supreme Force.

As might be expected, there are variations in the procedure of *pooja worship* offered to the different deities. These are particularly striking in the matter of food offered to the deity, the caste of the officiating priest, and the hymns or incantations recited in honour of the deity.

Each deity has its own favourite food which is generally offered to it by the worshipper. Most of the gods and goddesses of classicial Hinduism are believed to be fond of sweet food, milk and milk preparations which are offered to them at their *pooja*. Shiva is also a vegetarian god: he is believed to be fond of narcotics other than alcoholic drink, though; and devotees to Shiva offer him *bhang* and *ganja* and partake of the narcotics themselves. Ram Deo Ji is also a vegetarian and teetotal deity. On the other hand, Bhawani, Kalka. Sitala, Mari, Bari, Phoolmati and Lalbegi are deities who are believed to be extremely fond of animal sacrifices. The character of Behru varies according to the food habits of the caste with whom he is associated. By the vegetarian castes, a coconut is offered to him, whereas the non-vegetarian castes offer in his name sacrifice of a he-goat.

The caste of the priest also varies. The Brahmin serve only the Vaishnava gods and officiate at those rituals only where these deities are worshipped. Moreover, they serve only the 'clean' castes and the Nath Jogi. Vairagi Vaishnava and Gosain priests do likewise. At rituals observed in honour of other deities, the regular priest of the deity concerned officiates. The priest is generally drawn from the caste whose caste deity the god or goddess happen to be.

The nature of the incantations or hymn and the language in which they are spoken varies in accordance with the caste of the priest. Only the Brahmin, Vairagi Vaishnava and Gosain priests are eligible to chant scriptural incantations in Sanskrit. The others have to be satisfied with hymns in the local dialect. For every deity, there are different Sanskrit incantations and Hindi hymns and these have to be recited on appropriate occasions.

IV

Fasts and feasts form an important part of the religious life of village Hindus. They may be called 'fixed rituals', because the occasion and date for their performance is fixed on the local calender. They are observed as seasonal festivals. Their number is strikingly large, and their distribution over the year very irregular. Not all of them are observed by all castes of the village.

Given below is a chart listing the regular festivals observed by the Hindus of Patal, the month and date on which each is observed and the castes who observe it. The dates on which these festivals are observed are reckoned it terms of the Hindu calender. The months of the Hindu year are lunar months. Only the festival of Makar Sankranti also known a Til Sankrhnti is celebrated on a date reckoned in terms of solar calendar. The festival marks the transit of the sun at the Topic of Capricorn, and is popularly believed to be the beginning of the day of the gods and the night of the demons. Makar Sankranti may thus fall either in the lunar month of Poos or Magh. The festival is observed by 'clean' castes only, who bathe in cold water and give alms of rice and pulse grain to the Brahmin and temple priest.

An analysis of these 'fixed annual rituals' from the point of view of their religious import reveals that:

(i) three of them, viz., *Rama nomi, Krishna atham* and *Ganesh choth,* are celebrated to commemorate the birth of three of the principal gods of Hindu pantheon; two others, viz., *Shiva ratri* and *Anant chodas,* are also connected with two of the major Hindu gods;

(ii) three, viz., *Mahadeo Baba Ki jatra, Ganga dashmi,* and *Katik jatra* are pilgrimages to places considered to be sacred;

(iii) six of the these are by way of rituals devised to protect crops and cattle; these are *Akhati, Hariya goondiya, Hartalika, Keli pooja, Dewali* and *Annakot — Gobardhan*;

(iv) at six of the annual rituals (*Rishi panchami, Pitar Paksha, Nag panchami, Deva soni, Deva Uthni, and Teja ji ki jatra*), saints, ancestors and other local deities are honoured;

(v) the number of festivals observed by women alone is twelve; of these six are aimed at obtaining health and long life for husbands; the six are *Gangor, Bar ammavas, Bar satam, Hariyali, Garba and Karua atham;* on these occasions, they keep a day long fast, and offer *pooja* and prayers to the goddess Gouri, the *peepal* tree, the serpent god, or the Moon god for the perpetuation of their *suhag* (married state);

(vi) three rituals (*Bheru pooja, Mata poojan, and Narak chodas*) are aimed at procuring the welfare of one of the kin units — the family and the lineage;

(vii) the theme of at least four rituals is the dramatization of the brother-sister relationship, real or hypothetical; these are *Dewasa, Rakhi, Bhai beej and Ram nam*;

(viii) twice a year, rituals are observed to honour the mother goddes; on these occasions, the priest of the goddess worshipped goes into a trance and makes predictions for the half year — about crops, cattle, market conditions, disease, epidemics, and other topics of a general nature which are of interest. to the village people;

(ix) Lastly, there are the communal rituals, festivals in the real sense of the term, such as *Holi, Dol gyaras, Dashera, and Basant panchami,* when people observe a holiday from work and come out into the village lanes to sing songs and make merry.

Often the religious imsort of a ritual is differently understood by different castes. To the Palliwal bania of Patal and other Vaisya castes of neighbouring villages, Dewali is the day for the worship of the goddess of wealth; for the others, is a festival of lights, sweets and fireworks. Similarly, Dashera is a primarily Rajput ritual when they worship their arms and weapons. In feudal times this was called the day of *seemolanghan* ('violation of frontiers') when kings tried to extend the frontiers of their own domains by annexing land from neighbouring states. On the Rakhi day, adult Brahmin males keep a day long fast and change the sacred thread they wear on their shoulders.

Most of these rituals are purely domestic and private in character. The ceremonials are performed in the family house or in the village lane just outside the house, and they are presided over by the head of the household. In case of rituals observed by women exclusively, the *pooja* is supervised by the eldest female member of the household.

All these rituals are very similar in their formal features. The sequence of events is more or less the same. The participants observe a fast before the performance and undergo a ceremonial purification by bathing in the morning and donning washed garments. Sweets are cooked with care and special precautions. The girls and young women of the family paint traditional designs on the floor and walls of the scene of worship. Earthen lamps are lit, and the *pooja* is performed in the traditional way by pouring out libations of water presenting flowers and sandal paste, and finally offering the sweets in the sacred fire in the name of the deity who is worshipped on the ritual. This is followed by the recitation of sacred texts and singing of devotional hymns, and the distribution of the food offering (*prasad*).

V

To the common villager, Hinduism is more a way of life. It does involve some active worship, occasional visits and gift giving to temples, and observance of the annual fasts and feasts in the appropriate way. But more than that, for a Hindu, his *dharma,* prescribes what he should do and what he must not do. The latter, that is, the ritual prohibitions are more important to him since they constitute the character for his everyday actions.

In the first category, that is, the ritual prescriptions, coms such things as solemnizations and pilgrimages, giving of alms and gifts, and paying due respect to the Brahmin and other priestly castes. Thus, village Hindus are required to perform birth, sacred thread-giving, marriage, pregnancy and funeral rites in accordance with traditional rites. Of course, many of these rules vary from caste to caste and often from family to family, but the usual variations are only slight and often superficial. For instance, all Hindus observe some pollution on occasions of birth and death, though whether the pollution extends to the family circle or to the agnatic kin or to the entire kindred, and the actual nmber of days for which pollution is observed varied. Among the Rajput, for instance, death pollution affect the entire patrilineage of the deceased, whereas among the Malwi Brahmin, only the family members and near agnatic kin are involved in the ritual pollution caused by parturition and death. The Rajput observe death pollution and mouring for forty days, the Malwi Brahmin for thirteen days, the Khati and Mali for ten days, and certain 'unclean' Shudra caste like Malwi Balai, Malwi Chamar and Nath Jogi for three to seven days.

Similar is the case with menstrual pollution. In some measures all Hindus consider their women as impure during their menses. This is probably because of the fundamental Hindu religious belief that all bodily emissions (like saliva, perspiration, urine, faeces, menstrual blood and semen) are impure and polluting. But the actual observance of the taboos on menstruating women varies, in the number of days for which the pollution is observed and the restrictions the woman concerned suffers from. In this respect too, the Brahmin and Bania castes are the most rigid. In rural Malwa, Brahmin and Bania (both Vaishnava and

Jain) women observe menstrual pollution for a minimum of five days or for as many days as the flow actually lasts. During this period, they are required to remain in secluded quarters; they may not take a bath, cook food and attend religious observances; and on no account must they meet or sleep with their husbands. At the conclusions of the period, they have to take an elaborate purificatory bath to attain their normal ritual status.

Rajput women in Malwa do observe the menstrual pollution and taboos, but not with such rigidity as the Brahmin and Bania women do. They observe the pollution for three to four days and then keep on doing their domestic work; only they may not cook — during this period — for guests and offerings to deities. The Khati have only recently started observing menstrual pollution with any degree of seriousness. Many Khati women openly ridicule the very idea and say it is sheer waste of time and human energy for a woman to sit idle for a few days every month during her reproductive life. Among the 'unclean' Shudra castes, like the Balai, the Dhobi, the Teli, and the Dholi, there is very little evidence that such a taboo is observed at all through a few women from these castes assert that they do so. The caste elders, however, are definite that it is not a custom of the Shudra castes, and that it is enough for a woman to take a bath every day during her menstruation.

Rites and observances of the second category, that is, the prohibitive ones are much more important. These are related to the Hindu theory of pollution and are in reference with the ritual status of a person. According to the theory of caste which is one of the fundamental principles of Hindu social organization, the ritual status of a person is decided according to his caste, that is, his personal ritual status is the same as the ritual status of the caste to which he belongs. According to the prescriptions of the *dharma*, he is required to observe rules of his caste strictly, in order that his *karma* stock remains steady or there is some credit entry and he is able to get a better form in the next incarnation. Every Hindu believes in the doctrine of *karma* and *punarjanma* (transmigration of souls) and regards it as an active principle in the making of human destiny. Thus in order to improve his *karma* stock he is prepared to circumscribe his actions within the boundaries set by his caste traditions; that, so far as he is concerned, is his immediate *dharma*. The sanskrit idiom "that is the right path which has been trodden by great men" is taken to mean that the traditions of ones own caste are *the* right traditions for one to follow.

Caste rules lay emphasis on a "right behaviour" by their members. Particularly in matters of matrimony, sex relations, eating, drinking and smoking and in respect of friendship and visits, caste rules lay down the correct behaviour for their members.

Almost all castes require their members to marry within the caste, that is, castes are by rule endogamous. This requirement is for the purpose of maintaining the solidarity of the caste. Inter-caste marriages are still a rare phenomenon in villages, though they are becoming popular in many of our cities and towns. In villages, people still care to take their spouses from amongst their own caste members.

This is regarded with such sacredness and rigidity that inter-caste marriages cannot be performed while the persons live in their village environment. Also, since no Brahmin priest in villages would be willing to perform such a marriage, it can only be performed in a court of law according to the civil procedure or in an Arya Samaj temple which in Malwa are to be found only in towns. The result is that almost all marriages that one comes across in villages are intra-caste marriages. The punishment for offenders of the rules of caste endogamy are very harsh. They are summarily ex-communicated and are seldom re-admitted, so that they and their children have to be outside of the caste fold.

In matters of eating and drinking also each caste has its own rules, and if these rules are violated the caste council steps in to take severe action. In such cases they usually do no ex-communicate the offender, but demand for him a eating or drinking party and occasionally a contribution to the caste funds which may be utilised for the building of temples and dharamshalas or digging of wells and such other charitable purposes as the caste council may decide upon. One significant thing in this connection is that these rules are applied only which the person live in their village environment. It is found that when these same villagers visited towns like Indore, Ujjain and

Chart showing the annual cycle of festivals

Month Fortnight	Date of the fortnight	Festival	castes who observe
Chet 1st	Poonam	Samvatsar	Brahmin
	ekam to nomi (9 days)	Mata Poojan and Bari	Desha Chamar
2nd	edam to teej (3 days)	Gangor*	'Clean' Castes
	nomi	Ramnomi	'Clean' Castes
Baisakh 1st			
2nd	teej	Akhati	'Clean' Castes
Jeth 1st	ammavas	Bar mavas*	Purbi Thakur
2nd	dashmi	Ganga dashmi	All castes
	Poonam	Bheru pooja	All castes
	Poonam	Ram nam	'Clean' Castes
Asadh 1st	gyaras	Dev soni	'Clean' Castes
	gyaras	Hariya Goondiya	
2nd			
Sawan 1st	ammavas	Hariya Goondiya	'Clean' Castes
	ammayas	Dewasa*	'Clean' and 'Unclean' castes
2nd	Panchami	Nag Pooja	All Castes
	poonam	Rakhi	All Castes
1st	teej	Hariyali*	'Clean' Castes
	atham	krishna janam	'Clean' Castes
Bhadon	beej	Bhaibeej	All Castes
	teej	Hartalika*	'Clean' Castes
	choth	Ganesh pooja	'Clean' Castes
	panchami	Rishi panchami	' clean' castes
	chat	Hal chat	'clean' castes
2nd	dashmi	Teja ji ki Jatra	All Castes
	gyaras	Dol gyaras	'Clean' CAstes
	chodas	Anant chodas	'Brahmin

Month Fortnight		Date of the fortnight	Festival	castes who observe
Kuar	1st	ekam to amm avas (15 days)	Pitar paksha	'Clean'& Unclean' castes
	2nd	ekem to nomi (9 days)	Bari poojan	Malwi Balai & Gujarati Balai
		teej to nomi (7 days)	Mata pooja	All Castes
		dashmi	Daserah	All Castes
		gyaras to Poonam	keli pooja*	'clean' Castes
		poonam	Garba*	All Castes
Katik	1st	Atham	Karva atham*	Brahmin
		tears	Dhan teras	Brahmin and palliwal Bania
		chodas	narak chodas	All Castes
		ammavas	Dewali	All Castes
	2nd	ekam	Annakot-Gobardhan	'Clean' Castes
		atham	Gopashthami	'Clean' Castes
		nomi	Aonra nomi*	Brahmin
		Gyaras	Deva uthni	'Clean' Castes
		poonam	Katim jatra	All Castes
Aghan	1st			
	2nd			
Poos	1st			
	2nd			
Magh	1st			
	2nd	panchami	Basant	'Clean' Castes
Phagun	1st	teras	Siva Ratri	Brahmin, Palliwal Banja, Gosain, Nath jogi
		poonam	Holi	All castes
	2nd	poonam	Mahadev Baba ki jatra	All Castes

Dewas, they suspended the observance of caste rules about eating and drinking for the duration they were in the town.

These social rules are invested with ritual properties and sanctions by the Hindu society and *dharma*. Even though these are not concerned with actual worship, prayer or meditation, their observance is regarded as a ritual necessity by the Hindus and their violation leads to punishment or even ex-communication by the caste. The fact is that these rules and convetions are much more important for the persistance of the society in the traditionally integrated way and hence they are given by religious traditions the same sanction as is given to the formal religious rites and practices.

Bibliography

Bhattacharya, J.N. —Hindu Castes and sects, Calcutta, 1896.

Bouquet, A.C. —Hinduism, London, 1948.

Crooke, W. —Religion and Folklore of Northern India, Oxford, 1926.

—*Hinduism*, in Ency. of Religion and Ethics, vol. 6.

Dube, S.C. —Indian village, 1955.

Dubois, the Abbe —Hindu Manners, Customs and Ceremonies, (trans., by Beauchamp), Oxford.

Farquhar, J.N. —The Crown of Hinduism, 1913.

Ghurye, G.S. —Caste and Class in India, Bombay, 1951.

Masson-Oursel, P.G.&S. —Ancient India and Indian Civilization, pt. 2, London, 1951.

Mayer, A.C. —Caste and Kinship in a Village and its Region in Central India, London, 1960.

Monier-Williams, M. —Hinduism, Calcutta, 1951.

Morgan, K.W. (ed.) —The Religion of the Hindus, 1953.

O'malley, L.S.S. —Popular Hinduism, Cambridge,

1935.

Prabhu, P.N. —Hindu Social Organization, Bombay, 1954.

Srinivas, M.N. —Religion and Society among the Coorgs of South India, Oxford, 1952.

Stevenson, H.N.C. —*Status Evaluation in the Hindu Caste System,* J.R.A.I., vol. 84, Pts. 1 and 2, 1954.

Chapter-11

Herath : A Religious Ritual and its Secular Aspect

T. N. MADAN

Chapter-11

I

The indigenous Hindus of the Valley of Kashmir are Saraswat Brahmans[1]. They call themselves the Batta (बट्ट) and are known all over India, outside Kashmir, as Kashmiri Pandits. Batta is derived from the Sanskrit *bhatta* (भट्ट) meaning 'doctor', the designation of great scholars; and pandit (पंडित) is the Sanskrit equivalent for 'scholar' or 'learned man'.

The domestic life of Pandits is characterized by the performance of many rituals, secular as well as religious[2]. The Pandit domestic religious rituals may be classified according to their aim-content (intended purpose). The majority of these rituals commemorate some mythological event. The Pandits believe that the performance of such ritual increases the merit of the performers, averts untoward happennings and brings about divine blessings such as progeny, prosperity, health and happiness.

II

The most prominent and elaborate of the domestic religious rituals of the Pandits is *herath* (derived from the Sanskrit *hararatri* meaning 'Shiva's night'). The occasion is also celebrated all over India by Hindus as Shivaratri (Shiva's night) on the thirteenth day of a dark fortnight of the month of Phalgun (February-March). There are several versions of the mythological event which is celebrated on this occasion current among the Pandits. The Pandits are not worried by this lack of unanimity, nor does it abate their enthusiasm for the ritual. The most common popular version is that the god Shiva was married on this day (of the lunar calendar). In a village in South Kashmir[3] I was told the homely story of how Shiva once quarrelled with his spouse Paravati, who ran away from home and concealed herself in Sondar-nar, a gorge somewhere in the Valley. Shiva, repentant for his irascible temper, went searching for her. Other gods (with remarkable fellow felling !) came to his aid and he was finally reunited with Paravati on this day (of the year). Whereas the laity are satisfied with their own 'little tradition', the learned *literati* rely upon Sanskrit texts and the 'great all-India Hindu tradition'. The significance of this holy day is explained in several sacred texts including *Dharma Chintamani* and *Harihar Vasar Vinod* (see Shastri *et al* 1957). A Hindi commentary on the Sanskrit texts is also available (Bhatta 1931). It is written in the last mentioned of these books that when the world was crearted for human habitation Shiva looked for Shakti (his female counterpart) and, being omniscient, found that she was in a Himalayan forest, accompanied by her self-created female attendants (*yoginiyan*), preparing various utilities and food for the sustenance of human life. Shiva assumed a five-face, fifteen-eyes, eighteen-arm form and appeared in the form of Shakti, whose attendants were so frightened that they ran away. Shakti was greatly annoyed and she looked in anger at an earthenware vessel which she made for holding water. As a consequence of her angry wish an armed warrior arose out of the vessel, and he was followed by another armed but beautiful, rather than awesome, warrior who arose out of another vessel. The two warriors attacked Shiva but he took to his heels and vanished. Shakti blessed the two youths, whom she called Vataka and Rama, had them fed, and ordained that mankind should worship them on every anniversary of the day of their birth. Shiva wanted to be united to Shakti (without which happening there would be no mankind), and so he reappeared on the scene as a phallus of fire (*jwalalinga*). Vataka and Rama went up into the sky and down into the earth respectively but failed to find the two ends of phallus. Their pride was vanquished and they fell in prayer before it. Shakti absorbed into herself all her female companions and then was absorbed into the phallus. Shiva was thus united to Shakti. This is the event which is celebrated yearly by the Pandits as *herath*.

III

The religious rites on this occasion consist of offering prayerful praisem *arati* (waving of lighted lamps, incense and bells in front of an object of worship to the accompaniment of conch-blowing), flowers and food to Shiva, Shakti, Vataka and Rama represented respectively by a phallus made of baked clay and three earthen vessels containing water and walnuts. On the twelfth day of the fortnight Rama is worshipped in the morning. The next day the male head of every Pandit household observes a fast for the day and in the evening offers worship to Shiva, Shakti and Vataka. Several other gods and godlings also are worshipped on both days. On the morning of the fourteenth day there is a brief rite of offering prayer, bread and *arati*. The last rite takes place on the evening of the last day of the fortnight after sunset. The vessels are carried to a river, stream or spring and worshipped there. The water is then poured out but the walnuts are retained. These walnuts, regarded as sacred, are taken back home and eaten and distributed among kin and kith. The ritual being over, all the vessels and other earthen utensils are put to domestic use. Small saucers and the phallus are given to children who consider them as toys.

IV

The religious rites on the occasion of *herath* last four days. No other religious ritual commemorating an event in the life of gods is celebrated by the Pandits over as many days. For this reason alone *herath* stands out as the preeminent religious ritual in the Pandit calendar. But there is another reason also which invests *herath* with its unique importance. *Herath* is also the occasion for several secular activities and social transactions. These activities and transactions, spread over more than a fortnight, are to the Pandits an essential part of the celebration of *herath*. The secular activities associated with this occasion bring about a pronounced change in social interaction between kith and kin. Not only is there an increase in the rate of social interaction but there is also an emotional appeal which these activities have for young and old alike, so much so that every Pandit always looks forward to *herath* with enthusiasm. Let us now describe the more important of these secular activities and social transactions.

(1) Spring Cleaning. The winter in the Valley of Kashmir is long, cold and wet. The months of December, January and February are the coldest; a lot of snow falls and there are frequent frosts. Although the winter continues well into the month of March, the worst is usually over by the end of February, i.e. about the same time as *herath*. The months immediately preceeding *herath* witness the Pandits retiring into a shell of inactivity, their main concerns being to keep themselves warm and protected from cold. This is not a simple task in a society which does not know of centrally heated houses and geysers. The city (of Srinagar) and the towns are electrified but the villages do not have even the facility. Consequently domestic cleanliness, and to a certain extent personal cleanliness also, are neglected during these two or three months. The coming of *herath* means that the worst is over and it is time for house cleaning. This is done invariably (and almost formally) during the first nine days of the dark fortnight of the month of Phalgun (in the second half of February). The Pandit house is a big structure. It is a three or four-storeyed building with three to four rooms on each floor. The mud plaster floors are covered by matting. To clean the house the mats have to be removed from the rooms and beaten with sticks to rid them of dust. The rooms are then swept and washed with water and brown clay. The walls are also simply washed. As each room is cleaned, all the things taken out of it are restred into their former places. The whole house is agog with activity and everybody lends a helping hand to the women on whom the brunt of burden falls. In the city and the towns well-to-do families have the cleaning done by their servants or by hired labourers. The latter are invariably Muslims. But the sacred rooms in the Pandit house, viz., the kitchens and the 'worship-room' cannot be entered by Muslims as their touch is polluting. Even in those houses where servants are entrusted with the main task of sweeping and washing, women of the household supervise their work. The women who take part in this work are the daughters-in-law of many years' standing. Recently married women spend this time in their parental homes.

After the house, utensils are cleaned, followed by the washing of linen and other clothes. This is followed by the long personal baths. It taks a Pandit woman well over an hour to clean the mess out of her long hair neglected for several weeks. The cleaning is completed by the eighth day.

(2) Home-Coming. Every married woman visits her parental family on this occasion. As already stated, women recently married do not participate in the house-cleaning activities of their conjugal family. Others, of longer standing, take part in the cleaning activities for a few days and then go to their natal households. Even women who have been married many years and have grown-up children pay this visit to their natal homes, although it may last only a day, unless illness, distance (this holds good only in the countryside) or some extraordinary reason prevents them from doing so. This visit is regard as auspicious.

(3) Return of the Wives. Every woman goes back to her conjugal household on the ninth or the tenth day (of the fortnight). She receives gifts in cash and kind from her parents, or her brothers if the parents are dead. A young woman receives more gifts than an older woman. The minimum that even a growp-up woman receives is a *Khrav* (pair of wooden sadals), a *Kangar* (firepot),[4] some loaves of bread and a few rupees in cash. However, old women who have only brothers younger than themselves living in their natal household may not receive any gift. If it is the first *herath* after marriage, then a woman receives many gifts including new clothes.

(4) Ritual Gambling. Early in the fortnight children are given small cowrie shells by their parents, who buy these in the market. Each child gets a few dozen, and they play various games among themselves. All these games are regarded as gambling because the element of chance is decisive in winning or losing. Thus in one of the games every child contributes four cowries and then a toos decides who shall start the play. The child who wins the toos, picks up the cowries in his hands, closes the hands palm to palm, shakes the cowries between his palms, and then throws them on the floor. If an odd number of shells lie on the top side he wins all, if an even nummber he losses all,and has to pay a penalty. Schools remain closed in Kashmir during the winter and therefore all children, young and grown-up, are able to take part in these games. They enjoy themselves not only because they play, but also because such play is not permitted at any other time of the year. The Pandits lay a very great emphasis on prudence in matters pertaining to money, and therefore regard gambling with extreme abhorrence. They also believe in strict disciplining of children. But during this fortnight the child who shows rashness and skill in winning in the games is much praised in a lighthearted manner.

Adults take quite some interest in these games, and, if not earlier, then definitely on the tenth day they join the children in these games. This is a real climax. The Pandits have not heard of Freud and believe firmly in the time-honoured maxim of 'spare the rod and spoil the child'. In every-day life there is no show of friendly equality between parents and children. The parents are unmistakably the disciplinarians of their children. A parent may fondle his infant child and play with him, but as the child grows older there is a marked diminution in such behaviour, particularly so far as fathers are concerned. The Pandit men are not given to a free show of affection for their children. Consequently the children do not think of their parents as their playmates. But once the year, on the occasion of *herath*, the barrier between the generations breaks down. Children play with their parents; they gamble, and accuse their parents of cheating; and when a parent is caught in the act of cheating or is defeated, the children laugh out of sheer pure joy. And the parents join them. Every Pandit child carries fond memories of these days throughout the year to sustain him through less pleasant days. Many a Pandit will recall nostalgically how decades ago he used to play cowrie-shell games with his father.

The daughter-in-law who is spending her first *herath* with her conjugal family gets several hundred cowries with her from her parental home. On arrival in the home of her parents-in-law she is invited by her husband's siblings to play with them. The game begins and soon others may join in with the purpose of obtaining all the cowries from the new daughter-in-law. To make her 'cowrie-less', 'bankrupt', is the Pandits' idea of an excellent joke. A Pandit daughter-in-law who has been recently married (less than a year ago) is expected to be very reserved in her relation with her affines. However, on the occasion of *herath* she is faced with a dilemma: either she observes the norms of etiquette and allows herself to be humiliated of being deprived of all her cowries, or she becomes a bit bold, abandons some reserve and plays with caution. Most girls choose the former course, although they try to protect themselves from humiliation by carrying a large number of cowries with them. A kind of mock hostility, the desire to humiliate, is exhibited towards the new daughter-in-law on this occasion probably to emphasize her position as a partial stranger in the family.

Actual gambling between adult men, involving money (cowries are very cheap, 'worthless as a cowrie' being a common saying), may also take place on this tenth day, but this is rare.

Children are admonished if they continue playing cowrie games after the fortnight is over, and cowries may be taken away from them to be kept in stock for the next year. In most cases children lose their cowries and the few that are left are thrown away.

(5) The Potter's Burden. On the eleventh day the potter (invariably a Muslim), who supplies pottery to a number of fixed households on a hereditary basis, brings pots, vessels and other requirements of earthenware of his clients. Most of these earthen vessels and objects are needed for the performance of religious rites and for the use in the kitchen. The potter bring them in a huge basket on his head. His burden is not merely a head-load: he must bring the load on the right day and he must bring all the things required on the occasion. If any of the important objects, particularly any one to be used in the religious rites, is missing, he gest a scolding because such an omission on his part is regarded as a bad omen. The Muslim potter, no observer of *herath* and no believer, nor a literate person either, has to take great care in remembring the requirements of each of his client-households. The mutual interdependence of the Hindu and the Muslim is demonstrated on this as on many other occasions.

(6) The Priest's Dismay. Every Pandit household have available to them, on hereditary basis, the services of a priestly family who attend to their needs on ritual occasions such as births, deaths, marriages and propitiation rites. The male members of a priest household are able to look after all their client households with ease on all occasions except on the thirteenth day of the fortnight when the main *herath* ritual, the worship of Shiva, Shakti and Vataka is performed. Not all Pandits households perform the ritual on the morning of the twelfth day; they perform the worship of Rama also on the thirteenth day. The priests are not therefore put to any considerable trouble on that day. However, on the thirteenth day every Pandit household, without exception, perform the religious rites, and the presence of the priest is necessary because the priests alone know how to perform these rites. Moreover, every household want to perform the rites between sunset (about 6 p.m.) and midnight, the 'phallus of fire' having appeard, according to the mythological story, soon after sunset and disappeared at mid-night. A priest often finds it difficult to reach all his client-households before midnight. In the city a priest's client-households may be only four or five miles apart, but in the countryside they may be farther apart and in two or more villages. The delay in the performance of the rites becomes an ordeal. Not only is worship after midnight regarded as less meritorious, but the members of the household also suffer from hunger and lack of sleep because no food may be eaten unless the rites have been performed. The priest receives gifts in cash and kind for the services he renders. The members of such households where he reaches late angrily remonstrate with him. A priest told me of how he once heard curses being invoked upon him as he entered a house well after mid-night. In the past when there was no electricity in the city the priests, running from one street to another in the pitch-dark night, were often attacked by stray dogs or even thieves.

(7) Feasting, Dancing and Exchange of Gifts. *Herath* is the festive occasion *par excellence*. Feasting begins on the eleventh day when fish[5] must be cooked. The midday meal on the twelfth day and the evening meal on the thirteenth are also occasions for family feasts. The midday meal on the fourteenth day is, however, the principal feasting occassion. Fish and mutton are served with rice; those who can afford may also cook jungle fowls, ducks or other game. Brahmans all over India observe vegetarianism on this occasion, even those Brahmans who may not be vegetarians, but the Kashmiri Brahmans (the Pandits) are a law unto themselves.

The midday meal over, Pandit women of every neighbourhood collect together to dance and sing (in the open if it is sunny or dry). This practice of collective dancing and singing has died out in the city where it is regarded as typically rustic.

From early in the morning every Pandit household is visited by thier Muslim acquiantances who bring them gifts in kind to receive back gifts in cash. The potter brings a smoking pipe, the carpenter a pair of wooden sandals, the black-smith a knife, the basketweaver a basket, the milkman a jar of curd, and so on. Others like tenants and washerman come to offer greetings. All these people visit the houses of only such Pandit families who are their patrons, and receive gifts of money. In Srinagar beggars (Hindu and Muslim) and itinerant Muslim dancers and clowns also visit Pandit households indiscriminately to receive small gifts of money. Kith and kin also call on each other to exchange greetings. Children receive pocket money from their parents and from their mother's natal family. A newly married girl, her husband and parents-in-law receive gifts in cash and kind from her parents.

The concluding religious rites are performed, as already stated, on the evening of the fifteenth (and the last) day of the fortnight. During the following week every household send loaves of bread and walnuts to all the households of their close kin, affines, neighbours and friends. In a hamlet the gift may be sent to every other Pandit household, related or unrelated. The gift is called *herach-bogh*, 'the share of the *herath*'. The *herach-bogh* is portion of the walnuts and bread consecrated during the ritual performance on the thirteenth day. The closer their relationship, or the more intimate their mutual relations, the more the number of loaves of bread and walnuts sent by one household to another. If any family who have been sent such gifts in the past are not sent the gifts in a certain year, the import of the omission, whether deliberate or not, is serious. There will be complaints, and if no apology is forthcoming, retaliaton the next year. This then amounts to severence of social intercourse (*vartav chatun*). Not to send *herach-bogh* is to deny the obligations assotciated with kinship or friendship. No household, therefore, takes such a decision without sufficient cause. The exhange of *herach-bogh* (like the exchange of Christmas cards in English society) stands for the reaffirmation of mutual interest, particularly between distantly related households between whom there may be little other regular social intercourse. The man who carries *herach bogh* (well-to-do families may employ a servant for this purpose, particularly in contacting households who live far away) also carried with him news about the weal and woe of his own household, conveys greetings and makes enquiries about the welfare of the families he visits. The web of kinship (and friendship) is thus strengthened. And if Firth's statement about kinship being 'the rod of life on which one leans throughout the life' is true of any society it is, as we have shown elsewhere (Madan 1959), true of the Pandit society.

V

In the foregoing description of *herath* we have emphasized the secular activities because they are of far greater functional or sociological importance than the religious rites. Only the head of a household is directly involved in these rites as it is he who offers worship to the gods on behalf of the household. In the secular activities every member of the household — man and woman, child and adult — takes part. It may be maintained that the secular activities have no necessary relation with the religious ritual; they have an independence of their own and are not an aspect of the religious ritual. It is analytically possible to separate the two, but doing so would not only do violence to the reality but preclude a full understanding of the sociological significance of *herath*[6]. Looking for the trees one is apt to miss the forest. The basic fact is that the Pandits themselves do not make this distinction. Careful enquires have revealed that when they talk of *herath* it is the whole complex of activities, religious as well as secular, that is in their mind. However, it is the religious ritual of commemorating Shiva's union with Shakti (and the consequent birth of mankind) which occupies the central place in these activities. *Herath* is a religious ritual with a highly elaborate and socially important secular aspect.

The social importance of the secular activities lies in the fact that they are in effect the reaffirmation of social solidarity — between gods and human beings, kin, affines, parents and children, neighbours, co-villagers and friends. Even the Muslims with whom the Pandits engage in economic transactions participate in this mutual affirmation of social solidarity. The fortnight of *herath* is a time of intense social activities and religious performances. Not only is there an increase in the rate of social interaction; the quality of interaction also changes furnishing emotional stimulation. The Pandits live in close contact to each other and also in a sense to the Divine Being who, they believe, created and sustains mankind. It is an occasion when social (secular) transactions are merged with religious rituals in their experience.

Nadel (1954: 259--65) has mentioned four main 'competences' of religion, viz., explanation of the universe, economic ethics ('competence to guide 'the practical impulses of action"), support of social structure, and 'specific experiences and stimulations'. This brief ethnographic essay has indirectly been an attempt to show that the beliefs and the religious and secular actions associated with *herath* partly fulfil these functions, and do so in a remarkable manner considering the fact that *herath* is not the whole of Pandit religion but only one of its major rituals.

NOTES

1. Some Pandits say that Saraswat Brahmans are all those Brahmans who lives west of the underground river Saraswati, mentioned in the *puranas,* which joins the Ganga and the Yamuna at Prayag. However the majority of Pandits whom I questioned about this said that the Saraswat Brahmans of Kashmir are different from, and 'of course' (!) superior to other Saraswat Brahmans. They are the *bhatta*, they say of themselves, the favoured of Saraswati the goddess of learning.
2. To limit the use of the term 'ritual' to religious or sacred situations only is now out of date. The term 'religious ritual' is used by Radcliffe-Brown, Nadel, Firth and others. Benedict writes: 'Ritual....is a prescribed formal behaviour for occasions not given over to technological routine....The occasions which are ritualistically elaborated are usually solemn and are often therefore religious; but many secular occasions are similarly elaborated' (1934 : 396). Firth has

phrased the issue aptly and succinctly : 'Ritual may be defind as a kind of patterned activity oriented towards control of human affairs, primarily symbolic in character with a non-empirical referent, and as a rule socially sanctioned. When we are speaking of religious ritual in particular, the non empirical referent is ordinarily a god or other spiritual being or super-human force such as *mana*' (1951:222).

3. Part of the data used in this paper were collected by me in 1957 when I was doing fieldwork in Kashmir as a Scholar of the Australian National University to whom thanks are here expressed for financial support.

4. The *kangar* is a clay pot in a wicker contained which is filled with charcoal fire and used by Kashmiris to keep themselves warm. Every individual has his own *kangar*.

5. It is not quite clear why such a great emphasis is laid on the consumption of fish. The only explanation which I was given by the Pandits is that since fish are omnivorous, eating fish is very satisfying (in a mystical way).

6. In this connexion it is well worth pondering over what Firth has recently said: '...the search for meaning, for the social anthropologist, is a two fold process. He is concerned to discover the set of meanings within the religious system itself and also the correlates of the religious system with other aspects of the social system, and with the most general problems of society' (1950 : 133).

References

Benedict, Ruth 1934 'Ritual' in *Encyclopaedia of the Social Sciences.* Vols. XIII-XIV. New York.

Bhatta, Shiva 1931 *Shivarati Nirupan* (Hindi). Srinagar. Quoted in Shastri *et al* (see below).

Firth, Raymond 1952 *Elements of Social Organization,* London.

1959 'Problems and Assumption in an Anthropological Study of Religion.' Huxley Memorial Lecture 1959.

Journal of the Royal Anthropological Institute Vol. 89, Part II.

Madan, T.N. 1959 *Family and Kinship: A Study of the Pandits of Rural Kashmir*. Unpublished Ph.D. dissertation in the Australian National University Library.

Nadel, S.F. 1959 *Nupe Religion*, London.

Shastri, G.B. *et al* 1957 *Shivaratri Nirnay* (Hindi). Srinagar.

Chapter-12

Memorials, Temples, Gods and Kings. An Attempt to Unravel the Symbolic Texture of Vākāṭaka Kingship

H. BAKKER

Chapter-12

A recently found inscription of Prabhavāti Guptā, daughter of the Gupta emperor Chandragupta II, who was married to the Vākātaka king Rudrasena II, throws new light on a moot question regarding the genealogy of the Vākātaka dynasty. In his *Early History of the Deccan* Ajay Mitra Shastri informs us that "a grant of Prabhavāti Guptā engraved on a set of five plates is reported to have been found together with the ring and the seal a few years ago at Miregaon in the Sakoli Tahsil of the Bhandara District."[1]

Up to now two charters of Prabhavāti Guptā were known, her so-called Poona Plates, issued from Nandivardhana during the period of her regency over her minor son, and the Riddhapur Plates, issued from the *Ramagirisvamipadamula* in the 19th regnal year of her son Pravarasena II. In the seal attached to the Poona Plates Prabhavati describes herself as the "Mother of the *yuvaraja,* the ornament of the Vakatakas, who has attained royal fortune by inheritance" (CII v, 9). The name of this crown prince we learn from the inscription itself: Divākarasena. In the Riddhapur Plates, on the other hand, of which the seal is missing, the dowager queen describes herself as the mother of the illustrious Maharajas Dāmodarasena and Pravarasena (CII v, 36), Divākarasena had evidently disappeared from the scene and, since no inscription of Dāmodarasena has so far come to light, it was generally thought until recently, that Damodarsena might have been just another name of Pravarasena, so that we were actually concerned with one king only.

The Miregaon charter, however, which dates from the next year (i.e., the 20th regnal year of Pravarsena), though said to be 'similar in all respects' to the Rddhapur Plates, fortunately has preserved its seal, on which we read the following: "This is the enemy-chasting command of the illustrious Prabhavāti Guptā, who is the mother of two powerful Vākātaka kings."[2] These two kings are named in the inscription itself as Dāmodarasena and Pravarasena, of whom the latter was in power at the time his mother issued the charter.

The maternal discussed so far allows us to draw the following conclusions: 1. Rudrasena and Prabhavati had at least three sons, of whom the eldest, the *yuvaraja* Divākarasena, in all likelihood died before he had come of age. 2. The names of the Vākātaka princes, which all end in *sena,* were evidently not adopted at the time of their coronation.[3] 3. The *dvandva* compound *damodarasenapravarasena* should be interpreted as mentioning two brothers, of whom Dāmodarasena was the eldest (mentioned first in the compound despite his name being the longest). 4. The reign of Dāmodarasena must have been short, in view of the very long reign of his younger brother and the absence of inscriptions, or, for one reason or another, he was never allowed or able to exercise actual power.

The reign of Rudrasena II is characterised by a turn about in the religious affiliation of the dynasty. Whereas Rudrasana I in (later) inscriptions is described as a devotee of Svami Mahabhairava and Prithivisena I as 'intensely devoted to Mahesvara', Rudrasena II is said to have 'acquire an abundance of prosperity by the grace of Bhagvat Cakrapani,' i.e., Visnu (CII v, 12). Moreover, in an as yet unpublished inscription of Rudrasena found at Mandhal, a very important Vākātaka site, this king records his support to the Satvata branch of the Bhagavatas at the command of Mondasvamin, who is described as Sesasayin Visnu (Shastri 1987, 47). This change in religious affiliation is generally thought to have been instigated by Rudrasena's wife, who, like her father Chandragupta, professed to be an *atyantabhagavadbhakta* and who issued her charters from the Feet of the Lord, or the Lord of Ramagiri (CII v, 7, 35). This Vaisnava predominance lasted more than one generation, as is apparent from Pravarasena' support of the temple of the Footprints of Mahapurusa (CII v, 60)-despite the fact that he himself declares to be a devotee of Mahesvara (CII v, 19)-as well as from his grandson, Prthivisena II's profession to be an *paramabhagavata* (CII v, 81). Two inscriptions of the latter king have come to light in Mandhal, one of which was issued from a temple (*sthana*) at Ramagiri (Shastri 1977-78, 162), but of his father, Narendrasena, no documents have been found.

As appears from the dynastic names—Rudrasena II named after his grandfather, Prithivisena II after his great-great-grandfather, and Pravarasena II after his great-great-grandfather —the names of these kings were largely handed down within the family with the sole exception of Pravarasena's two brothers and son: Divākarasena, Dāmodarasena and Narendrasena. Consequently, no certain conclusions with regard to religious affiliation can be dawn from them, although Rudrasena I may point to an original Śaiva milieu and Dāmodarasena to a Vasnava one.

Let us nevertheless, for reasons that will become clear later, read these names as could have been done in a Vaisnava context, and try to associate them with different forms of Visnu, that is, let us try to solve a kind of cryptogram.

It is natural that Prithivisena could be associated with the Varaha incarnation of Visnu. The boar's connection with the earth is well-known. In *Taittiriyasamhita* 7.1.5.1 it is said of Prajapati, Visnu's predecessor in this respect:

> This was in the beginnings the waters, the ocean. In it Prajapati, becoming the wind, moved. He saw her, and becoming a boar (*varaha*), he seized her. Her, becoming Visvakarman, he wiped. She extended, she became the earth (Prithvi) and hence the earth is called 'the extended one' (*prthivitvam*). (tr. Keith).

Rudrasena is more difficult at first at sight. Gonda in his *Visnuism and Sivaism* notes that: "It is, to begin with, interesting to notice that in the *Rgveda* Rudra and Visnu, excepting two cases one of which is insignificant, maintained no direct relations with each other."[4] However, a little further Gonda remarks that: "Visnu's Man-lion aspect—the main exception to the general preponderance of kindly, human traits of this god—corresponds to Siva's shape of terror" (o.c. 122). Of all the Vaisnava myths it is especially the one Narasimha that has frequently been translated into a Śaiva version.[5] And, similarly, Eschmann's research in the tribal background of the Jagannatha deities led her to conclude that:

> Narasimha is the *ugra* aspect of Visnu par excellence and therewith also that aspect of Visnu with the highest

> affinity to Siva. [...] It has been shown, that the worship of Narasimha can be integrated into Śaivism, [... and] it can therefore be assumed that the worship of Narasimha not only continued, but perhaps even was emphasised under Śaiva predominance, because it was acceptable to both Vaisnavas and Saivas.[6]

A name as Rudra-Narasimha would express such an ambivalence.

Divākarasena refers of course, in Vaisnava semantics, to the solar aspect of Visnu. Of all forms of this god Trivikrama best represents this side of his nature. As Gonda remarked in his *Aspects of Early Visnuism:*

> The general idea underlying the three strides of the god is in all probability [...] the diurnal course of the sun through the tripartite cosmos in his ascent from the horizon through the atmosphere to the zenith, which might, at least occasionally, have been considered a sort of heaven.

And he goes on to specify this view to the effect that the "the steps refer to the diffusion of light by the sun, rather than the luminary proper [...],"[7] a characteristic that could well be denoted by the word *divakara,* makers of light.'

The connection of Damodara with the Vaisnava patheon is evident, since the name refers to Krsna who was tied up to a mortar by his angry mother in order to check his appetite for butter. The early play of Bhasa, *Balacarita,* which relates this episode, consequently refers to the two brothers Krsna and Balarāma as Damodara and Samkarsana.

Finally, we are left with Pravarasena, whose name does not yield an easy clue, neither to the Śaiva nor to the Vaisnava pantheon. However, in view of Pravarasena's predominance over his brother Dāmodarasena, and the latter's association with Krsna, the word *pravara* could, artificially it is true, be taken to refer to the 'principal' or 'elder' of the two, i.e., to Balarāma, despite Pravarasena's actually being, in all likelihood, the younger brother.

In order to avoid misunderstanding, I am not arguing that these connotations were all intended when these princes received their names, but only, that in a special ritualistic Vaisnava context, this eponymous signification could have appeared meaningful in retrospect.

We now return to the ritual centre of the Vākāṭaka dynasty, Ramagiri or modern Ramtek Hill, 6 km north of the royal residence Nandivardhana. The main sanctuary on top of the hill was, no doubt, a Vaisnava one, and there are good reasons to believe that it was a temple enshringing Visnu's or Rama's footprints, situated on the spot that is occupied today by the 13th-century Rama temple.[8]

On a less prominent site of the hill, about 350 m east of the main temple complex, is a group of five temples that date from the 5th century. I have described these temples elsewhere.[9] On the basis of archaeological and stylistic arguments I proposed the following chronological development, which, I am happy to say, has gained approval of a leading art-historian, Prof. Joanna Williams (University of California) in a personal communication.

The oldest construction is probably the pavilion enshrning a stout theriomorphic image of Varaha. It should be dated in the 1st quarter of the 5th century. Not far from this Varaha Mandir are two very similar Narasimha temples enshringing virtually identical images of the Man-lion. These temples are traditionally known as the Rudra-Narasimha and the Kevala-Narasimha Mandirs and are separated from each other by a distance of about 100 m. The older of the two appears to be the Rudra-Narasimha temple, which may date from about the same time as the Varaha shrine or somewhat later. On account of its more polished workmanship and stylistic refinement the so-called Kevala-Narasimha temple can be said to have been built after the Rudra-Narasimha temple and, consequently, should be dated in the 2nd quarter or about the middle of the 5th century.

The remaining two temples are one dedicated to Trivikrama, preserving the Trivikrama image, despite most of the *mandapa* being in ruins, and the so-called Bhogarama temple. They are both later than the Kevala-Narasimha temple, yet it is hard to tell which is the younger of the two, owing to the fact that the Bhogarama temple no longer contains the original idols. Both temples should be dated in the 2nd half of the 5th century.

The Bhogarama temple has the peculiarity that it consists

of two parallel *garbhagrhas.* In a forthcoming article I have argued on archaeological and literary grounds that the two brothers Vasudeva and Samkarsana, alias Krsna and Balarāma, are the best candidates amongst the Vaisnava deities for having been installed originally in the two cellas. The name of the temple, which is attested in a 13th-century inscription (Bakker 1989b, 487), may refer to the, at the time more important of these two, Balarāma, to whose serpent coil or hood the word *bhoga* originally may have referred (Bakker forth. a).

The archaeological heritage of the Ramagiri hill thus allows us to distinguish, by and large, three stages of building activity and to picture an evolution of historical constructions as given in the appendix.

We now come to the central question as to the accommodation of these sanctuaries to their religious and cultural environment, that is to say, the question regarding their 'Sitz im Leben.' In all articles dealing with these temples so far, including my own, it has simply be assumed that these sanctuaries were just built there. Yet, their rather peripheral location, grouped in a cluster (with one exception), demands an explanation. In this regard the recently discovered Vākātaka inscription in the Kevala-Narasimha temple may be of great value.

This inscription, which has been severely damaged, has been briefly discussed by Ajay Mitra Shastri (1987) and, very unsatisfactorily, published by A.P. Jamkhedkar in the same year. We are presently preparing an edition of it on the basis of detailed photographs which are studied with the aid of stereoscopic techniques. The interpretation that we intend to propose is that the text was made by the children, and in all probability, especially by the daughter of Prabhavati on the occasion of the consecration of the temple in which it is found. The name of this royal daughter (*manujendraputri*) has become illegible. The inscription also speaks of the brother (*bhratr*) of this princess, who, according to our interpretation, must be Pravarasena II. The mother obviously is dead and the inscription purports to bestow the merit ensuing from the construction of the temple on her in the hereafter. The crucial verses could be translated as:

A temple [...], considering [...] transitory, she [i.e., the

> princess]
> free of sins, for the sake of a mass of merit for her mother alone,
> [...] stone, [...], resembling [...], for a long time [...].[10]

The name of the mother may be inferred from the name of the deity to which the temple is said to have been dedicated:

> [...] the Lord of the Earth and Master of Prabhavati; for the sake of everlasting merit she [i.e., the princess] has made [...].[11]

We know from an inscription of Prabhavati herself that shed used to refer to god as the 'Lord of Ramagiri' (*ramagirisvamin*) (CII v, 35). The naming of an image or deity, in this case Visnu/ Narasimha, after a (deceased) person was quite common in ancient India,[12] a practice which be also exemplified by the temple of Pravaresvara.[13]

We therefore come to the conclusion that the so-called Kevala-Narsimha temple was a 'memorial' shrine, constructed after the demise of the great dowager queen, keeping in mind that a 'memorial' in the Indian context should be conceived of as a building which is constructed primarily with the aim of transferring merit to the deceased. This would imply that the temple was built after AD 440—herd last inscription dates from the 20th regnal year of her son (Shastri 1987, 51)—but not much after, since the queen must by then have been very old indeed. The epigraphical testimony thus agrees with the archaeological dating.

If, so we may ask, one of the Narasimha temples turns out to be a sort of memorial building, could the other temple not be likewise? We may recall that temple is traditionally known as Rudra-Narasimha. Could the affix 'Rudra' somehow preserved an ancient tradition? It must be observed that there is nothing in the two Narasimha temples that makes one into a Rudra- and the other into a Kevala-Narasimha sanctuary, since both images are virtually identical. But provided the name Rudra-Narasimha, the other temple may, for ease of distinction, have come to be designated Kevala-Narasimha, according to the other, peaceful, aspect of the god.[14]

If we assume that the Rudra-Narasimha is a shrine, erected after the demise of king Rudrasena II, a pertinent question may be answered: why two more or less identical Narasimha temples next to each other? The Rudra-Narasimha temple was erected by the devout spouse of Rudrasena, who outlived her husband for at least 35 years and for whom Narasimha was the most appropriate form of god to be associated with the deceased king.[15] He really was the 'Lord (*svamin*) of Prabhavati,' and after her own death a similar monument was erected in her memory too. Side by side they must have called to the minds of their contemporaries the conjugal unity that once was the mortal couple Rudrasena and Prabhavāti Guptā.

The idea of enlarging the sacred complex on top of the hill to include temples of the most popular forms of Visnu of those days, temples that were at the same time monument which bore testimony to the greatness of the kings of the Vākātaka lineage, may first have occurred to Rudrasena and his wife after the former had succeeded his father Prthivisena to the throne of Nandivaradhana. As we have argued in the beginning, the linkage of Prthivisena with Varaha is an obvious one within a Vaisnava context and, consequently, the shrined of Varaha might well have been designed at the turn of the 4th century, not only to worship this god, but also to transfer merit and to pay homage to a king whose name designated him as 'Ruler of the Earth (*prthivi*).'

The third generation of Vākātaka princes coincides with the third stage of building activity described above. Divākarasena, the crown prince, died young, before he could ascend the throne. The Royal Family may have decided to build the Trivikrama temple for the sake of his merit. This temple is situated somewhat apart from the other temples which all lie within a cluster, a special position that may signify the exceptional case of a 'memorial' for one who never really was Māhāraja. According to the above-quoted inscriptions the two remaining brothers, Dāmodarasena and Pravarasena, both bore the title of Māhāraja of the Vakatakas.[16] However, considering the lack of Dāmodarasena inscriptions, their rule became somehow intertwined. To commemorate this dual rule no temple may have seemed more suitable than one dedicated to the Satvata brothers, Vasudeva and Samkarsana, i.e., Krsna/Damodara and Balarāma. In addition to the ancient Vaisnava triad of Trivikrama, Varaha and Narasimha,[17] the Bhagavata mode of worship centering around the Vrsni or Satvata deities was popular in the Vākātaka realm, as is clear from the above mentioned Rudrasena II inscription in which he pledges support to two monasteries of the Satvata school.[18] The name of the temple, Bhogarama, referred to the more important (*pravara*) of the two, Balarāma, whose sideway connection with the Rudra-Siva cult,[19] although a Vaisnava deity, may have played a part in the choice of the relatives of Pravarasena, devotee of Mahesvara. These associations, the popularity of the dual deities Krsna and Balarāma, the particular historical circumstances of the somehow combined rule of two royal princes, and the Vākātaka tradition of building temples for the sake of merit for the deceased members of their lineage, these factors taken together explain the origin of such an unique monument as the Bhogarama temple.[20]

We may summarize the results of our investigation by connecting the two parts of our scheme, the pedigree and the archaeological chart, as is done in the appendix.

Elsewhere I have argued that the images installed in these Vākātaka sanctuaries should be seen, apart from obviously symbolising the divine, as a kind of metaphor, representing the qualities of the kings by ritual analogy (Bakker forth *b*). Thus the image of Narasimha is not particularly ethereal or heavenly, not hieratic, but expresses powerful supremacy, which is accentuated by its relaxed friendly, even sweet playfulness. The theory expounded here is meant to support this interpretation and should not be conceived as implying divinity of the kings involved. That does not alter the fact, that these monuments were also designed to produce the effect desired, viz., to commu-nicate the prestige and sovereignty of the Royal Family that had built them.

By the assimilation of popular cults like that of the boar and the man-lion, a dual aim was served, viz., to unite the subjects of the realm into a community of worship, and, secondly, to confirm the Royal Family's sacrosanct, leading role in this community (cp. Stein 1983, 89 f.). In this way the symbolic texture of Vākātaka kingship was given shape in the heyday of its rule.

Postscript

After this article had been completed, further study of the inscription in the Kevala-Narasimha temple shed new light on the crucial passage quoted in not 10. We now propose the following reading.

> *prasadam dayi(t)(a)(dh)atur vicintya tam asasvatam /*
>
> *matur edva samuddi*(sya pu)nyaugham aghavarjjta */30/*
>
> sil(a)lasan(k)asam(ci)ra(ya) ⏑ ⏑ ⏑ ⏑ ⏓ /
>
> ⏓ ⏓ – ⏓ ⏓ ⏓ ⏓ – ⏓ //31//
>
> Reflecting that temple for her beloved (begetter) is transitory, she free of sins, for the sake of a mass of merit for her mother alone, [...] stone [...], resembling [...], for a long time [...]. (30-31)

The conjecture *dayitadhatur* ('of/for her beloved begetter') is based on the fact that the syllables 4 and 5 of 30a reading dayi practically only allow the word *dayita* ('beloved'), which one would expect to be used exclusively for close relatives, and this is in accordance with syllable 8 °*tur*, which may be a genitive of a nomen agentis or noun of relationship probably different from matr found in 30c. The root dha with preposition a in the sense of 'to impregnate', 'to make' is attested, e.g., in *Bhagavatapurana* 9.24.52: *vasudevah sutan astav adadhe sahadevaya//*. The more usual *pitur* is excluded by the long a's we read in syllables 6 and 7 would also yield a metrically incorrect verse in view of the short fourth syllable. Another metrically possible conjecture *dayitabhratur* is rejected because 30b seems more appropriate if we assume that the temple was built already some time ago, *matur eva* (30c) suggests 'father', rather than 'brother' and, last but not least, °*bhratur* is palaeographically almost impossible in view of the absence of the subscript 'ra that should have been sivible in the undamaged part of the stone belows the syllable. If this conjecture is accepted it would mean that we are here dealing with a temple of/for the beloved father of the princess (i.e., Rudrasena), of which the transitoriness is realized. In other words, *prasadam* (30c) refers not to the Kevala- but to the Rudra-Narasimha Mandir, of which it has been argued above that it was built for the sake of Rudrasena's merit, an argument that is now substantiated, it would seem, by the inscription in the adjacent temple itself. It is plausible that the main clause in verse 31 contains a reference to the stone (*sila*) temple that is the find spot of the inscription, built by the princess, daughter of Rudrasena and Prabhavati, in emulation of the adjacent Rudra-Narasimha temple, exclusively (*eva*) for the sake of her mother's merit. Hence the appropriate designation of its image as Prabhavatisvamin (verse 21a). The word *ciraya* (31b) may indicate that the princess, aware of the dilapidation of the old Rudra-Narasimha temple, wished this new temple for her mother to be (more?) durable.

NOTES

1. Shastri 1987, 51.
2. Shastri 1987, 51: *vikkrantayor jananyas tu vakatakanarendrayoh sriprabhavatiguptayah, sasanam ripusasanam.*
3. Cp. Shastri 1987, 52.
4. Gonda 1970, 87.
5. See Gonda 1970, 105 ff.
6. Eschmann 1978, 104, 112.
7. Gonda 1954, 60. This interpretation is in accordance with the prevailing view (see Kuiper 1983, 41 n. 1). Kuiper 1983, 43 argues that "one can hardly evade the conclusion that in the *Rgveda* Visnu has no particular connections with sun. It is possible that the sun, when in the zenith, was associated with Visnu just as the rising sun was a manifestation of Mitra and the setting on of Varuna." This does not, however, affect our argument, since we are here concerned with the traditional (classical) associations of this deity.
8. See Bakker 1991.
9. Bakker 1989a; cp. Jamkhedkhar 1988.
10. *prasadam dayi - - tur viciintya tam asasvatam / matur*

eva samuddi(sya) (pu)nyaugham aghavarjjita / 30 / / sil(a) - - lasan(kasam (ci)ra(ya) ⏑ ⏓ ⏑ ⏓ ⏑ */ / 31 / /*

11. prabhavatiisvaminam ca lokana(tha)m adha / punyam aksayam uddisya ma (a)k(a)raya(t) //21//.

12. Cp. Shastri 1986-87; Shastri 1987, 52.

13. CII v, xli, 19.

14. Rao I I, 149 f. Cp. Eschmann 1978, 106. That the name 'Rudra-Narsimha' could be a reminiscence of king Rudrasena was first suggested to me by Dr Chandrashekhar Gupta (Nagpur).

15. Compare, for instance, Prabhavati's brother, the emperor Kumaragupta, who liked to compare himself with Narasimha on the coin with the legend: "The Lion-king who resembles Narasimha is always victorious" (Altekar 1957, 189).

16. CII v, 36: *vakatakanam maharajasridamodaras-enapravarasena.*

17. Cp. Harle 1974, 11 f.; Williams 1982, 90 f,; Berkson 1978; Gail 1977, 127 ff., Bakker 1990, 78 f.

18. Shastri 1987, 74: *satvatacaranadhivasadvayasya.*

19. See Jaiswal 1967, 53 ff.

20. That the Bhogarama temple could have been some sort of memorial shrine was first suggested to me by Dr. A.P. Jamkhedkar (Bombay).

APPENDIX

Chronological chart
of the Vākātaka temples
on Ramagiri
(Ramtek Hill)

Vākātaka genealogy
(Nandivardhana branch)

AD

(*c. AD 360-385)*

Prthivisena I (~Varaha) ....Varaha temple

------- 425

(*c. AD 385-405*)

Rudrasena II (~ Narasimha) .... Rudra Narasimha temple

x(*c. AD 405-419*) .... Kevala Narasimha temple

-------- 450

(*+before AD 419*)

Divākarasena............................. Trivikrama temple
(~Trivikrama)
(*c. AD 420-452)*

Dāmodarasena
(~Krsna)

Pravarasena II.. Bhogarama temple
(~Balarāma)

------- -475

BIBLIOGRAPHY

Altekar, A.S. (1957), The Coinage of the Gupta Empire (and its imitations). Varanasi. Corpus of Indian Coins IV.

Bakker, Hans (1982a), 'The Antiquities of Ramtek Hill, Maharashtra', in: South Asian Studies 5, 79-102.

—, (1989b), 'The Ramtek Inscriptions', in: *Bulletin of the SOAS LII, 467-496.*

—, *(1990), 'Ramtek: an Ancient Centre of Visnu Devotion in Maharashtra', in: The History of Sacred Places in India as Reflected in Traditional Literature. Edited by Hans Bakker, Leiden 1990, pp. 62-85.*

—, *(1991), 'The Footprints of the Lord', in: Devotion Divine. Bhakti Traditions from the Regions of India.* Studies in Honour of Charlotte Vaudeville. *Edit. by Daina L. Eck and Francoise Mallison, Groningen 1991, pp. 19-37.*

—, *(forthc. a), 'The Manbhaus' Seat on Ramtek Hill', in:* Devotional Literature in South Asia: Current Research, *1985-8, Cambridge 1991.*

—, *(forthc. b), 'Throne and Temple. Political Power and Religious Prestige in Vidarbha', in: The Sacred Centre as the Focus of Political Interest. Proceedings of the Symposium held on the occasion of the 375th anniversaryd of the University of Groningen*, 5-8 March 1989. Edited by Hans Bakker, Groningen 1991.

Berkson, Carmel (1978), 'Some new Finds at Ramgarth Hill, Vidisha District', in: *Artibus Asiae* XV, 2/3, 215-232.

Bhasa, *Plays ascribed to Bhasa: original thirteen texts in Devanagari.* Crit. ed. by C.R. Devadhar, Poona 1962, Poona Oriental Series 54.

CII, *Corpus Inscriptionum Indicarum.* Vol. V Inscriptions of the Vakatakas. Edited by Vasudev Vishnu Mirashi. Ooctamund 1963.

Eschmann, A. (1978), 'The Vaisnava Typology of Hinduization and the Origin of Jagannatha', in: *The Cult of Jagannath* and the regional Tradition of Orissa. *New Delhi 1978, pp.*

99-117.

Gail, Adalbert J. (1977), 'Visnu als Eber in Mythos und Bild', in: Beitrage zur Indien-forschung Ernst Waldschmiidt zum 80. Geburtstage gewidmet, *ED. Hartel, Berlin, pp. 127-168.*

Gonda, Jan (1954), Aspects of early Visnuism. *Utrecth.*

—, *(1970),* Visnuism and Sivaism. A Comparison. *London.*

Harle, J.C. (1974), Gupta Sculpture. Indian Sculpture of the Fourth to the Sixth Centuries A.D. *Oxford.*

Jaiswal, Suvira (1967), The Origin and Development of Vaisnavism (Vaisnavism from 200 BC to AD 500*). Delhi.*

Jamkhedkar, A.P. (1987), 'A Newly Discovered Vākātaka Temple at Ramtek, Dist. Nagpur', in: Kusumanjali. New Interpretation of Indian Art & Culture. Sh. C. Sivaramamurti Commemoration Volume, *ed. by M.S. Nagaraja Rao, Delhi 1987, Vol. I, 217-223.*

—, (1988), 'Beginnings of North Indian Style: Early

Vidarbha Style, c. A.D. 350-500. Vakatakas (Main Branch)', in: Encyclopaedia of Indian Temple Architecture. 2, I North India: Foundations of North Indian Style. Edited by M.W. Meister, M.A. Dhaky, K. Deva, American Institute of Indian Studies, Delhi, pp. 59-72.

Kuiper, F.B.J. (1983), Ancient Indian Cosmogony. Essay selected and introduced by John Inwin. *Delhi.*

Rao, T.A. Gopinatha, Elements of Hindu Iconography. *Intr. and editorial notes be K.K. Das Gupta, Varanasi, etc., 1971 (Indian Reprint). 4 vols.*

Shastri, Ajay Mitra (1977-78), 'Mandhal Utkhanan', in: Vidarbha Samshodhak Mandal Annual, 142-174.

—, *(1986-87), 'Some Aspects of Personal Names in the Vākātaka Inscriptions', in:* Journal of the Oriental Institute, *36, 257-264.*

—, *(1987), Early History of the Deccan. Problems and Perspectives. Delhi.*

Stein, Burton (1983), 'Mahanavami: Medieval and Modern Kingly

Ritual in South India', in: Esasays on Gupta Culture. *Edit. by Bardwell L. Smith, Delhi, etc., pp. 67-90.*

Taittiriyasamhita, The Veda of the Black Yajus school, entitled Taittiriya Sanhita. Transl. from the original Sanskrit prose and verse by Arthur Berriedale Keith., Cambridge (Mass.) 1914, 2 vols., Harvard Oriental Series 18, 19.

Williams, Joanna Gottfried (1982), The Art of Gupta India. Empire and Province. Princeton.

Chapter-13

Vedic Mythology: A Rethinking

Some Dual Divinities in the Rgveda

R.N. DANDEKAR

Chapter-13

The occasion for the present rethinking of the Rgvedic mythology has been the urge to seek a satisfactory rationalization of the concept and nature of dual-divinities in the *Rgveda.* I should like to start with the following postulates: (1) The Rgvedic mythology cannot be said to have assumed a finite and finished form at any given moment. It would, therefore, be wrong to study that mythology as if it was a static phenomenon. Rgvedic mythology had been throughout reacting and responding to the various vicissitudes in the cultural history of the Rgvedic age. (2) A particular Vedic god is seen to have been dominant in a particular period, because the personality and character of that god adequately reflected the ethos of the period. (3) Even after Rgvedic god had been once conceived, his character did not remain unchanged. His personality, as it were, 'grew' - it often assumed a heterogeneous character on account of the different elements which came to be assimilated into it in conformity with the mythological ideology which had been undergoing constant modification. (4) The relationships among the various Rgvedic gods were governed by certain culture-historical compulsions.

Before I proceed let me make it clear that I am not going to examine critically the views of other scholars regarding the topics which I shall be dealing with in the course of this paper. I have already done so at great length elsewhere.[1] I shall take for granted my own views in this regard and shall endeavour to set them forth in a new frame-work. Further I shall be taking into account mainly the original character of the Vedic gods who form the subject-matter of my discourse and not the subsequent development of their personalities.

On this background. I propose to discuss in this paper three Vedic gods, namely, Varuna, Indra, and Visnu. I think that there are indications in the *Rgveda* of a broad chronological sequence in respect of the ascendancy of these three gods.

The ninth verse of the ninetieth hymn in the first book of the *Rgveda* reads:

> *šaṁ no mitrah saṁ varunah*
> *šaṁ no bhsvatv aryama/*
> *šaṁ na indro brhaspatih*
> *šaṁ novisnur urukramah.//*

> "Propitious unto us Mitra; propitious varuna; propitious unto us may Aryaman be. Propitious unto us Indra; Brhaspati,[2] propitious unto us Visnu, the widestrider."

Whether it is deliberately intended or not - in view of the significant recurrence of the verse in various Vedic texts,[3] I for for one should like to believe that it is deliberately intended - this verse reflects the three main and consecutive phases of the evolutionary mythology of the *Rgveda,* some of the principal features of which I have set forth above in the first two quarters, the first phase of the definite realization of the cosmic (moral) order established by the 'binder' god Varuna and his two alter egos Mitra and Aryaman; in the third quarter, the phase of the mythologization of history as represented by Indra and his purposefully concocted counterpart Brhaspati; and in the fourth Quarter, the phase of the hierarchisation of popular religious cults as symbolized by Visnu.

It may be presumed - and this presumption gets adequate confirmation from the history of later Hinduism - that independent religious sects grew round these gods. A mutual confrontation among those religious sects was also inevitable - and, indeed, quite understandable. Therefore, in order to avoid any probable schism in the Vedic religion that might arise out of such confrontation, the Vedic seers contrived the concept of dual-divinities and thereby sought to establish a kind of rapprochement among these gods, based mainly on the principles of complementariness, conciliatory adjustment, and hierarchisation.

The conception of dual-divinities in the *Rgveda* is certainly of great moment in the early Vedic evolutionary mythology. As pointed out earlier, the relationships among the various Vedic gods were governed by certain religous-cultural compulsions. I believe that the conception of dual-divinities—at least in some major cases - has originated out of such compulsions. In the first phase of the Rgvedic mythology, which had developed in the Proto-Arvan period in the region round about Balkh, great emphasis was put on the belief of the sustenance and regulation of the cosmi phenomena and incidentally of the affairs of human life, having been brought about through some kind of 'bondage.' There must have also developed, during that period, some kind of simple ritual involving agni and Soma. But the predominant mythological concept was definitely that of the cosmic law *Rta*[4] and the sovereign administrator of that law Asura Varuna. As far as the Vedic mytology was concerned, the mythological concepts of Mitra and Aryaman represented merely an extension of the Varuna-concept - they were obviously minor and late. Broadly speaking, mitra was conceived of as being in relation to the affairs of men what Varuna was in relation to the cosmic phenomena. Mitra was *yatayajjana,*[5] the organizer and regulator of human relationship through the bonds of contract and friendship. Aryaman's function was still more restricted in scope. He may be said to have been responsible for establishing amicable relations with 'strangers.' In course of time, however, Mira's function must have come to be regarded as being as important as that of Varuna, for, the ethical-moral order in human affairs was believed to be as essential as in cosmic phenomena. The two gods representing the two different aspects of the same basic concept of ethical bond, namely, Asura Varuna and *yatayajajna* Mitra, were combined to form a single divinity Mitravarunau. Indeed, as far as the *Rgveda is* concerned, the dual-divinity Mitravarunau has more hymns dedicated to it than to each of the two god individually. Twenty-three whole hymns and parts of several others celebrate Mitravarunau, while Varuna has twelve hymns addressed to him and Mitra only one. In the case of Mitravarunau, the concept of dual-divinity served the purpose of religio-mythological complementariness.[6]

The concept of Indravarunau is, however, of far greater consequence. The dominant religious cult of the Proto-Aryan period was the Varuna cult. The last years of the Proto-Aryan period witnessed the migration of the Proto-Tryans towards Iran on the one hand and towards Saptasindhu or the Land of seven Rivers on the other. The migration towards Saptasindhu meant for these people, whom we may now call Vedic Aryans, a drastic change in their way of life and thought, particularly after their fairly long sojourn in the region of Balkh. It was now a life of lateful confrontation with Vrtras—human foes and environmental impediments—and of consequent warlike adventures. This new life of conquest and colonization called for a new religion and a new god. The cosmic religion of the world—severeing Asura Varuna could no longer adequately meet the exigencies of the new age. The Vedic Aryans Naturally creaved for a heroic god could bless and promote their onwards march towards Saptasindhu and beyond. So was Vrtraha Indra 'born' in the Vedic pantheon. And soon after he had been born, he became the foremost among the Rgvedic gods—*yojata eva prathamah.*[7]

Numerous Rgvedic references would make it clear that originally Indra was not a god, but that he attained god-head through his own achievements.[8] It is noteworthy that the Rgvedic poets have not emphasized the human traits, in form and character, of any other god to the extent to which they have down of Indra. The human elements in Indira's personality are really basic and essential and not merely the result of the anthropomorphization of a natural phenomenon. Verily, Indra was a human hero, who was characterized by some human weaknesses but who, at the same time, possessed the capacity for superhuman exploits.

After the mythological deification of the human hero Indra, all conceivable exploits—historical or otherwise—came to be attributed to him. It is the period of the warlike adventures of the Vedic Aryans and their subsequent conquents and colonization under the victorious leadership of Indra, which is largely reflected in the *Rgveda.* This explains why the Rgvedic mythology is so conspicuously Indra-dominated.

In course of time, there developed in Vedic religion two major cults, presumably rivalling each other,namely, the more ancient cult centering round Asura Varuna and the newly evolved one centering round Vrtraha Indra. A headlong conflict between these two cults could have adversely affected the solitarily of the Vedic community. The impending schism within the Vedic Aryandom had to be avoided at all costs. This was achieved by the evolutionary Vedic mythology through the conception of the dual-divinity Indravarunau.

There are in the *Rgveda* eight whole hymns and parts of two hymns which have Indravarunau as *devata*. Out of these, the four hymns in the seventh book of the *Rgveda*, which, indicentally form the largest single group of the Indravarunau hymns, are particularly significant. Vasistha, the seer of the seventh book, was a devoted protagonist of the Varuna cult.[9] But, transcending all thought of bigotry, he assumed a very practical and realistic attitude and deliberately sought to co-ordinate and harmonize the two religious cults.[10] He studiously emphasised in his Indravarunau hymns that the spheres of activity of Varuna and Indra, though separate, were essentially complementary and that an active collaboration, on equal terms, of these two gods would alone ensure the properly integrated and amicable operation of the world-process in its cosmic and socio-political aspects. All thought of antagonism between Varuna and Indra was vigorously discountenanced, and an attitude of religious conciliation became quite transparent. This, Vasistha accomplished in various ways. For instance, he identified the specific spheres of sovereignty of these two gods by characterising Varuna as *samraj* or primeval world-sovereign and Indra as *svaraj* or one who won his divine suzerainty through his own prowess.[11] In the course of the development of the Vedic religious ideology, Varuna, the administrator of cosmic law, also came to be represented specifically as the god who enforced moral order within the human community. In his Indravarunau hymns, Vasistha has taken special pains to reiterate that Indra, the war-god, sponsored the Vedic Aryans' exploits of conquest and colonisation (*prtanasu*,) while Varuna, the moral governor, blessed their efforts in connection with the establishment of law and order (*ksemasya prasave*).[12] Both gods were great (*mahantau*) in their respective roles; having duly recognised this, all other gods, in the highest heaven, subserved Indra—Varuna by consigning into them their splendour and their strength.[13] But Vasistha's main slogan in his efforts to bring about conciliation between the Varuna-cult and the Indra-cult may be said to have been embodied in *RV* VIII.83.9 ab: *vrtrany anyah samithesu jighnate vratany anyo abhi aksate sada.* "One of the two gods", proclaims Vasistha, "vanquishes the enemies in battles, while the other over sustain the socio-ethical laws." In other words, Indra *conquers* and varuna *rules.*

Brhaspati-Brahmanaspati (I take the two divinities, Brhaspati and Brahmanaspati, to be identical), obviously owes his origin to the tendencies which were inevitably engendered by the Indra-dominated mythology. In a sense, therefore, this god may be said to belong conceptually to the second phase of the evolutionary mythology of the *Rgveda.*

Brhaspati is celebrated in eleven entire hymns of the *Rgveda,* while in two hymns (IV.49, VII.97) he forms a dual-divinity with Indra. Though some kind of distinction appears to have been made between Brhaspati and Brahmansapati in the Vedic ritual and in the ancillary Vedic texts,[14] the two words are used almost indiscriminately in the *Rgveda.* Etymology also seems to suggest the identity of the two gods.[15] Incidentally it may be noted that only one name, namely, Brhaspati, is generally retained in later literature. Rgvedic references to Brhaspati clearly indicate that he has by no means grown out of naturalistic mythology. Nor is he an outcome of the mythologization of a historical human personality. Again the suggestion that *Brhaspati* was originally an epithet of Indra and was later separated from him and established as an independent god does not seem to be warranted. There is no indication in the *Rgveda* of this kind of evolution in his personality—he already appears as a full-fledged independent god in that Veda as is clearly testified by II.24.11-13. At the same time, there can hardly be any doubt that he is a later addition to the Vedic pantheon. The facts that Brhaspati has no Indo-European or Indo-Iranian cognates, that his name is artificially coined as a compound with *pati* as the latter member, that the hymns relating to him rarely contain any internal repetitions, and that sometimes a suspicion is expressed regarding the genuineness and originality of his personality[16] would seem to confirm such an assumption.

The over-all impression that one might form in the light of what has been said so far would be that Brhaspati was a deliberate artificial mythological creation, that he was conceived at some later state in the evolution of the Rgvedic mythology to serve some specific function. Without discussing the various aspects of the personality and character of Brhaspati, I shall address myself to only one question: why did Brhaspati come to be introduced in Vedic mythology?

We have seen that the changed conditions in the life of the Proto-Indo-Aryans necessitated a transition from the consmic-ethical phase of the Rgvedic mythology to the Indra-dominated heroic phase. During their migration from Balkh to Saptasindhu and their subsequent colonization in that region, the early vedic Aryans had to confront many Vrtras, both natural; and human. History came to be mythologized, and as the result of this the victorious warlike leader of the Vedic Aryans was born' in the Vedic pantheon as Indra and forthwith become the foremost among the gods - *yo jata eva prathamo manasvan.*[17] This naturally eventuated in the general glorification of the cult of military prowess. The socio-religious reprercussions of the newly evident domineering stance of the cult of militarism against priestcraft - of Ksatra against Brahman—are seen to have been reflected in several Vedic passages. In *Rgveda* X.109, for instance, there is a reference to *brahmajaya,* the wife of a priest, having been kidnapped.[18] The same topic is dealt with at greater length in *Atharvaveda* V.17. That hym contains a clear threat that the kidnapped wife of Brahman is fearful and causes great disaster.[19] It is hinted that there will be nothing but sheer misfortune in the kingdom in which a Brahman's wife is kept away from him.[20] *Atharvaveda* V.18 refers to the robbing of a brahman of his cow. "Her," it is said, "the gods did not give thee for thee to eat, O king; do not thou, O Rajanya, desire to devour the cow of the Brahmana, that is notto be eaten."[21] The degraded military potentate becomes addicted to dice, is evil and self-ruined, and eats up the Brahman's cow, for, he only thinks: let me live today; I don't care for the morrow—*adya jivani ma svah.*[22] He forgets that the Brahman, like fire, is not to be harmed by one who holds himself dear, for, Some is Brahman's heir and Indra his protector against imprecations.[23] We are told that the military rulers, Vaitahavyas, who usurped the Brahman's cow (that is, the Brahman's belongings), perished.[24] Elsewhere it is reported that the Srnjaya-Vaitahavyas, who prospered excessively, who just did not quite touch up to the sky *(nodiva divam asprsan),* having molested the Brahman, bhrgu, suffered utter mortification.[25] those who spat upon a Brahman, we are further told, or who sent their mucus at him - they sit in the midst of a stream of blood, devouring hair.[26] A king who thinks himself formidable and who desires to exploit a Brahman - his kingdom is laid waste where a Brahman is scathed.[27] The derisive attitude of the Pajras towards Brhaspati may also be mentioned as being indicative of the growing brahman-Ksatra antagonism.

Obviously the need must have been felt, even at an early stage, for counteracting such militarist arrogance. Passively, the Vedic poet-priests used to insist that, in order to prove efficicacious, the military prowess (as symbolished by Indra) had to be supplemented by the magically potent *mantra.* For instance, the credit for the victory of Sudas in the War of the Ten Kings *(Dasarajna)* is said to have largely belonged to Vasistha (Sudas's Purohita) who, through his *mantra*-power, had brought about Indra's intervention in Sudras's favour.[29] When, in that war, the Prtsu-Bharatas had become disrupted and weak, their Purohita Vasistha assumed the leadership and goaded their patrons on to victory.[30]Elsewhere it is said: O Indra-Varuna, invulnerably you overpowered Bheda by means of your deadly weapons and thus aided Sudas in the Dasarajna battle; for, you listened to the magically potent prayers of the Bharatas even i the midst of the urgent rival-invocations.In all this, indeed, there clearly became evident the supreme efficacy of the priest-craft of the Trtsu-Vasisthas - *satya trtsunam abhaavat purohitih.*[31]

Another step in this process of asserting the claim of priest-craft by the side of—or, in some cases, eve against—military prowess was more positive. A veritable new god was concived and came to be introduced in Vedic mythology—Brahaspati-Brahmanaspati, the lord of *brahman, of mantra*-power and priest-craft. Understandably, there was little anthropomorphism in the make-up of this god—the 'function' aspect of this god was definitely more prominent than the `individuality' aspect. It is emphasised that that king along would indeed prevail over his adversaries who held Brhaspati in high esteem and regard.[32] Brhaspati is the sage of sages *(kavim kavinam),* the supreme king of prayers *(jyestarajam brahmanam).*[33] He promotes the yoking of devotion, and without him sacrifice does not succeed.[34] As a pathmaker he makes good the access to the feast of the gods.[35] He awakens the gods with sacrfice.[36] Wise gods themselves attain their share in sacrifice through mighty Brhapati; he is the creator of all magically potent *mantras.* Whoever makes offerings unto him will never be subjected to suffering; but of the Brahman-hater he is a veritable scourage.[37] Verily, Brhaspati is the most godly of the gods *(devanam devatama)*[38]

Besides such conventional glorification of Brhaspati, attempt seems to have been deliberately made to present that gods as being on par with Indra, the victorious warlike hero who had become the foremost among the Vedic gods. Brhaspati Angirasa, the first-born holy one, cleaver of rocks, roars as a bul at the two worlds, slays *vrtras,* shatters forts, overcomes foes.[39] No one can overpower him in great fight or small.[40] He is to be invoked in combats,[41] and is a priest much praised in conflict.[42] Brhaspati shares with Indra the epithets *vajrin* (wielder of the bolt),[43] *maghavan,*[44] and *somapa.*[45] He is sometimes represented as the companion and ally of Indra,[46] but, what is far more significant, Brhaspati is individually credited with great heroic exploits in the celebrated Vala-myth. The mountain is said to have yielded to Brhaspati's splendour when he opened the cowstall. Accompanied by his singing host, he rent Vala with a roar and shouting drove out the lowing cows. he won treasures and the great stalls full of cows; the irresistible Brahaspati slew his foe with flames.[47] Brhaspati's conquest of Vala was regarded to be so characteristic that it almost became proverbial.[48]

There can hardly be any doubt that such warlike character was tendentiously superimposed on Brhaspati. Indeed, in their enthusiasm for counteracting the ascendancy of the Kstra-power over the Brahman-power, the Vedic myth-makers have gone to the other extreme. Indra's role, even in warlike exploits, is sometimes said to have been secondary to that of Brhaspati.[49] Presumably, therefore, in order to avoid a new impending conflict between the Brahman-cult and the Ksatra-cult, the evolutionary Vedic mythology conceived the dual-divinity of Indra-Brhaspati, who is celebrated in the two whole hymns, *RV* IV.49 and VII.97.

Besides complementariness (as in the case Mitravarunau)and conciliatory adjustmnt (as in the case of Indravarunau and Indrabrhaspati), the third purpose which the conception of the dual-divinities served was religio-mythological elevation or hierarchisation.

It needs to be emphasised hat the *Rgveda-Samhita,* as we have it today, does by no means constitute the entire literature which had been produced in the *Rgvedic* age. Nor can the *Rgveda* claim to reflect the life and thought of all the strata of the Rgvedic community. For instance, the cults, which had developed round Varuna-Mitra-Aryaman and Indra and Brhaspati and which we have briefly surveye so far, have to be understood as representing mainly the religio-mythological ideology of the class of the Rgvedic poets, priests, and warriors. But there must have then existed also some forms of these 'popular' cults could possibly not be by-passed altogether. In course of time, after the life-conditions of the Vedic Aryans had in general become more settled and secure, the peculiar pressure of circumstances must have compelled the Vedic poet-priests to grant cognition to these gods, albeit with some reluztance. But while granting such recognition, those poet-priests took care to change the original character of those gods in such a way as to bring those gods in line with the hieratic religio-mythologicalideology. However fortunately for us some indications about the original character of those gods have remained unobliterated in the *Rgveda.* A typical example of this phenomenon is the evolutionary mythologyrelating to visnu.[50]

For instance in a few passages of the *Rvedeva,* Visnu is characterized as *sipivista.* It is noteworthy that these passages are—perhaps deliberately—shrouded in obscurity. Apparently the vedic poets were straining themselves to refer to Visnu's character denoted by the epithet *sipivista* in as guarded and vague a manner as possible. Etymologically, the word *sipivista* denotes an expanding, active male organ, Presumably, the concept of *sipivista* must have been regarded by the sophisticated poet-priests almost as taboo. In the *Nirukta,* Aupamanyava describes Visnu's epithet *Sipivista* as *kutsitarthiya* - "having a censurable implication." This would explain why the Rgvedic poet-priests mentioned it (when they were at tall required to mention it) almost grudgingly. That epithet signifies Visnu's connection with the concepts of virile power, procreation, fecundity, etc. In other words, Visnu must have originally been a god of virility and fertility. In confirmation of this hypothesis, attention may be drawn to the *Vrsakapi*-hymn in the *Rgveda*[51] wherein the *Vrsakapi* is said to have invested the exhausted Indra with fresh virile power. The identity of Vrsakapi with Visnu is proved by considerable literary evidence. Visnu's connection with virility, procreation, and fertility is further confirmed by some other, incidental references in vedic literature and ritual, such as, Visnu's association with Sinivali, the guardian goddess of wombs, his epithets *nisiktapa*[52] and *sumajjani*[53], and the formula, *visnur yonim kalpayatu,* employed in a rite connected with conceiving.

Anthropological research has shown that many primitive communities have conceived their fertility-gods as having 'bird' as their symbol. Some traces of this trend are to be seen in Vedic ritual also. For instance, the divinity which plays a very significant role in the Mahavrata rite, which is obvisouly a fertility-rite,is represented in the form of a bird. Similarly the *mahadukthya* altar used in that rite has the shape of a bird. The word *visnu* is to be derived from the root *vi* 'to fly,' to which is suffixed the termination *snu* (as in such words as *jisnu, ksesnu).* Thus, Visnu, the god of virility and fertility, was also conceived as having the form of a bird.

When, however, the Vedic poet-priests were constrained to admit Visnu into their mythology, they shrewdly shifted their emphasis from the concept of the bird as the symbol of a fertility-divinity to that of the bird as the symbol of a solar divinity. As a result of this, Visnu appears in the *Rgveda* mainly as the wide-striding sun-god. In the Rgvedic mythology, Visnu is thus seen to be steadily developing from his original character as a popular fertility-divinity to an artificially sophisticated solar divinity. In course of time, the Rgvedic mythology sought to validate this elevated mythological status of that god. It brought this about by associating Visnu with Indra in howsoever superficial and artificial a manner. Indra had become the very hallmark of the hieratic Rgvedic religion, as is amply testified by the conspicuously Indra-dominated Rgvedic mythology. He served as a catalyst, as it were, in the process of the hieratic elevation of 'popular' gods. Intrinsically Visnu had nothing in common with Indra - he had hardly anything to do with Indra. But Vedic mythology-makers made him a subordinate ally or an equal partner or sometimes even a superior associate of Indra in his heroic deeds and eventually confirmed his elevated status by combining him with Indra to form the dual-divinity Indravisnu.[54]

NOTES

1. *Dandekar, Vedic Mythological Tracts (VMT),* Delhi, 1979.
2. On account of the single occurrence of the word *same* in this quarter it is sometimes suggested that *brhaspath* is to be understood as an epithet of Indra. But the general tenor of the context makes it clear that the mention of two separate divinities, Indra and Brhaspati,is intended here. Moreover, in no sense can *brhaspati* be regarded as a distinctive epithet of Indra (in the way in which *urukrama* can of Visnu).
3. *AV* XIX,9.6; VS 36.9; TA 7.1.; TU 1.1.1; 12.1; Man SS 6.1.5.
4. Cf. *RV* V. 1.7; IV. 42.3; II.27.8.
5. RV III.59.5; VIII.102.12. Also cf. III.59.1.
6. The dual-divinities Dyavaprathivi and Suryacandramasau, though generally suggestive of complementaryaness, are 'physical (naturalistic)' rather than mythological' concepts.
7. *RV* II.12.1.
8. *VMT* 141-198.
9. See "A Vedic god and a Vedic Seer", *VMT,* pp. 312-350.
10. Se Vasistha sas religious conciliator" in *Dandekar, Exercises in Indology,* Delhi, 1981, pp. 122-132.
11. *RV* VII.82.2.
12. *RV* VII82.4 ab; 5 cd; 6.
13. *RV* VII.82.2bcd.
14. Cf. *TS* II.1.7; 2.6; 8.2; *Nirukta* X.11.12; *Brhaddevata* 1.12.2; 11.2.3. The word *brahmanaspati* is sometimes employed as a gloss on *brhaspati* (TB II.11.4.2).
15. *Brahman-* and brh- are derived romthesame root *brh* which means "strengthen" or "make firm."
16. Cf. *RV* 1.190.5.
17. *RV.* II.12.1.
18. *RV.* X. 109. 2.5,
19. *AV* V. 17.6,7.
20. *AV* V.18.1.

21. *AV.* V. 18.1.
22. *AV* V. 18.2
23. *AV* V. 18.6.
24. *AV* V. 18.10.
25. *AV.* V. 19.1.
26. *AV* V. 19.3
27. *AV* V. 19.6.
28. *RV.* I.190.5.
29. *RV* VII.33.3.
30. *RV* VII.33.6.
31. *RV* VII.83.4.
32. *RV* IV. 50.7-9.
33. *RV* II.23.1.
34. *RV* I.18.7.
35. *RV* 11.23.6,7.
36. *AV* XIX. 63.1.
37. *RV* II.23.4.
38. *RV* II. R4.3..
40. *RV* 1.40.8.
41. *RV* II.23.13.
42. *RV.* II.24.9.
43. *RV* 1.40.8; AV XI.10.12,13.
44. *RV* 1.24.12.
45. *RV* IV. 49,50.10.
46. *RV* II.23.18; 24.2; VIII.85.15.
47. *RV* II.23.18; IV.505; VI.73.3.
48. *AV* IV. 3.2.
49. *RV* X. 108.6,11; II.24.3.
50. See "Visnu in the Veda", VMT, pp. 68-90.
51. *RV* Z. 86..
52. *RV* VII.36.9.
53. *RV.* I. 156.2.
54. One whole hymn, namely *RV VI.69*, is dedicated to *Indravisnu.* This dual divinity is also referred to in many other passages. Incidentally it may be mentioned that the history of the dual-divinity Indrapusanau has much in common with that of Indravisnu.

Chapter-14

The Goddess with the Severed Head : A RECENSION OF SADHANAMALA 232, 234 AND 238 ATTRIBUTED TO THE SIDDHACARYA VIRUPA

M. NIHOM

Chapter-14

During a stay in Kathmandu in the winter of 1986-87[1], Dr. John Locke, learning of this writer's interest in the literature of the *Hevajratantra,* kindly allowed me to make a xerox copy of a manuscript in his possession. Consisting of 75 folia, numbered 1 to 73[2], it contains four texts written in *devanagari* in a modern hand. Only the last may be said to belong unambiguously to the literature of the *Hevajra* cycle. The first three are texts on meditative praxes associated with Vajrayogini.[3]

Only the first of these four texts is presented here. The second and third, also attributed to Virupa and containing much interesting material on the nature of the goddess, will be edited separately. The study below is in three parts. The first section will discuss the problem of the authorship of this *sadhana,* the second presents the edited text as compared to the *Sadhanamala* recension and the third treats of some problems evoked by he text.

I

Arguably the most important source for the knowledge of particular Buddhist tantric deities is the collection of *sadhanas* published some 65 years ago by B. Bhattacarya under the title *Sadhanamala.* Among the 312 items, seven, nos. 232-238, all anonymous,[4] are explicitly dedicated to Vajrayogini. This goddess comes in two colours, red and yellow. Bhattacarya (158: 247-249) holds that there are in fact two yellow Vajrayogini, represented respectively by SM 232 ad 234. However, Mallman (1975: 432) points out that Sm 234 is an abbreviated version of 232. Indeed, 234 consists primarily of mantras also found in 232. As for 238, Bhattacarya supplies the colophon *Vajrayoginya balividhi.* The two mantras, themselves the entire body of the text, are with minor variations identical to mantras found in the manuscript.

The presence of these 4 texts in one, albeit modern,

manuscript, encourages one to ask if this Vajrayogini might be associated with the hevajra cycle, thereby motivating the presence of all four texts in one document, or whether, if taken as a form of Vajravarahi, the consort of Samvara, her consanguinity mus rather be to the cycle of the *Samvaratantra*?[5] In the event of the latter, we must wonder about the reason for her presence in one document consisting of the three short texts attributed to Virupa, and devoted to Vajrayogini and a commentary on the *Hevajrasadhana*.

In fact, the problem of the association of the yellow Vajrayogini here with one or other of what became the cycles of the *anuttaratanra* class of texts and one or more of the *'dhyanibuddhas'* is perhaps irrelevant: whichever the century to which Virupa ought be dated, his position as preceptor vis a vis Dombi Heruka who is said to have proceeded Saraha and Kampala—the 'finders' of the *Hevajratantra* (Snellgrover; 1959: 12-13) — means he must have lived during an early period in the development of what became the class of *anuttarayoga* tantras. Virupa became an exceedingly important figure not only for the *yogini* or mother tantra in general, but especially in the lineage tradition of the *sa skya pa,* a sect which especially emphasises the traditions of the *Hevajratantra* and developed meditations methods associated with this *siddhacarya*.[6] This state of affairs, that Virupa came to be especially associated with the Hevajra cycle, might itself be seen to explain the constitution of the manuscript, regardless of any scholastic determination as to the Buddha family (*kula*) to which the yellow Vajrayogini should be held to belong.

There is as such no reason to impose features of distinct *anuttarayogatantra'* cycles to these texts on the yellow Vajrayogini. The goddess herself is not assigned to a given Buddha family in the available texts. She may in due course have come to be so affiliated, but explicit evidence for this is not forthcoming in the 3 *sadhanas* on the yellow Vajrayogini of the *Sadhanamala*, in the three Virupa texts of the Locke manuscript, nor in Virupa's *Chinnamundasadhana* located in the Tibetan canon. Rather than worrying about the affiliation of the goddess, one might therefore propose that if *Sadhanamala* 232, 234, and 238 are indeed authored by Virupa, then, i the absence of additional Sanskrit texts on the yellow Vajrayogini, the possibility exits that Virupa himself may have been responsible for introduction of the yellow Vajrayogini alias Trikayavajrayogini.[7]

But should one accept the manuscript's attribution of authorship? As noted by Bhattacarya (1958: 1; 1968: cxlii-cxlvii), this yellow Vajrayogini is analogous to the Hindu deity Chinnamasta, also known as Chinnamunda. Abhayadatta in his *Caturstitisidhapravratti.* (f. 95,3) has the *siddhacarya* Kanha call her P'ag mo dbu bcad ma, *Chinnamunda Varahi.[8] The goddess Chinnamunda is explicitly represented by two texts in the Tibetan Buddhist cannon (Meisezal 1965-6:266-7). Srimatidevi entitles her work the *Chinnamundavajrava- rahisadhana.* The other work on this goddess in the canon is the *Chinnamundasadhana,* one of some 14 works in the canon said to be authored by Virupa,[9], himself one of the traditional 84[10] *siddhacarya* of the Buddhist tantric tradition. Consequently, to find a version of SM 232 attributed to Virupa where Vajrayogini has much the same iconography as the Chinnamunda of the retranslated text in the Tibetan canon definitely written by this savant, is reasonable. Yet, the question arises of whether there is any internal evidence for acquiescing in this determination of authorship. I believe there may be, but it is indirect.

Most of the text below is found, in a slightly different version, in SM 232. Those fragments which are not consist in the main of 3 sets of mantras. The first, the *japamantra - om sarvabuddhadakiniye om vajravamaniye om vajravairocaniye hum hum hum phat phat phat svaha*-is also to be found in SM 236, a text devoted to the red Vajrayogini, where, however, it is the *mulamantra.* We also find it in SM 233, again of the red Vajrayogini. It is not named,but inasmuch as it is here the first of a set of mantras which are given names, it may also be seen as the *mulamantra* for this SM 233. Interestingly, our text repeats the mantra towards the close, where this time it is deemed *mulamantra.*SM 232 here yields the same mantra—deemed *japamantra*—save that the three om are placed at the beginning (*om om om sarvabuddhadakaniye...).* This version *(om om om .. hum, 3 phat 3 svaha(* is also spelled out in verse in the Tibetan translation of Virupa's *Chinnamundasadhana.*[11]

The text below contains two mantras absent from SM 232, which are in fact the entire text of SM 238. From the second mantra it is clear that these are for the *bali* ritual.

There remains a block of text (f. 3a, 5-3b, 4) which is found in SM 232, but in a severely compromised form. Our text has *om odiyanavajra puspe hum svaha* and so on with *purmagiri, kama-ksa* and *srihata*. There are the four *pithas*. SM 232 reads: *pascat punar* [i.e. in the form *om ... hum svaha] api odiyan pumagiri....ity anena pujayet*. Likewise, our text has *om dharmakayavajrapuspe hum svadha*, and so on with *sambhogakaya, nirmanakaya* and *mahasukhakaya*. SM 232 reads *api dharma sambhoganirm-anamahasukha ity anena*. In other words, our text explicitly associates 4 *pithas* and the 4 bodies of the Buddha with a flower, *vajrapuspa*, in two sets of 4 mantras and these associations are absent from SM 232. With the exception of SM 234 which treats of the *kanakasyama*[12] Vajrayogini and which is, as noted, primarily a compendium of the mantras of 232 (see infra), the association of *pithas*—and indeed the 4 bodies *(kaya)* of the Buddha with the *vajra*-flower is found in no other of the remaining 310 texts of the *sadhanamala*.

Mantras with the term *'vajrapuspa'* are found explicitly in at least 12 other texts of the 312: SM 3, 7, 15, 35, 36, 50, 80, 128, 129, 131, 159, and 266. In all of these, the mantras, although differing in detail, are associated with the worship *(puja)* of the divinity or divinities. Their names occasionally may (SM 3, 35, 36, 159) or may not be found as part of the mantra, also often known as a *pujamantra*.[13] In most instances this mantra is found as first of a set of five, each pertaining to one of the five gifts *(pancopacara*[14]*)* used in the *puja* ritual.[15] In such standardized contexts the honorific prefix *vaajra-* may also be omitted (e.g. SM 12, 67, 142, passim). Consequently, the presence of *yajrapuspa* alone in these *sadhanas* is not as such significant, even while its frequent occurance in the *Sadhanamala* makes its co-incidence with the *pithas* and *kayas* within a mantra in SM 234 and the ms. all the more exceptional.

The situation is therefore that the text below associates 4 *pitha* with *Vajrapuspa* and that, while the *vajrapuspa* is absent from Sm 232, the four *pitha* are found associated with worship (*ity anena pujayet)* and the terminus *vajrapusapa* in 234 which is as 232 devoted to the yellow Vajrayogini. Because the fourth *pitha, srihatasrihatta / sirihatta,* as one of a set of four is unusual in Buddhist tantric contexts, we may propose that co-occurrence of this *pitha* and *vajrapuspa* within a mantra used in *puja* appears for reasons yet unknown to be a diagnostic of the yellow Vajrayogini and/or an identifying characteristic of the author of SM 232, 234 and edited text. In short, on the co-occurrence of *vajrapuspa* and a *pitha* would appear unique to the yellow Vajrayogini, possibly but not necessarily without regard to Virupa's putative authorship of her *sadhanas.*

In the absence of additional *sadhanas,* that this use of *vajrapuspa* is definitive of the yellow Vajrayogini is effectively untestable. As for the second possibility, knowledge of the person of Virupa is scant, effectively limited to hagiographic works much as Abhayadatta's *Caturasitisiddhapravrti.* This twelfth century author says that virupa was born in the city of Tripura in the East. We may observe that Sircar (1973: 96) identifies the *pitha srihatta* as modern Sylhet in Assam. Virupa is said to have gone to the monastery Somapuri in the South of India. After twelve years as a monk he was accused of drinking wine and eating pigeon meat and as a consequence expelled. From a lake next to the monastery he cut a lotus and, having offered the blossom to the Buddha, stood upon the leaf and crossed the water of the lake. This miracle impressed the inhabitants of Somapuri. Virupa, denying that the pigeons had been killed, brings them back.[16] At this point in his life, Abhayadatta says, he quit the monkhood and became a yogin.[17]

Worship of the Buddha and 'miraculous' events are the meant of this text. Even so, this incident provides an hagiographic connection of Virupa with flowers within the context of yoga independent of the *vajrapuspa* data of the Trikayavajrayogini *sadhanas.* A check of biographies of the other 83 *siddhacaryas* in Abhayadatta's work shows that the association of a gift of a flower to the Buddha resulting in a miraculous 'crossing to the other side' is, for this Indian author, unique to virupa. Confirming the theme, in the second text of the Locke manuscript (f. 6a,5), Virupa calls the goddess *tirayogini,*[18] "the yogini of the (other) shore" as well as *samsaratarini* (f.6b,1).

A further association of flowers with Virupa may be determined from iconography. The 84 *siddhacaryas* are occasionally depicted in series of thanks or in sculpture. The specific iconography of Virupa is various—he is often shown with a turban, a mustache, a beard, holding a skull, with earplugs and so on. But most important for our purposes is the "*cemahasiddha* porte toujours, comme ici, un collier de fleurs" *Dieux et Demons* 1977: 152).[19]

We therefore have three associations:

1. The presence of a *vajrapuspa* associated with *pithas* in a *sadhana* attributed to Virupa and its absence in similar context in *sadhanas* attributed to Virupa and its absence in similar context in *sadhanas* attributed to other authors;

2. The story of the offering of a lotus to the Buddha resulting in a miracle and Virupa's enlightenment in the *Caturastitisiddhapravrtti;*

3. The fact that iconographicly Virupa is always shown with a necklace of flowers.

These there data together support the view that the text below, and *Sadhanamala* 232, 234 and 238, are in all probability authors day this Buddhist tantric master.

II

Ms. Locke (f.1)[20]	SM 232
namah srivajrayoginyai *om ah hum phat*	*namo vajrayoginyai /* *om ah hum /*
[Bhavana]	
prathamam tavan mantri *kasminn api pradese* *kasminn apy asane upavisya* *trikayavajrayoginibhavanam arabet /* *tatra svanabhau vikasita-suklavamapamkaraparinanam* *sitapadmam satadalam vibhavayet* *tatropari raktavamam rephejam*	*prathamam tavan mantri* *kvacit kasminn api pradese* *kasmin apy asane upavisya* *vajrayoginibhavanam arabhet /* *tatra svanabhau vikasitam suklavamam* *padmam bhavayet /* *tatropari* *atiraktavamasuryamandalam*

suryyamandalam
bhavayet
bhavayet /
tatropari[21] sinduravamam

dharmodayam[22] ca vibhavayet

tatrapi ca madhye pitahr-
imkaraja
pita svayam eva
kartya karttitam[23] svamastakam
vamahaste sthitam
dharayanti
daksinahastastha (2a) karttya
sahita[24]
urddhavistrtavamabahvi
adhonamitadaksinabhuja
vasahsunya[25]
prasaritadaksinapada
akuncitavamacarana

kabandhad avadhrtivartmana
nihsrta[26] srgdhaara
tasyamukhe prapatati pravisati va
apare lalanarasanabhyam ca
nihsrta
parsveyor yoginyo mukham
pravisati iti bhavyam
tatra vamaparsve sysmavamani
vame karttidaksine kapalam
bibhraa
prasaritavamapada
samkucitadaksinacarana
muktakesi nagna
daksinaparsve de (2b) vya pita
vajravairocani daksinena karttim
vamena kapalam bibhrati
muktakesi
nagna vistrtadaksinapada
vamasamkoca iti bhavyam
ubhayoh parsveyor yoginyor
antarikse tibhayakulam
smasanam bhavayet iti bhavana

tatropari sinduravamam
madhyahrimkarastithamdhamodyam
bhavayet /

tatrapy upari bhattarikam
vajrayoginim
tatra sthitahrimkaraparinatam
;itavamam svaya eva
svakartrikarttitasvamastaka-
vamahastasthitam

daksinahastakartrisahitam

urddhavavistravamabahum
adhonamitadaksinabahum
vasahsunyam
prasaritadaksinapadam

sankucitavamapadam
bhavayet /
kabandhan
nihsrtyasrgdhara

svamukhe pravisati
apare ubhayoh
parsvayoginyor mukhe
pravisati iti bhavayet /
vamadaksinaparsvayoh
symavamavajravamani
pitavamavajravairocanyau
vamadaksinahastakartrisahite
daksinavamahastakarparasahite
prasaritavamapadaprasarita-
daksinapade
samkucitetarapade
muktakesyau bhavayet /
ubhayoh parsvayor ubhayor
yoginyor
madhye antarikse atibhayakulam
smasanam bhavayet iti bhavana

om sarvabuddhadakiniye	*(453.5)*
om vajravamaniye	*[cf. SM 233, 454.10-12 where*
om vajravairocaniye	*mulamantra]*
hum hum hum phat 3 svaha iti japamantrah	

[Puja]

idanim pujocyate mandalam caturasram	*pujocyate mandalam krtva*
tatra yryopari tallagnam dharmodayam	*dharmodayam suryyalayalagnam*
likhitva	
likhet	
tanmadhye hrimkaram vamayam	*madhyahrimkarasahitam*
li (3a) khya pujayet	
tadbhavam va purvoktarupam[27]	*tatah purvoktabhavanaya*
bhagavatim madhye aropya	*bhattarikam madhye aropya*
tatra dharmodaya madhye	
om sarvabuddhadakiniye ity	*om sarvabudhadakiniye ity*
adina mantrena prathamam[28]	*adimantrena dharmodayamadhye*
arcayet	
tad anu	*pujayet/*
om sarvabuddhadakiniye hum phat	*pascad arghah/*
	om sarvabuddhadakiniye hum
svaha	*svaha*
ity anenarghodayah	*iti mantrena*
vame	*pascad vamaparsve*
om vajravamaniye svaha	*om vajravamaniye hum svaheti mantrena*
daksine	*pascad daksinaparsve*
om vajravairocaniye hum svaha ity	*om vajravairocaniyehum*
arcayet	*svaheti anena*
om odiyan[29] *vajrapuspe hium svaha*	*pascat punar api odiyana pumagiri*
om purmagirivajrapuspe hum svaha	*kamakhya sirihatta*
om kamaksavajrapuspe hum svaha	*ity anena pujayet*
punar madhye	
om srihatavajrapuspe hum svaha	[Compare SM 234]
(3b)	

om dharmakayavajrapuspe hum svaha	*punar api*
om sambhogakayavajrapuspe hum svaha	*dharmascambhoganimanamaha sukha*
om nimanakayavajrapuspe hum svaha	*ity anena*
punar madhye	
om mahasukhakayavajrapuspe	
hum svaha	
punar madhye	
om namah sarvagurubuddhabo-dhisattevebhyo	
vajrapuspe hum svaha	

[Japa]

dyanat khinno mantram japet	
tatryama mantrah	
om sarvabuddhadakiniye	*om om om sarvabuddhadainiye*
om vajravamaniye	*vajravarmaniye*
om vajravarocaniye	*vajravairocaniye*
hum hum hum phat 3 svaha	*hum hum hum phat phat phat svaha*
tatrayam mulamantrah	*ity japamantrah*
	vajrayoginishadhanamsamaptam
om vajravairocaniye hum paht	
hrdayamantrah	
om vajrayoginiye (4a) upahrdayamantrah	
omkaradisvahantena pujayitva	
puravavad visarjayed[31] *iti*	

[Bali]

om srivajrayogini	*SM 238*
sarvabhutapisacadin[32]	*om srivajrayogini*
sodhya 2 hana 2	*sarvabhutapretapisavadin*
	sadhaya sadhaya hana hana daha daha grasa grasa
sarvasiddhipradhani	*sarvasiddhisadhanani*
prayaccha arvasam[33] *me paripuraya svaha*	*prayaccha sarvasam parjpuraya svaha /*
srivajrayogini sarvasiddhi	*om srivajrayogini sarvasiddhim*

kuri 2
sarvavinayakha
hana 2
samyaksambodhaye mam idam
balim ghmantu 2 hum 3 phat 3
svaha
sadhanam vajraayoginyam iti
tvaya[34] *yat punyam acitam tena*
lokabhavattavena
samyaksambodhilabyi nasati ity
aryabhagavatitrikayavavajrayogin
(4b) sadhanam
samaptam subham
krttir ayam siddhacaryavirupam
danam iti

kuru kuru
sarvavighnavinayakan
hana hana
samyaksambodhaye mama
balim tgrhna hum hum hum
phat phat svaha/

III

This short text may be divided into six parts: a) introduction, b) meditative-production, c) worship, d) recitation, e) *bali* offering, and f) conclusion. The discussion which follows cannot be exhaustive either philologically or culture-historically, but will strive to indicate that the praxis is an internal yoga and a reflex or counterpart to the (external) rite known as *savasadhana* in Hindu texts.[35] In addition, an instance will be given of the well known connection between Samvara and Siva.

(a) Introduction, f. 1,1: The manuscript starts with a salutation to Trikaya Vajrayogini. The stipulation *trikaya-* is also found in the two other Virupa texts (not edited here), but not in the *Sadhanamala.* There follows the mantra *om ah hum phat,* thereby distinguishing it from what is elsewhere called the *kayavakcittadhisthanamantra, om ah hum.*[36] *Phat* is also added to the *arghamantra* as found in 232.

(b) *Bhavana,* f. 1,1-2b,5: This specifies the iconography of the yellow Trikaya Vajrayogini. The substance is identical to SM 232. After the usual preliminaries, one meditatively produces in the naval a yellow Vajrayogini, in the *Pratyalidha* posture and carrying her own severed head in her right hand and a knife in her left. On her right and left are the attendants Vajravarnani and Vajravairocani, nude, in *lidha* and each bearing a knife and skull. From Vajrayogini's headless trunk three streams of blood issue from the three (yogic)veins *lalana, rasana* and *avadhuti* - here named *avadhrti*[37] - and enter the mouths of Vajravarnani, Vajravairocani, Vajrayogini respectively.

There are a few details meriting attention. SM 232 specifies that the stream of blood *(asrgdhara)* enters *pravisati)* the mouth of Vajrayogini. Our text reads *prapatati pravisati va.* Both attendants make do with *pravisati.* Whether this formulaic alternative might be taken as evidence that our text is older than that of SM 232, is unanswerable. It is nevertheless of interest, for this implies that the status of the streams of blood directed to the attendants is different from that of Vajrayogini, as it indeed must be, since *lalana* and *rasana* represent sun and moon, vowel and consonant, Insight and Means.[38] Hence, the gross iconography of the yellow Vajrayogini is a depiction of an internal yoga. Indeed, the goddess who has three bodies abides in these three paths (f. 71, 6-7b, 1: *(trimarge samsthita devi trikayavajrayogini).*[39]

This proposition, that the distinction of *pravisati/prapatti* might have meaning and that it may refer to yogic practises of the Buddhist tantric literature often associated with the figure Candali and Vasantatilaka, is supported by the Nepalese painting from the collection of the Musee Guimet reproduced in black and white by Mallman (1975: plate XII).[40] The streams of blood do seem to enter the mouths of Vajravarnani and Vajravairocani - whose teeth are visible.This is not discernible for Vajrayogini, the mouth of whose severed head is closed. Assisting interpretation of the three figures, the middles of the disks of the sun and moon high in this miniature are *precisely* aligned with the open mouths of the two attendants. Further, the tip of the topmost flame of the *prabha* is an iota higher the upper rims of the sun and moon, and is aligned not with the center of the headless body of Vajrayogini, but with the point of conjunction of Bhairava and Kalaratri on whom she treds. Consequently, vajravarnani and Vajravairocani might be seen to represent *lalana* and *rasana* - often associated with the sun and moon- and Vajrayogini and Bhairava and Kalaratri their union on a white lotus in the navel, the locus for the meditative-production of the goddess (f. 1,3: *svanabha...sitapadmam ...vibhavayet)*[41] . A fundamental similarity with yogic praxes connected with Candali is evident.

Our hypothesis is that the Nepalese minature, and by implication the manuscript, treat of an internal yoga of the three primary *nadis* whereby the fusion or choking off of the two side veins (that is, duality) results in the achievement of a symbolic death by self-decapitation. The logic of the meditation in question seems to require that the *sadhaka* himself becomes deceased (abolishing duality), and doubtless reanimated,[42] by identification with the visualized goddess. From this perspective the subject matter of the meditation might be seen as an internalized *savasadhana* whereby the practioner makes himself into the means (the corpse) of this gruesome rite.

(c) *Puja,* f. 2b. 5-3b, 4: his section provides mantras (also found in SM 232 and 234) for worship of the deities of the mandala. Although the dedication of the ms. is to Vajrayogini, the chief deity is addressed as Sarvabuddhadakini. Mallman (1975: 339) notes that this women occurs in SM 234 236 and 249 (overlooking the loci in 232 and 233). Because Sarvabuddhadakini in SM 249 is one of a set of five *dakini* well knownfrom the mandala of Mahamaya [Heruka] (see NSP no. 9), we remove it from further consideration. Of the remaining four *sadhanas,* SM 232 and 234 treat of the yellow and SM 233 and 236 of the red Vajrayogini. Mallman further suggests (ibid.: 133) that there are three separate devinities named Buddhadakini. The third "est invokee sans etre decrit dans 232, 233, 234, 236 SM 234 Jui attribue simplement la couleur jaune et semble la localiser a I'E. de (ou devant Vajrayogini, et elle peut aussi etre appelee Sarvabuddhadakini. There are some misunderstandings here. Collating SM 232, 234 and our ms., it is evident that the four mantras may be divided into groups of one and three. The first Sarvabuddhadakini in all three texts must refer to Vajrayogini as Trikayavajrayogini, the subject of the meditative-production *(bhavana)* of the three deities in the ms. Trikaya-' refers to the Vajrayogini who has three bodies, namely sarvabuddhadakini/ Buddhadakini, Vajravarnani and vajravairocani. From this perspective, *'tad anu'* and*'pascad'* respectively in the ms. and SM 232 indicate that three mantras temporally follow that of "Trikayavajrayogini'. In SM 234 *agratah* then means that the second (of 4) mantras is invoked as first among the second set consisting of three items. Both Sarvabuddhadakini and

Buddhadakini are invoked in the center. Buddhadakini here is the central and as Sarvabuddhadakini the comprehensive figure of the three-bodied Vajrayogini. As for a distinction of colour, in SM 234 Buddhadakini is yellow *(pitavarna);* Sarvabuddhadakini alias [Trikaya] vajrayogini is deemed *kanakasyama.* A possible signifificance of this will be discussed below. In the table, M stands for the mantra.

Ms.	SM 232	SM 234
tatra ... madhye M	*M...dharmodayam adhye*	*M madhye*
[Sarvabuddhadakini]	[Sarvabuddha dakini]	[Sarvabuddhadakini]
tad anu M	*pascad...M*	*agratah M*
[Sarvabuddhadakini]	[Buddhadakini]	[Sarvabuddhadakini]
vame M	*Pascad vamapa rsve m*	*daksine M*
[vajravarnani]	[Vajravarnani]	[Vajravarnani]
daksine M	*pascad daksinaparsve M*	*pascime M*
[Vajravairocani]	[Vajravairocani]	[Vajravairocani]

In contrast to these sequences of a set of 1, both introduced by (SM 232, 234) and introducing (ms.) a mantra, and a set of 3, introducing a mantra, the third group of 4 mantras, mentioning the 4 *kaya,* is to be segmented into a group of 3 followed by 1, the *mahasukhakaya.* In the manuscript it is not clear whether the second group of four mantras containing the 4 *pitha* are to be sectioned according to the first or second method. However, SM 234 groups both the second and third set of 4 mantras into sets of 3 plus 1, whereby because of the presumed analogical structure of the *sadhanas, srihatta* may be considered connected to the *mahasukhakaya.*[43]

pitha	*kaya*
odiyana	dharmakaya
purnagiri	sambhogakaya
kamarupa[44]	nirmanakaya
srihatta	mahasukhakaya

Associated with the summum of th efour bodies of the Buddha, the presence of *srihata/sirihatta* as a *pitha* evidently not attested elsewhere in Buddhist tantric texts is suggestive.

Perforce finding succor in non-Buddhist sources, the sixteenth century *PIthanimaya* provides an apparent equivalence of *srisaila* and *srihatta (*Sircar 1973: 52). The text is a comprehensive catalogue of *pithas* associated with the Hindu Goddess Sakti. Each place of Pilgrimage is given a corresponding body part of the Goddess, a *devata,* and form of Bhairava (the *pithadhisa):*

> srisaile (srihatte) ca mama griva mahalaksmis tu devata.
> *bhairavah sambaranando dese dese vyavathitah//*
>
> In Srisaila *(Srihatta)* is my neck, Its presiding divinity is Mahalaksmi. Sambarananda is theBhairava [Siva] who abides in each place.

A number of 'co-incidences' are manifest; first, the *pitha* is associated with the neck. We recall that the yellow Vajrayogini carries her own head, severed at the neck. That the neck of itself has some import is also indicated by the Nepaleses enminiature discussed above where the edges of the three skull-bowls in the miniature of Vajrayogini are held on the level of the necks of Vajravairoeehi, Vajravairrocani and the headless trunk of Vajrayogini (cf. Mallman 1975: plate (XII).

Next, the presence of Sambara (var. ms. E. *sambara-):* Sircar, invoking the Bengali version of the text, prefers the (hypometric) reading *sarvananda,* but Skt. ms. E *sambarananda* suggesting an allusion to a form of Siva to be assiciated with the Buddhist divinity (cf. Snellgrove 1987: 153) is not unattractive. As Snellgrove (1987: 150, 153-9) clearly states, the practises represented by these fierce divinities are in origin neither Hindu nor Buddhist. Indeed, Siva and his consort are pesent in the *Samvaramandala* of the *Nispannayogavali* (no. 12) where Samvara and Vajravarahi tred upon Bhairava and Kalaratri, as does the yellow Vajrayogini in the Nepalese miniature.

Further, of the set of 16 paired figures in the eight directions of the first circle (*cittacakra)* of the Sambaramandala, we find in the east Khandakapala and his consort Pracanda.[45] In the *Kathasaritsagara* of the eleventh century Somadeva, there is a Khandakapalika who, as his name suggests, is a member of th eSaiva sect of the skull bearing Kapalika-s. This character, in order ot win the princess Madanamanjari, engages in rituals involving a corpse *(savasadhana)* ina cemetery (*smasana).*[46] This might be considered of little relevance for our purposes were it not that Vajrayogini holds a skull, her own, and the *Sadhana* specifies the presence of a cemetery. More importantly, a cemetery considered as a the market place of the dead (*mrtabhatta),* in immediate textual proximity to a fierce form fo Siva holding skull and sword, may be noted within the context of a *savasadhana* in the Hindu *kaulavalinimaya*[47] xiv. 228-230. Teh praxis proper beginning at xiv.219c, at this point the practioner has taken his seat on the corpse and has effected conjunction with the divinity by means of mantra recitation *(tatra sakrjjapitva devatamelanam bhavet,* vs. 227 cd).

> *tatra natva mahadevam mahadevin ca sadhakah/*
> *tadbhasmatikakam kritva svayam viresvaro bhavet//*
> *nisayam mrtahatte ca unmattanandabhairavah/*
> *digvasa*[48] *vimali bhasmabhusano muktakesakah//*
> *kapali khadgahastas ca japen matrkaya sudhih/*
> *tada tasya mahasiddhir jayate satajapatah//*

> Then, having bowed to Mahadeva and Mahadevi, the practitioner, having applied such a *tilaka* of ash, himself becomes a lord of heroes, And at night in the marketplace of the dead, he who is the Bhairava Unmattananda, nude, immaculate, havin ash as ornament,with deshelved hair, with skull and sword in hand, he, insightfl, ought recite the *matrka.* Them after a hundred recitations, great success is born for him.

The presence of the reading *mrtahatta* deserves attention. A possibility, although most unlikely, is a correction to **mrte hatte.* In this event the practioner recites the mantra seated, one assumes, 'on a deceased, in a marketaplace'. However, the text has specified a cemetery *(smasane)* at xiv.225c, so this may be discarded. Another interpretation is suggested by English idiom, namely a `dead,' that is empty, marketplace. however, to my knowledge this meaning for *mrta* is not Sanskrit. Nevertheless, *Kaulavalinimaya* xiv.92 does mention the empty marketplace *(sunyagara)* as one of the suitable loci for a *savasadhana.* Instead of this, I propose that *mrtahatta* refers to a 'fair', that is, an gathering place of the dead, a cemetery. From this perspective, we may ask if the import of the unique preence of the*pitha* called *srihatta* in the *sadhanas* of the yellow Vajrayogini is as much geographic - as identified as modern Sylhet in Assam - as it might be topological, given the term *mrtahatta* as an expressionfor a cemetery in the *Kaulavalinimaya.* The latter is indirectly supported by *Hevajratantra* I.vii.18, where lists are given of th etwelve categories of places of pilgrimage, *pitha, upapitha,* etc. Instead of toponyms, for the category *smasana* the text supplies two descriptions of which the first is *smasanam pretasamhatam,* "a cemetery is a gathering place of *pretas.*"[49] We may recall that the ms. reads *srihata:* it remains speculation, albeit justified, to hazard that this aberrant name of a place of pilgrimage could hence also mean '*the* illustrous gatherign place', scin. a cemetery. Because it may seemingly be equated with the *mahasukhakaya (supra)* and because in Buddhist texts its presence in *sadhanas* of the yellow Vajrayogini is unique, this would but further distinguish *srihatta* from the other three places of pilgrimage in the *sadhana.*

(d) *Japa,* f.3b, 4-4a, 1: This section provides various mantras for recitation *(japa),* after which the practitioner is enjoined to discharge the divinity "as before" *(purvavad).* Unfortunately, the manuscript does not record this activity elsewhere. Moreover, the mantra which is here identified as the *mulamantra* is found deemed the *Japamantra* immediately subsequent to the description of the *bhavana*and directly preceding the instructions for drawing the *pujamandala.* Although missing at the corresponding locus in SM 232, in its parallel to this section the *Sadhanamala* refers to the mantra as the *japamantra.* Precisely where the intiall dismissal of the divinity is meant to have taken plae is obscure: after the*puja* would seem most likely.

The divinity having been discharged, she would have to be generated anew. Therefore, the manuscript asserts the presence of two meditative-productions. The first is called a *bhavana:* the second, a *dhyana.* The question now arises whether the *dhyana* is didentical tot he previous *bhavana.* It may very well be. However, *Sadhanamala* 234 provides another meditative-production of the yellow Vajrayogini whom it specifies as meditatively-producted in the heart, unlike the *bhavana* above which is positioned in the navel. I suggest that this might perhaps be the *dhyana*b mentioned in the manuscript. This proposal woudl appear supported by teh datum that SM 234 begins directly with the passage cited below and lacks theusuall preliminaries of an introductory verse, the finding of an appropriate seat or generation of the four *brahmavihara,* as well as any introductory phrase, such as *prathamam* (compare SM 232, 233, 236 passim) whatoeer. An absence of some or all of these is not unknown in the *Sadhanamala,* but not common amogn the prose *sadhanas.* In addition, because Vajrayogini is visualized in the heart, this meditation may perhaps be regarded as a more advanced practice insofar as the internal yoga which the initial *bhavana* may represent - a meditation implying th efusion or choking off of the breaths in th eside veins resulting the meditative-prodution of the goddess at the level of the navel - might proceed to a meditation in the next of the 4 Buddhist *cakra* up, in the heart. *Sadhanamala* 234, 1.2.2 - 7:

> *hrdi nanavarnapamkaraparinamena visvapadmam bhavayet / tatropari raktavarnarephaparinamena suryamanadale dharmodayamsamadhikaraktavamam bhavayet / dharmodayopariraktavamamhrimkaram / hrimkaradibhih purvoktaih samastaih parinamenavajrayogini kanakasyamam suryasane padmamadhye tathatra parsve dakinidvayam bhavayet katrtikarotakadharam alidhapadasamsthitam*
>
> By transformation of a syllable *pam* of various colours in the heart, one should meditatively-produce a *visvapadma.* On top of that on a sun disk,by transformationof a red-hued *ram*, one should meditatively-produce an intensely red *dharmodaya* [triangle]. On top of the *dhamodaya* [one produces) a red syllable *hrim.* By transformation by means of all the abovementioned - the syllable *hrim* and so on one should mediatatively-produce the golden thorn-apple [hued] vajrayogini in the middle of a lotus situated on the sun and, likewise there to [either] side, the two *dakini* who bear a knife and skull [cup] and abide in the *alidha* position.

Clearly, this meditative-production is very similar to the earlier one. That this indeed a second meditation mightbe indicated by the fact that the procedure described is mostly that of the preliminaries. The iconography of Vajrayogini is presumed. One difference, if such it truly be, is that Vajrayogini is deemed to be *kanakasyama* rather than *pita.* The former is an uncommon color term whose only other attestationis in *Sadhanamala* 15 as an attribute of Tara *(kanakasyamvama).* Meisezahl (1981: 530) observes that "Yar lo Grags pa rgyal mchan ubersetzt *gser sngon po'i mdog lta bu dkar zing,* 'wiiss wie die Farbe der stechapfel-[Blute]....' ... Gemieint ist wohl der zweifarbig, ausserlich violett *(nilohita)* and innerlich weiss *(sveta)* bluhende *dhattura* (datura fatuosa, Fam. Solanacenae) den Sivadatta auch *kanaka, Kanakahvaya, suvarma* order *hema* nennt.." However, although *kanaka, kanakahvaya, suvama* oder h*hema* nennt..." However, although *kanaka,* which is usually to be rendered 'gold' or 'golden', is a name of a species of datura, the same is valid for the terminus *syama.*[50] Hence, *kanaka* may well be an adjectival modification of *syama* and the compound may refer to a golden (or yellow) thorn-apple. This has the advantage that one may maitain, the accordance with the manuscript and SM 232, a yellowish colour for the Varayogini of SM 234.

There is another reason why *kanakasyama* as "the golden thron-apple [hued]" is appropriate. We proposed that the practise enjoined by the manuscript was, in fact, an internalized yoga understood as a self decapitation whose external reflex is a *savasadhana.* in the passage cited from the *Kaulavalinimaya* above, the practitioner, holding,as does the (Buddhist,), yellow Vajrayogini a skull and knife, becomes identified with Unmattanandabharava, a ferocious form of Siva. The term *unmatta* alone has the meaning of "thorn-apple", that is, a species of datura, as well as "furious, mad, intoxicated" that is, a species of datura, as wellas "furious, mad, intoxicated" (Monir-Williams 1899: 193) The practioners of *savasadhana* are said to experience most horrific hallucinations(Gupta 1979: 162). The sado-masochistic fantasies and allucinations inherent inthe use of datura are well-known and documented,[51] so that such as might be hypothesized as the (historical) ground for the meditative-production of th e yellow Vajrayogini need not have been literally fatal to the practioner. Be this as is may, the presence of *kanakasyama* as colour term is in itself not sufficient to establish the use of solonaceous alkaloids in Buddhist tantric circles, although its presence here is suggestive.[52]

In any event, the *dhyana* SM 234 is to be distinguished from the initial *bhavana.* The manuscript furthe rappears to note that the practioner is sweating *dhyanat svinno mantram japet).* This statement, if left standing, is remarkable. In fact, *svinno,* albeit the lectio difficilior, shoudl be emended to *khinno* since the *Sadhanamala* furnishes numerou sloci where the practitioner is told to continue with the meditative-production until fatigue sets in, whereupon which he should recite a mantra.[53]

(e)*Bali,* f. 4a, 2-4a, 5: This section suplies to *balimantras* which are substantively identical to those of SM 238.

(f)Conclusion, f. 4a, 5-4b, 1. This section signals the close of the *sadhana* provides an exhortation and specifies that the author is the *siddhacarya* Virupa.

NOTES

1. This stay in Nepal was funded by the Deutsche Forschungs-gemeinschaft, to which I should like to express my thanks.
2. There are two folia numebred 18 and 19.
3. The fourth text is Suratapada's *Hevajrasadhanasya Vajradipanama tippani.*
4. SM 235's colophon ascribes the *sadhana* to the school *(mata)* of the *siddhacarya Sabarapada (evam nandyavarttena siddhasavara padiyamatavajrayoginya-radhanavidhi).* See Bhattacarya 1958:247-249.
5. The two texts in the canon treating of Chinnamunda are considered by Meisezahl to belong to the writings on Vajravarahi (Meisezahl 1956-6: 259, 266-7).
6. For the exegetic lineages of the *Hevajra-, Dakarnarva* and *Yamaritantras* deriving from Virupa, see the *Blue Annals* (Roerich 1949: 207-8; 390- 379; 1046). On the meditations of Virupa known as the four *lta ba, *drsti* (?) see the brilliant exposition by Ruegg (166: 58-64).
7. To my knowledge - but the literature of the tantra is vast-only Virupa of the'early' *siddhacaryas* is identified

with the yellow Vayrayogini. Bhattacarya (1964: 159 ff.) notes that SM 235, a *sadhana* of Vajrayogini, credits the *siddhacarya* Sabarapa "with the introductin of a new cult of Vajrayogini" (but cf. supra, note 4) However, this text does not specify the goddess as yellow.

8. Virupa and Kanha are the only *siddhacarya* with whom Chinnamunda Varahi is explicitiy associated by Abhayadatta. Virupa is said to have recited the mantra of Vajravarahi,but neither the mantra nor the form of the goddess is given. Cf. Robinson 1979: f. 9,3; 95,3.
9. PTT 2263, 2873, 2874, 2875, 2876, 2878, 2900, 3129, 3130, 3133, 3172, 3197, 4691, 5026 (Robinson 1979: 289-290).
10. The number is apocryphal. See Das Gupta 1969: 202-210; Snellgrove 1959: 12.
11. CF. PTT volo. 52, p. 206, p. 206-51/5/7.
12. See infra.
13. E.g. SM 15 (44.17-19), *tatra Pujamantrah om vajrapuspe hum* .. SM 12 (36 (36.3-4), *pujamantrah.* [mss. ABNC *pujamantras tu] om lokesvara puspam praticcha svaha evam dhupam dipam ityadi boddhavyam;* see also, *Hevajratantra* II.i.4.
14. A lucid presentationof the *pancopacarapuja* as practised by Newari Bajracaryas is found is Locke 1980: 76-78.
15. The occurences of *vajrapuspa* in the *Sadhanamala* are of two types. Thefirst may be exemplified by SM 35 (*Oddiyanakramena Trailakyavasamkararalokesvaras-adhana)* 79.13-15 where a flower is presented to the divinity:...*mandalamadhe trailokyavasankaralokesvar-abhattarakam pujayed anena mantrena om trailokyavasan-karaya vajrapuspe hum praticcha svaha.* No other gift save the flower is presented and the text continues with the description of the meditative production of the divinity.I these cases (e.g. SM 35, 36) such a mantra is located towards the beginning of the text.

    The second variety is *vajrapuspa* embedded in a mantra which is the first of five, each corresponding to one of the five presentations *upacara).* As noted by Mk'as grub rje, variation in the sequence in accordance with the class of text (*kriya-, carya-, yoga- and anuttarayogatantra)* is not unknown (Wayman and lessing 1980: 179). For the the *kriya* and *caryatantra* classes this is *gandha puspa, dhupa, naivedya* and *dipa* ibdi.: 181-83. Interestingly, absent *naivedya,* the identical sequence is to be located in the Hindu *Kulacudamanitantra* III.2.) absent *naivedya,* the remaining four offering materials are also found in the sequence *dhupa, puspa, gandha, dipa,* as four of the eight *pujadevatyah present in may mandals of the fundamental text of the yogatantra, the Tattvasamgraha* (cf. 91-25-6; '35.1-8; 193.25- 194.5; 287.12-13; 308-12; 326.10-327.4; 359.8-11; 368.5-8; 392.15-393.2; 427.4-7; 463.13; 515.6). In the *anuttarayogatantra* clss, as for example *Hevajratantra* II.i.4 and in almsot all the relevant texts of the at *Sadhanamala,* the *pancopacara are puspa* (flower), *dhupa (*incense), dipa (lamp), gandha (Perfume) and naivedya (food-offering). Variation in terminology is easily found: for example, *Samvarodayatantra* 8.18 substtutes *candana* (sandalwood) for *naivedya* [mss. BCEP reverse the position of *dipa* and *gandha]* and *Sadhanamala* 15 (*Khasarpanasadhana)* 44.17-19 replaces *Dipa* by *aloka* (mirror) and *naivedya by dhara* (food offering).

16. A further example of the revivification of a pigeon is found in the biography of Marpa (Bacot 1976: 39-40, 94-5). See infra note 41.

17. Robinson 1979, f. 11,3-4: *c'u de'i t'og na p'ar padma'i 'dab ma la zabs bzag nas padma'i me t'og c'u (4) ma nub pa sbyang nas/sangs rgyas la mc'od pa byas te p'a mt'ar songngo//* The religious meaning of the story is transparant: because Virupa engages in tantra, consumes wine and meat, he obtains the possibility of supernatural accomplishments (*siddhi).* This possibility is activated by worship of the Buddha—the offering of the lotus. The result is a 'miracle', the walk across the water of the lake of existence, as a result of which he attains the other shore, enlightenment.

18. For *timayogini?* Or is *tira* a reference to the side *nadls-lalana* and *rasana?*

19. On the various representations of Virupa, see Robinson 1979: 265- 266; *Dieux et Demons* 177: 152 (no. 150); *Tantra*

Art 1972: %* (no. 223).

20. The rubrics between brackets are for convenience only and are not found in the texts. In the transcription of the manuscript, readings such as *mamtra for mantra* and *samyaktam for samyak* have been regularized.
21. Ms. *tatopari.*
22. Ms. *dharmodaya.*
23. Ms. *karttitah.*
24. Ms. *sahita urd-.*
25. For ms. *vamasunya,* unless one understands 'devoid of daulity' via *vama* (masc.), "female breast" (Monier-Williams 1899: 941). Thi sin the absence of furthe rconfirmation is not likely.
26. Ms. *nihsrtah.*
27. Ms. *purvoktarupa.*
28. Ms. *prathamamam.*
29. Ms. *odiyane vajra-.*
30. For ms. *svinno,* seeinfra.
31. Ms. *visarjayad.*
32. Ms. *pisacadin.*
33. Ms. *sarvasam me.*
34. Ms. *tvayat.*
35. What appears to be an example of a particularly virulent Tibetan adaptation of this rite may be found,as a meditation, with as tutelary deity a red, three-eyed Vajrayogini holding skull and knife, in Evans-Wentz 1958: 311-312. The red Vajrayogini usually holds a skul and *khatvanga* (cf. mallman 1975: 432). This rite is put in terms of self-flaying and by implication autocannibalism, that is, as a tantric feast, rather than in terms of a *homa,* as one finds in the Hindu *Kaulavalinimaya* (chapt. xiv).
36. f. 9b,6: *om. ah hum iti kayavakcittadhisthanamantrah.*
37. Compare f. 5b, 6-6a, 1: *lalanarasanayogad eva* (sic) *dhrti mahasukha.*
38. Cf. Dasgupta 1974: 156 ff.
39. Cf. *Yogaratnamala* (Snellgrove 1959: 110) on *Hevajratantra* I.i.31. See also Virupa's *Chinamundasadhana* (vol. 52, 206-4-4/4-7) *lam gsum nas ni k'rag 'dzag cing// rtsa gsum nas ni byung nas ni// rtag tu 'byung bar bsgom par bya// a*

ba dhu ti gyen du 'gro// g'yon dang g'yas kyi gnis kyang/ de ltar myur due bsgom par bya// sku gsung t'ugs kyi rang bzin gyis// rtsa gsum gyi ni gno bor gnas// ses rab ngo bo la la na// ra sa na na t'abs su gnas//dbu ma gnas a ba dhu ti ni// bde c'en mam pa't rang bzin no//

40. Mallman (1975: 433) describes the painting as follows: "L'essentiel de la description s'y trouve illustr'e, mais: a) la tele tranchee est dans un coupe cranienne doree; b) les assistantes sont respectivement rouge a droite et bleue a gauche, leur m. dr.sont faisant le geste de menace, la g, tenant la coupe cranienne; c) il n'y a pas de Cimetieres' d) la lune et le soleil sont figures en haut de la composition; e) enfin, Vajrayogini est fendue vers la go. sur Bhairava blanc et Kalaratri verte etroitement unis, sur un louts blanc a plate-forme noire."
41. Dasgupta (1974: 155) states that the two side veins enter the navel region from the right and left. The question of the exact place for the joining of the two veins in the Buddhist tantra seems confused. See Wayman 1977: 67, 237 on the "lower orifice" of the*avadhuti.*
42. Reanimation of a corpse is parcel of the Hindu ritual (Gupta 1979: 162) and is also known as *parapurakayapravesa* (cf. Eliade 1969: 393-4). In Tibetan Buddhism it is known as *grong' jug* and is a teachign of the lineage represented by Marpa and Milarepa and deriving from Naropa (Wayman 1973: 145). See Evans-Evas-Wentz 1951: 145-147: 158: 254-259. The Sanskrit equivalent would seem to be *parakayapravesa* Chandra 1976: 394), but see Wayman 1977: 281. See also Locke ms. f. 7a, 2: *paramcittakayapravesabh-ijna-.*
43. That is, for both the second and third sets of four in SM 234, first three mantras, and then *punar madhye* after which the fourth mantra.
44. SM 234; ms. *kamaksa.;* SM 232, *kamakhya.* See Sircar 1973;: 87).
45. *Nispannayogavali* p. 27: *tatah cittacakrasya purvasminnare khandakapalapracande...khandakapaladayo viras trinetr-aikavaktra jatamukutino lalatanivistavajramalankit-avirapattas caturbhujah alinganabhujabhyam vajravajragh-*

ante vamena khatvangam savyena damanum bibhrana brahmasutrakeyurayukta damstrakaralavadanah pancamudrina alidhasthah.

46. Lorenzen 1972: 62-63. On the *savasadhana,*see Gupta 1979: 161 ff. which refers here to a pasage in the *netratantra* 18.1-12). Further, the *Vinasikhatantra* 190cd-193. Additional references may be foudn via the (always very useful) index in Goudriaan 1981.
47. On this text, authored by Jnananandagiri Paramahamsa and dated to the sixteenth century, see Goudriaan 1981: 144.
48. For printed *higvasa.*
49. See Snellgrove 1959: 70 note 1. On the *pithas,* cf. Tsuda 1971,1973; Snellgrove 1987: 163-167.
50. Monier-Williams 1899:1094.
51. See especially Harner's fascinating study on hallucinoggens (flying ointments) in European witchcrat in Harner 1973.
52. I hope to demonstrate the presence of these substances in the *hevajratantra* elsewhere.
53. The phrasing is found both with *dhyana* and *bhavana,* cf. *Sadhanamala* p. 109-16, 112.2, 122.4, 173.12, 175.16, 177.16, 382.16, 426.4, 454.9, 468.9, 469.15. Note especially 396.13-17 *tatah ... drstva tavad bhavayet yavat khedo na yayate / khede sati svahrccandre kuktaharopamam mantram pasyan japet om ...)* and 398.1-4 *(tatah svahrdayat pujadevih samspharyya pujayitva sataksaramantram avarttyat pujadevih samspharyya pujayitva sataksaramantram avartta ca tavad bhavayet yavat khedo na jayate / khinne citte sati mantram japet om...).* On the other hand, 'sweat' in combination with a yoga of breath control in a cemetery, and ina Buddhist tantric context with the goddess holding skull and knife, may be found in the old Javanese holding skull and knife, may be found in the Old Javanese *Sutasoma* (cantos 10-11, Soewito 1975: 172-175). This deserves further study, if for no other reason that most of the items in the *Sadhanamala* lack the prerequisite of Weariness before directing engagement in mantra recitation. Instead, after directing engagement in mantra recitation. Instead, after completion of the meditative-

production of the divinity, the practioner is enjoined to recite the appropriate manttra(s). See, for example (taken at random), SM 214, *tato mantram japet,* or 268, *tadanu mantram uccarayet.*

BIBLIOGRAPHY

Caryagiti (Kverne 1977)

Abhayadatta's *Catursitisiddhapravrtti* Tibetan translation, cf. Robinson 1979)

Virupa's *Chinnamundasadhana* (Tibetan translation, PTT vol. 52, pp. 206-2-6/207-3-2)

Hevajratantra (Snellgrove 1959)

Kaulavalinirnaya (Avalon)

Kunjarakamadharmakathana (Teeuw 1981)

Nispannayogavali (Bhattacarya 1972)

Pithanimaya (Sirvcar 1975)

Sadhanamala (Bhattacarya 1968)

Samvarodayatantra (Tsuda 1974)

Sutasoma (Soewito 1975)

Tattvasamgraha (yamada 1981)

Vinasikhatantra (Goudriaan 1985)

Tantra, hayward Gallery, London 30 Sept.-14 Nov. 1971, Arts Council of Great Britain, 2nd ed., 1972.

Dieux et Demons de l'Himalaya, Grand Palais, 25 Mars-27 Juin 1977, Secretariat d'Etat a la Culture, Editions des Musees nationaux, Paris, 1977.

Avalon, Arhur (ed.), *Kaulavalinirnaya,* Calcutta, no date (Tantrik texts vol. xiv).

Bacot, Jacoques, *La Vie de Marpa le 'Traducteur',* Paris, 1976 (orig. 1937) (Documents ct Travaux pour l'etude du Bouddhisme, 1e serie, tome vii).

Bhattacarya, B.T., *The Indian Buddhist Iconography,* 2nd ed., Calcutta, 1958.

——, *An Introduction to Buddhist Esoterism,* Varanasi, 1964 (Chowkhamba Sanskrit Studies vol. xlvi).

——, *Sadhanamala,* 2 vols, Baroda, 1968 (Gaekwad's oriental series no. 26 (vol. 1, 1925), no.41 (vol. 2, 1935)).

——, *Nispannayogavali of mahapandita Abhayakaragupta,*

Baroda, 1972 (rep.) (Gaekwad's Oriental Seires no. 109)

Chandra, Lokesh, *Tibetan-Sanskrit Dictionary,* 2 vols, Kyoto, 1976 (rep. of orig. ed. 1961).

Dasgupta, Shashi, *Obscure Religious Cults,* 3rd. ed., Calcutta, 1969

——, *An Introduction to Tantric Buddhism,* Berkeley, 1974 (orig. 1958)

Edgerton, Franklim, *Buddhist Hybrid Sanskrit Dictionary,* reprint, Delhi, 1070.

Eliade, Mircea *Yoga; immortality and Freedom,* 2nd ed., Princeton, 1969 (rep. 1970).

——, *Shamanism: Archac Techniques of Ecstasy,* Princeton 1964 (rep. 1972)

Evans-Wentz, W.Y. (ed.), *Tibet's Great Yogi Milarepa,* 2nd ed., London, 1958 (rep. 1969).

Furst, Peter T. (ed.), *Flesh of the Gods: The Ritual Use of Hallucinogins,* New York, 1972.

Goudriaan, Teun, *The Vinasikhatantra: A Saiva Tantra of the Left Currant,* Delhi, 1985

Goudriaan,Teun and Sanyukta Gupta, *Hindu Sakta and Tantri Literature.*

Gupta, Sanjukta and D.J. Hoens, To Goudriaan, *Hidnu Tantrism,* Leiden, 1979 (Handbuch der Orientalistik, vereter Band, zweiter Abschnitt)

Harner, Mechael J., "The Role of Hallucinogenic Plants in European Witchcraft:, in M.J. Harner (ed.), *Hallucinogens and Shamanism,* Oxford, 1973, pp. 125-150.

Jaeschke, H.A., *Tibetan-English Dictionary,* London, 1972 (rep., orig. Publ. 1881)

Kvaerne, Per, *An Anthology of Buddhist Tantric Songs: A Study of the Garyagiti,* Oslo, 1977 (Det Norske Videnskaps) Akademim II. Hist.- Filos. Klasse Skrifter, By Serie no. 14)

Locke, John K., *Karunamaya: The Cult of Avalokitesvara-Matsyendranath in the Valley of Nepal,* Kathamandu, 1980.

Lorenzen, David, *The Kapalikas and Kalamukhas: Two lost Saivite Sects,* New Delhi, 1972.

Mallman, M.-Th. de, *Introduction a l'Iconographie du tantrisme Bouddhique,* Paris, 1975.

Meisezahl, R.O., "Die Gottin Vajravarahi: Eine Ikonographische

Studie nach einem Sadhana-text von Advayavajra", in *Oriens* vol. 18-19 (1965-66), pp. 228-303.

——, "Drei Miszellen zur Farbenlehre der Buddhistischen Ikonographe," in *Oriens* vol. 27-28 (1981), pp. 522-537.

Monier-Williams, Sir Monier, *Sanskrit-English Dictionary,* Oxford, 1899

Robinson, James B. (trans.), Buddha's Lions: *The lives of the Eighty-Foru Siddhas,* Berkeley, 1979

Roerich, George N., *The Blue annals,* 2nd ed., Delhi, 1976

Ruegg, D.S, *The Life of Bu ston Rin po c'e,* Roma, 1966 (Serie Orientale Roma xxxiv).

Sircar, D.C., *The Sakta Pithas,* 2nd rev. ed., Delhi, 1973

Snellgrove, D., *The Hevajra Tantra,* 2vols, London, 1959

——, *Indo-Tibetan Buddhism,* London, 1987.

Soewito, Santoso, *Sutasoma: A Study in Javanese Wajrayana,* Delhi, 1975 (Sata-Pitaka Series no. 213)

Teeuw, A., And S.O. Robson, *Kunjarakama Dharakathana: Liberation Through the Law of Buddha,* The Hague, 1981 (Bibliotheca Indonesica no.21).

Tsuda, Shinichi, "Theory of Pitha in the Samvara Literature," (I) in *Buzan Gahuko* no. 16, 1971 and (II) in no. 17-18, 1973.

——, *Samvaraodayatantra: Selected chapters,* Tokyo, 1974.

Wayman, Alex "The Nine Orifices of the Body", pp. 139-150 in Wayman, Alex, *The Buddhist Tantras: Light on Indo-tibetan Esotericism,* London, 1973.

——, *yoga of the Guhyasamajatantra,* Delhi, 1977.

Yamada, Isshi, *Sarvatathagatatattvasamgraha nama Mahayanasutra,* New Delhi, 1981 (Sata-Pitaka Series vol. 262).

Chapter-15

The Chief Currents of Contemporary Indian Philosophy

RAMA SHANKER SRIVASTAVA

Chapter-15

A Background

After the dark age and the decadence of Indian Philosophy in the medieval times we have the resurgence and renaissance in the modern India. The Indian philosophy, religion and culture became stagnant and dead due to the Muslim and British rule for centuries. We may preceive two main reasons for the fall of Indian philosophy. *Firstly,* the British domination precede by the Muslim rule ruined our culture and civilization. Political domination resulted into the mental slavery of India. The orthodox Indians, on the one side, created walls of customs, rites, ceremonies and many social distinctions in order to preserve their indigenous thought and life. Because of the insecurity and attacks from the outside, they wanted to live in the closed walls of their religion. They grew more conservative. They searched and planned for security instead of taking bold adventures in the realms of thought. The desire for preservation of the old and traditional philosophy was their first concern. If any bold spirit did ever breathe the fresh air or tired to come out, he was ostracised immediately. The Indian thinkers began simply to codify their philosophy and religion. They erected walls of segregation, distinction and exclusiveness. They preferred closed walls to fresh air. They adhered to ancient traditional philosophy and desired security rather than progress. They wanted to be secure, closed and integrated. They were afraid to go out and breathe the fresh air of the environment. If anyone tried to break up the walls, he was ruthlessly tortured. They became very narrow in outlook. Everyone desired security to progress. In a closed society and religion the rites, cereminies, customs and the like governed most. People became less introspective and the spirit within the temples was reduced to a dead existence in the medieval age. Underneath the walls lay the dead spirit of India.

The intelligentsia class began to imitate the West in fashion, culture, speech and thought. They neglected their indigenous philosophy, morals and ways of life and imitated the West in all branches. They devoted their time to the European philosophy and literature. In order to gain high positions and service in the slave India, they put their nerves in aping the European and especially the British. The intelligentsia class did not contribute towards their indigenous philosophy and religion, rather they desired to engraft the West on the Indian thought. Evidently this resulted in the downfall of Indian philosophy than to their own. They thought the Western philosophy to be superior to their own.

Secondly, the Indians tried to compensate their present inferiority by singing the glory of their past Vedic and Upaniṣadic philosophy and culture. They thought that the Vedas and the Upaniṣads give to us the highest systems of philosophy and that their scope and extension were so wide that there can be no development of any new thought. The highest and the loftiest idea were contained in the scriptures and all thoughts and knowledge are contained in them. How can any new thought emerge, when there is such a wide and extensive literature in Indian thought? The Indian thinkers conceived that the Vedas and Upaniṣads are the highest, the best and the widest in the realms of philosophy. It is so vast that there is absolutely no scope for the Indian philosophy to grow in an independent line. The medieval people looked to the past for guidance. The attitude was regresive rather than progressive. The medieval age began to trace all scientific advances, like aeroplane, bomb, cars, etc., from the Vedas. They conceived that all kinds and branches of knowledge viz., economics, politics, physics, chemistry, engineering, mathematics, etc., are contained in the Vedas.

The renaissance of Hinduism started with the powerful thinker, Raja Ram Mohun Roy. He was a great patriot, social reformer, and political worker. He abolished many extraneous elements from Hinduism. The evils of Satiprathā, child marriage, untouchability, casteism, superstition and other ceremonies were removed by him. He founded the Brahmosamaj. He stood for the open, dynamic and progressive religion. For Brahmosamaj, everyone is capable of God realisation. Its religion and philosophy conceive the reality of impersonal Brahman and therefore, it has very few religious performances. But the Brahmosamaj movement influenced only Bengal most and it could have no hold on the mind of India as a whole.

The Chief Currents of Contemporary Indian Philosophy

The present age is the age of renaissance. We are passing through the days of intense change and growth. The renaissance not only means the revival of the past but it also conveys the evolution of new thoughts and systems of philosophy. The past lives in the present and there is the revival of the past heritage. But the content and texture of philosophy differ widely. The modern age has evolved divergent and emergent principles, but its development is the natural and continuous growth and manifestations of the ancient truths. The modernists have new configuration of the essential truths of the past, and they also discard the many accepted principles of the past, which in course of ages, were thought to be untruth, unreal and dross. The new philosophy is not engrafted on the past but emerges out of it. The modern Indian philosophy has in its growth, synthesis and evolution of the principles, flowering of the new concepts, morals and outlook. Whereas the basic values were in crude form, the modern Indian thought creates and manifests new values. It gives new importance and significance to the ancient truths. It assimilates new values. It changes the form and texture of the materials of the past. It opens the ancient truths. It is also impossible to establish the old truths without effecting suitable changes in order to adapt them to modern conditions of scientific advancement, Western environment and social evolution. Hence inevitable and necessary changes are made in the past to suit the present. While the contemporary Indian philosophy is a native growth, it has certain basic features. The chief currents of contemporary Indian philosophy may be elucidated in the following points :

1. Positive attitude towards the world.
2. Cosmic and spiritualistic outlook.
3. Integral and synthetic view.
4. Reconciliation of theism and absolutism.
5. Monotheism or monoism of Spirit and Matter.
6. Evolution of Superman or Gonstic Being.
7. The new approaches to salvation.

8. Dynamism, openness and catholicity.
9. Humanistic tendencies.

1. *Positive attitude towards the World*

The basic feature of the ancient Indian philosophy has been spiritual and individualistic in outlook. It does not conceive the world as Divine. The universe is either considered to be material or illusory and, therefore, not a fit abode for the individual self. The spirit of ancient Indian philosophy is ascetic. It lays much stress on the renunciation of the world.

The modern thinkers conceive that the world is real and spiritual. God has created it out of His own existence. They discard the negative attitude to the world and also asceticism. It was Swami Vivekananda who first of all emphasised the positive aspect of the world and laid much stress on the realistic and practical teaching of Sankarācārya. The positive approach to the world reaches to its zenith in the philosophy of Mahatma Gandhi, who preferred service to salvation, action to mere teaching and a way of righteous life to this ascetic escape from duties and refuge in the forests. The modern thinkers refute the illusrioness and the unreality of the world advocated by the Advaitins. They develop the philosophy of humanism, bread-labour, equality, brotherhood, world-economy and world-government. The world is not evil and self-realisation is not a state of loneliness of the self, nor is it a condition of freedom and escape from the world. For the modern thinkers, self-realisation, is not possible by the dissociation of self with the universe. When one is dissociated from the world, one leads a life of passivity, indolence and narrowness. Then there is no hope for the salvation of mankind. If there is any spiritual evolution of man, it is a state of higher life with greater powers of consciousness and omnipotence. When the individual self attains perfection, he transforms the world and changes its very structure. His life is a dedication to the service of humanity.

2. *Cosmic and Spiritualistic outlook*

The thinkers to-day take the cosmic view of things. As against the individualistic character of the past, we have conviction in the cosmic evolution and salvation. An individual self can not attain liberation until the entire humanity realises it. The ancient systems of Sankhyayoga, Nyāyā, Mimāṁsā and Śanker conceived that the salvation of an individual is not possible in an imperfect environment of fallen selves kept in bondage and ignorance. The modern Indian thinkers conceive that the salvation of an individual is possible only when there is a spiritual environment. If the environment is evil, ignorant and base, there can never be any perfection of the individual self. The self cannot attain perfection in an imperfect environment. Unless the nature is Divine, no perfection of the individual self is possible. Hence it is conceived that the ascents of the individual self and the world go together. If nature is not sufficiently evolved, it cannot manifest, refine and perfect the individual selves. Again, when the individual selves realise perfection, they disperse their force and consciousness and illumine the fallen selves. For Sri Aurobindo and Radhakrishnan, salvation is only possible when the world becomes spiritual. So long the lower prakṛti is not transmuted into the Parā prakṛti, there can never be the salvation of man. Conversely, whenever there is the ascent of the individual to the greater powers of consciousness and omnipotence, the world is uplifted and spiritualised. When an individual self attains perfection, he transforms the world, and changes its very structure. The salvation of the individual is not possible till the entire mankind evolves to a high spiritual stage. Hence it is evident that the cosmic salvation or the realisation of God by the entire community of man must take place. The individual realises salvation with other selves that are in bondage today. The modern Indian philosophy is cosmic in outlook as against the individualistic outlook of the past. It denies the view that the individual self remains always individual. With the increase of spiritual powers, the self becomes unlimited in extension. It becomes infinite. Therefore it is very logical to suppose that the salvation for the individual self lies in the union with the Cosmic Spirit viz., Saccidananda.

3. *Integral and Synthetic*

The modern Indian philosophy is integral and synthetic. It is a synthesis of the East and the West because the modern

Indian philosophy has grown up in the environment of the West. While its development has been native to its soil, it has to grow in the climate of the Western civilisaion and philosophy. Every modern philosopher of India has deep study of the Western philosophy, culture and religion. The man today cannot dissociate himself from the environment, and the West encircles us and deeply influences Indian thought. The great modern Indian thinkers viz., Radhakrishnan, Rabindranath Tagore, Vivekananda, Aurobindo and K. C. Bhattacharya, had sound study of the Western religion and philosophy. These are synthetic personalities. The Western thoughts are so immensely imbibed in the minds of the Indian revivalists that they neither narrowism nor orthodoxy with them. The ancient Indian philosophers could not take the advantage of the different systems of philosophy developed in other countries of the world. Due to the lack of communication and communion with foreign people their knowledge was narrow, seclusive, parochial and stagnant. The modern Indian philosophy is not narrow in its outlook. It conceives of cosmic salvation, world government, world brotherhood and world humanity. With the lack of the development of science in India, it was more introspective. The modern Indian thinker has his roots in the past but he also assimilated the modern Western thought in him.

The contemporary Indian philosophy is very synthetic in outlook. It combines not only the East and the West but also the realism and idealism in intimate union. It is idealistic in the sense that all philosophers think that salvation is the ultimate end of human endeavour. It is humanistic and realistic also, because it envisages the salvation of the entire community of man. Cosmic salvation is the ultimate destiny of mankind. It is synthetic not only of the past historical systems, but it also assimilated the philosophies of the leading thinkers in the world.

4. *Reconciliation of theism and absolutism*

The most remarkable trend in modern Indian thought is found in the endeavour to reconcile both theism and absolutism. The personal God and the impersonal Brahman have very nicely been adopted in their systems. The Brahman is impersonal, pure existence, being, truth, reality and consciousness. But God is personal, creative, omnipotent, just, merciful, creator, manitainer and destroyer. God is immanent in the world and is the Supreme Person. All modern thinkers conceive and include both the personal and impersonal, dynamic and static, immanent and transcendent aspects of God in their systems of philosophy.

We observe that Radhakrishnan, Rabindranath Tagore, Ram Krishna, Mahatma Gandhi and Sri Aurobindo, all these thinkers conceive that the supreme Reality has double aspects, the creative and the non-creative, the static and dynamic, transcendent and immanent, the impersonal and personal aspects of God. But these modern thinkers are more inclined to propound the view that God is higher to Brahman. In His supreme existence, the Absolute is comprehended. There is a tendency towards belief in theism more than the absolutism of the past. But they swindle in their systems adjusting both the aspects of God. While the emphasis is on theism and the Supreme Person as the highest reality, there are passages while lead us to think that they are absolutists. There is an attempt to reconcile Sankara and Rāmānuja in all modern philosophers. The philosophers namely, Tagore, Gandhi and Sri Aurobindo conceive Saccidānanda as the highest reality which include the impersonal Brahman. But Vivekananda, Radhakrishnan, K. C. Bhattacharya, adhere to the absolutism of Brahman. It is evident that all the modern thinkers are dominantly theistic and imperceptibly absolutistic. When we go into the details we find that in some systems, theism is inclusive of absolutism, and in few others the impersonal Brahman is more than personal God. Whether absolutism is dominant or theism in any system, the truth is that all modern Indian thinkers try to reconcile both absolutism and theism in their own systems of philosophy in a unique way. For Radhakrishnan and Vivekananda, Brahman is impersonal, absolute, transcedent and universal consciousnss. The forms of Brahman in the shape of Kāli, Kṛṣṇa and other gods vanish with the emergence of divine consciousness in man. The sāmādhī consciousness reveals that Brahman is the advaita consciousness. Radhakrishnan accepts the reality of both God and the Brahman. For him the Absolute is the precosmic God. God is the Absolute from the cosmic point of view. God is the projected and creative aspect of the Absolute. He creates the universe, guides, maintains and evolves it. But after the cosmic salvation, God has no purpose. God lapses into the Brahman and creation is dissolved. Brahman again manifests another creative aspect, which creates another type of universe, unknown and inconceivable to the world. Radhakrishnan has very ably reconciled the duality of God and the Absolute in his synthetic and dynamic philosophy. All the modern Indian thinkers have endeavoured to reconcile and construct a comprehensive system of philosophy inclusive of God and the Absolute in their systems of philosophy.

5. *Monotheism or Monism of Spirit and Matter*

The dominant feature of recent Indian philosophy is this that it has demolished the fundamental dualism of Matter and Spirit. Modern Indian philosophy is essentially monotheistic and monistic. Matter is Brahman, observes the great Indian sage, Sri Aurobindo. Matter is the lowest manifestation of God or is God. From the superficial point of view the duality between Spirit and Matter disappears when we conceive that the manifestation of the Spirit has different grades. Spirit is God. It is the native or explicit reality of God, whereas Matter is the implicit, latent and involved aspect of God. There are degrees of manifestation between Matter and Spirit. We have between them the principles of life, soul, mind, higher mind, intuition, overmind, supermind and other divine grades of consciousness and reality from Supermind to Saccidānanda. Matter evolves into life, life into mind, mind into higher grades of consciousness, and finally into the complete and explicit existence of Spirit in its full manifestation. The duality between Spirit and Matter is only apparent. The modern thinkers do not endeavour to establish monism by thinking the hierarchical grades of reality as unreal. The true monism is not devoid of all duality and manyness. The realities in the universe belong to hierarchical grades. Those who dismiss matter life and mind as illusory or mere dreams have not the proper insight into the nature of reality. The realities of the universe are the revealed aspects or modes of God. The manyness of modes of God are real. The realities are similar to God as well as different. There is, however, unity in diversity. While all the realities are made of the divine substance, they have different modes and degrees of Divine expression.

6. *Evolution of Supermen or Gnostic Beings*

The modern Indian thinkers conceive the emergence of Superman or Gnostic being in course of cosmic evolution. For them man is not the highest product of cosmic evolution. The evolution of superman or gnostic beings is the next higher emergence that has yet to take place. Man is not the highest, most perfect and ultimate end of cosmic evolution. The grades of consciousness and power, have yet to be embodied in some higher beings. Sri Aurobindo and Dr.Iqbal conceive that man will in course of time evolve into Supermen. The animal has evolved into man and the man is to be transformed into the Superman. Man is not the end of evolution. The cult of supermen is gaining belief today. Henri Bergson conceives that in course of evolution, many mystic beings will emerge and form a society. Sri Aurobindo also conceives that the Supermen will greater powers of consciousness and will, must emerge in the world soon. Our mind is limited, ignorant, and erroneous. The intuition comes to us momentarily and passes away. But in the Supermen, the Supramental consciousness will be the permanent consciousness in us. The spiritual and supramental grades of consciousness are much higher than the mental consciousness. The continuous and ceaseless evolution of man will transform him into the spiritual and supramental being.

7. *The new approaches to Salvation*

The conception of salvation has taken altogether a different turn. The modern thinkers conceive that salvation is the rebirth of the soul in the individual. The individual is so spiritually transformed, that he becomes spiritualised and divinised. To realise salvation is to be God or Kṛṣna having divine body, life and mind. Such gnostic begins have the highest powers of consciousness. The soul finds its union with the consciousness of nature. Salvation does not mean today the cessation of rebirth or freedom from the world of nature. Such supramental beings take birth and rebirth in order to purify the world and make it divine. Salvation means the realisation in us of greater powers of consciousness, omniscience and omnipotence. They yield more powers of consciousness and ceaselessly endeavour for transforming the cosmos. The realised souls do not merge into the universal Brahman in order to lose their individuality in it but get transformed into the divine life of Saccidānanda. The Supreme realisation has not yet been achieved to humanity. There are, again, other thinkers like Rabindranath Tagore, who think that salvation is the realisation of constant communion, presence and enjoyment of the munificence of God. Salvation lies in bondage and not in freedom. Tagore wants to enjoy the vision of God. The realised man enjoys in play with Him. One likes to enjoy sugar and not to become sugar. Similarly, the realised individual receives the greatest happiness and blessedness in the pursuit of transforming the lower material nature into the Divine Supernature.

The salvation of an individual lies not in freedom, liberation or other worldly existence. It is not a state of escape from the world. It is a condition of higher birth, when man is reborn anew and takes a new supermental life, body, consciousness and energy. The highest realisation of universal consciousness, will, energy and gnostic life is called salvation.

Though the conception of salvation vastly differs in modern Indian thinkers, yet they all conceive that this is a stage of highest realisation of the individual self which makes him omniscent and omnipotent. They establish constant communion with God and are ever engaged in the spiritualisation of the world. They are immortal by their conduct and serve as example to others. Thus they bring about spiritual transformation in nature. While for Rabindranath Tagore, salvation means the purified state of the individual self in constant communion with God, for Mahatma Gandhi it is a state of God realisation in which man is completely dedicated to the services of the world, and for Sri Aurobindo, it is a spiritual rebirth into the supramental. We observe that all modern Indian thinkers are of the view that the perfected souls takes higher births and serve as leaders of society in moral, ideal and spiritual pursuits. The supermen take births and rebirths for the good of the world. They transform the world and ceaselessly spiritualise it. Sri Aurobindo conceives that the gnostic consciousness is all pervasive. It is connected with the earth consciousness, and thereby shapes and spiritualises the universe. The realised souls according to Sri Aurobindo, Rabindranath Tagore, Mahatma Gandhi and Dr. S. M. Iqbal, do active service to humanity and endeacour to lift up the masses and make them sublime, ideal and spiritual.

8. ***Dynamism, Openness and Catholicity***

The modern Indian philosophers are very liberal and dynamic in outlook. They do not believe that in credal or sectarian religion, and teach the gospel of universal religion comprising the best of all religions. Ramkrishna—Parmahansa, Tagore, Gandhi and Radhakrishnan visualise the advent of a catholic religion, which is open dynamic, universal and all embracing. Thus Mahatma Gandhi says "My religion is Hinduism which for me, is religion for humanity and includes the best of all the religions known to me" (Contemporary Indian philosophy, 2nd Edition, p. 21). Ramkrishna Parmahansa emphatically says that all religions are true and they all serve as different pathways to the realisation of God. The same truth runs in the heart of all religions. There is essential unity in all religions and yet there is diversity. While the renascent leaders have faith in the truth of all religions, they all hold, that one particular religion should not be engrafted on another religion. Each religion has its value and serves society in a particular manner. The solace and satisfaction can be derived from religions only when it grows on indigenous lines. There should be growth in all religions, which should flower independently on their own pattern. It will be harmful to reduce all religions to a colourless form of one particular religion.

In the history of India, it is for the first time that Swami Vivekananda, Sir S. Radhakrishnan and Mahatma Gandhi called on the Indian masses to break their narrowness and lead the life of religon based on their religious experience. The modern Indian thinkers preach that the soul of a religion is different from its body. The myths, castes, rites constitute the body of the religion which is perishable. The spirit of Indian religion is that of an open religion based on the intuitive experiences of God. A religious man is a social reformer, a truc Karmayogin like Raja Ram Mohun Roy and Mahatma Gandhi.

9. ***Humanistic tendencies :***

The renaissance in India has given immense emphasis to

the life on earth and well-being of society. They lay more stress upon the values of life and the realisation through social service, feeling of brotherhood an righteous action. We can realise our salvation only by performing our duties. The revival of the Gītā's teaching of selfless action, dedicated service and flight against evil, ignorance, poverty and misery has resulted in the release of a large fund of religious energy for social work in the present times.

The modern Indian thinkers are excessively traditional. They have their roots in the past and they hardly deviate much from the ancient systems. All the truths and values inculcated by the contemporary thinkers are traceable to one or the other systems. Being essentially synthetic in outlook, and given too much to inheritance, there is hardly a system in modern Indian thought which carves out new paths and developes new channel of thought. This has led many scholars to the view that there is no modern Indian philosophy as such. These thinkers reinstate the ancient truths and values and they can hardly be called creative philosophers. The philosophy of recent thinkers is moer or less a synthesis of different systems. But there is undoubtedly the difference in interpretations, systematistations and above all in the angles of synthesis which are of immense value. Amongst the great modern mystic thinkers, Sir Aurobindo may be called as the most exalted thinker who has built up an integral advaitism. There is the meeting of the East and the West in Sri Aurobindo's philosophy which also opens up new lines of thinking.

The basic elements of modern Indian thought are contained in its positive outlook, cosmic view, integralism, reconciliation of theism and absolutism, monism of Spirit and Matter, emergence of gnostic beings or supermen, new approaches to salvation, dynamism, openness and humanism. These are the chief characteristics of modern Indian philosophy propounded by the pioneers of contemporary Indian thought. The impact of the West, the scientific advancement and human values mould the mind of Indian renaissance thinkers. We also observe that Indian renaissance movement is still in infancy. The modern Indian philosophy is yet to grow to maturity and if it has to regain its prestige today in the philosophical world, it has to be creative, revolutionary and progressive in the realms of metaphysics and social philosophy.

BIBLIOGRAPHY

Aurobindo	The Life Divine, New York, Sri Aurobindo
1949	Library, Inc., Reprint edition.
Bose, N.K.	Selections from Gandhi, Navajiwan Publishing House, Ahmadabad
Gandhi M. K. 1956	An Autobiography of My Experiments with Truth, Navajiwan Publishing House, Ahmadabad.
Iqbal, S. M. 1920	The Secret of Self, Macmillan & Co., Ltd.,
Iqbal, S. M. 1960	The Reconstruction of Religious thought in Islam. Shaikh Muhammad Ashraf & Co. Lahore. Reprinted.
Radhakrishnan, S.	An Idealist View of Life, Geroge Allen & Unwin Ltd. London,
Radhakrishnan	Contemporary Indian Philosophy, George Allen
and Muirhead 1952	& Unwin Ltd., London, Second Revised Islam.
Tagore, R. N. 1949	The Religion of Man, George Allen & Unwin Ltd., London, Third Impression.
do 1954	Sadhana, Macmillan & Co. Ltd., London, Reprinted.
do 1956	Gitanjali, Macmillan & Co. Ltd., London, Reprinted.
do 1948	Personality, Macmillan & Co. Ltd., London.
Vivekananda :	The complete works of Swami Vivekananda,
1955	Eight volumes, Advaita Ashrama, Mayawati; Almora.

Chapter-16

Sociology of Religion in India. A Trend Report

SURAJIT SINHA

Chapter-16

In this report, I am concerned with a review of the published literature on 'Sociology of Religion' with reference to the people of India and also of the trends of research in the broad field of sociology of religion by Indian scholars. I will not make a distinction between 'Sociology' and 'Social anthropology' of religion, although I am aware that the anthropological approach is distinguished by its holistic and cross-cultural perspective.

An examination of various definitions of religion is beyond the scope of the paper. For our purpose, however, religion will be defined as "beliefs and practices related to supernatural entities, spirits and powers, who/which are considered as the ultimate concern of all mundane existence among different human groups". In sociology of religion we are concerned with the forms and processes of articulation between religious beliefs and practices as defined above and society. A proper sociological study of religion will take into consideration the three components of the organic complex, *viz.* (a) beliefs in supernatural entities, (b) specialists who create such beliefs and (c) laity who receive it in various forms.

Early Studies

1. *The Pioneers:* While generations of Brahman Pundits have been interested in preparing commentaries on the basic religious0-cum-philosophical texts of Hinduism, including those concerned with social norms, there was no indigenous tradition for systematic analysis of social behaviour in relation to ideal textual norms. It was the European travellers, missionaries, natural historians and humanistic scholars who began the systematic recording and study of religious texts and behaviour of the people of India. The initial spadework of recording religious behaviour was done during the 18th and the 19th centuries. European scholars were immediately impressed by the culture-shock of contrasts with monotheistic Christianity—polytheism, idolatry,

animal sacrifice and plethora of rituals. They became interested in three broad areas-a complete description of the diversity of religious beliefs and practices; a search for the primitive base of Hinduism in archaic folk rituals and tribal customs; and bringing into relief the higher philosophical thoughts and rich symbolism in pantheistic/monistic Hinduism.

From the very beginning, however, two distinct approaches could be observed among these European scholars interested in Indian religions. One group, the classicists, were mainly interested in textual analysis of symbols and philosophical concepts, while the other took up the task of recording contemporary ethnic beliefs and rituals—the 'folk customs' or 'popular religions'. The initial emphasis of the latter group of scholars was on describing standard beliefs and rites rather than on relating them systematically to group behaviour. It was, however, realised very early that the basic theme of 'purity—pollution' and *karma* were intimately connected with *Vama-Jati* base of Hindu society.

Among the scholars of this pioneering phase may be mentioned Dubois (1928), Buchanan (1925) and Wilson (1958). The list could be multiplied. The Census Reports from 1872 onward and the various 'Tribes and Castes' volumes pursued this original impulse for recording the diversity of ethnic (tribe/caste) and sectarian customs throughout the length and breadth of the country and an image of Indian society emerged as an agglomeration of numerous social groups whose behaviour was moulded by distinct magico-religious customs. Apart from the mapping of diversity, the nature of continuity between 'tribal primitivism' and 'folk' or popular Hinduism as well as the contrast between tribal religions and the philosophical traditions of Hinduism were the main theoretical interests of these scholars. Risley's famous characterisations of Hinduism as "animism more or less transformed by philosophy" or as, "magic transformed by metaphysics" (Risley, 1915: 233), provide the keynote to the intellectual concern of this period. Fraser's famous *Golden Bough,* with its evolutionary bias, absorbed a good deal of the information on archaic customs of the peoples of India. Indian scholars like J.N. Bhattacharya, Rajender Lal Mitra and S.C. Roy shared similar perspectives in their study of religious customs.

At the turn of the twentieth century we find that the concern for description of the religious customs was further elaborated in the form of ethnographic monographs. S.C. Roy's *Mundas and Their Country,* (1912) is an important example of this. Later on, in Bodding's three volumes on Santal folklore and medicine (1925, 1927, 1940) we already see the beginning of an attempt to correlate religious beliefs and rituals to social life. Among later scholars involved in regional mapping of popular religious forms, the studies by Elmore (1915) and Whitehead (1921) on village gods of South India deserve special mention.

2. *Diffusionists:* During 1929-40, we find a few Indian scholars responding to the contemporary interests in diffusion studies in British, German and American Anthropology. Chattopadhyaya studies on *Dharma Puja* and *Chadak Puja* (1935, 1942), Das's article on "Sun Worship among the Tribes of Eastern India" (1927) and Bose's study of "Spring Festival in India" (1927) belong to this category.

Slater made an attempt to identify the 'Dravidian elements' in Indian culture (1924). An attempt to differentiate the so-called Dravidian, Austric, Negrito, Tieto-Chinese and Aryan elements of India cultural amalgam is seen in Hutton's classic monograph, *Caste in India* (1961).

3. Acculturation studies Although earlier scholars like Rislev had already writtend in general terms about transformation of 'magic' and 'animism' loadedd tribal customs under the impact of Hinduism, the credit for the first field study of acculturation in religion among the tribes goes to S.C. Roy. In his classic monograph *Oraon Religion and Customs* (1928). Roy analyses the nativistic and reformist Bhagat movements among the Oraon as a response to the pressures of acculturation. Bose's important article "Hindu Method of Tribal absorption" (1941) indicates how incorporation of Hindu religious symbols has followed the economic and power gradient from the dominant Hindu peasantry to the tribes.

Recent Developments and Trends of Research

1. *Max Weber and Religion of India:* When Max Weber's famous book on *Sociology of Hinduism and Buddhism* was first published in German in 1920-21, it did not attract the attention

of contemporary Indian as well as Anglo-American scholars. As late as 1951 there is no mention of Weber by Hutton in his bibliography on "Caste in India" (1961). It is only after Gerth and Martindale published the English translation in 1958 that Weber's ideas on the role of religion, particularly Hinduism, in the process of modernization of Indian society started attracting attention.

It is now widely known how Weber has tried to construct a Hindu ethic based on two cardinal dogmas, "the *samsara* belief in the transmigration of souls, and the related *karma* doctrine of compensation". According to Weber, these two cardinal doctrines worked together to form the theodicy of the caste system which was unable to generate a this worldly rational ethic. Milton Singer has critically reviewed, in great detail, Weber's analysis of sociology of Hinduism (1961). Although I agree with Singer that Weber's sociological hypotheses, largely based on extrapolation of textual notions of Hinduism, were considerably over-drawn and that more recent studies suggest the need for some revision in Weber's major conclusions regarding traditionalism and irrationality of Hinduism he has to be credited as being the first systematic sociologist of Hinduism who has directly addressed himself to the issues like religious/ ideological bases of *Varma-Jati* order, sects and tribalism and their relationship with the process of modernization, nationalism, industrialization and bureaucracy.

2. Religion and Society among the Coorgs of South India: The decisive boundary-marker in the modern trend in Sociology of Religion in India is Sriniva's classic Religion and Society among the Coorgs of South India (1952). In this monograph, Srinivas relates Coorgi joint family or Okka, caste and local group, village or Nad. For a broader understandingof Coorgi religion int he wider context of Hinduism. Srinivas introduces the concept of 'spread' of varying order: 'local,' 'peninsular,' 'all India.' The social functions of religion are analysed in terms of two sets of solidarities — vertical (i.e., local) and horizontal along caste lines. On eof the major contrbutions of Srinivas is to bring into relief how social mobility along caste rank is achieved through 'Sanskritization. (Sec also Srinivas 1956).

3. *Caste and Social Structure*: Among the other important publications correlating religion with social structure may be mentioned the works of Gough (1959), Mathur (1964), Harper (1957a, 1957b, 1959, 1963, 1964a), Beteille (1964-1965) and Nicholar (1967).

In *Caste and Ritual in a Malwa Village* (1964), Mathur demonstrates in detail how religious rites and ideas regarding purity and pollution determine caste hierarchy and caste behaviour (see also Stevenson, 1954).

In an interesting paper on Hindu village pantheon in a Mysore village, Harper demonstrates how there is a broad reflex of three-class caste system in three grades of deities (1959). In another paper relating to the Havik Brahmans of the same village, Harper demonstrates relationship of male dominance in social strucutre and utilisation of spirit possession as a stress-reducing mechansm (1957).

Andre Beteille observes how participation in Pongal religious festival symbolises differential positions of various castes in the social structure and does not generate larger cohesion or integration (1964). In another paper 'Social Organization of a Temple in a Tanjore Village,' Betteille shows that the different cults in the village tend to be autonomous and unconnected and do not directly contribute to village or caste solidarity (1965).

The binary opposition of the religious notions of pure and impure has been assumed to the basis of the Indian caste system both by Dumont and Pocock. In his famous book *Homo Hierarchicus,* Dumount attempts to bring into relief the underlying opposition in Hindu thought between world renouncing Sanyasi and Man-in-the-world, between pure and impure, between priesthood and possession and between status and power (Dumont, 1970). Pocock's article on caste hierarchy in Gujarat also emphasizes the theme of a series of binary oppositions inherent in the Varna order (1957). Levi-Straus's important article on "Bear and the Barber" suggests how primitive totemism can be structurally transformed into caste-based Hindusism by reverseing the rules regarding the exchange of food and women (1963). The theme of opposition of purity and pollution implicit in the Dharma sastras have been made explicit by Orenstein by what he describes as `grammar of defilement' (1968).

4. *Religion and Indian Civilization:* In 1954 Redfield and Singer wrote an important article "Cultural Role of Cities" in which the concepts of `primary or orthogenetic civilization' as the product of interaction of `Great and Little Traditions' was first spelt out (Redfield and Singer, 1954). This was further elaborated by Redfield in the chapter on "Social Organization of Tradition" in his book *Peasant Society and Culture* (1956).

Marriott used the concept of Great and Little Tradition in analysing the cultural strata and processes in the village of Kishengarhi in Uttar Pradesh (Marriott, 1955). According to Marriott, Little Traditions of the village find a place in the Great Tradition by a process of "universalization", whereas the Great Traditions are converted into Little Traditions by a process of "parochialization". He further points out that certain elements of the local Littled Tradition may be conceived as strictly local `residual category' unaffected by the two way interaction process of universalization and parochialization (ibid). Redfield's ideas about social organization of civilization were further elaboratedd by Marriott and Cohn in developing the concept of "Networks and Centres in the Integration of Indian Civilization' (Marriott and Cohn, 1958). The emphasis of this mode of analysis is on studying the role of cultural specialists and channels of cultural communication. Merriott writes that the channels of cultural communication as well as the contents are becoming more and more centralized and standardized in modern India (Marriott, 1959, 1963).

Milton Singer experimented with Redfield's ideas on 'social organization of tradition' in his study of religious behaviour in Madras city. In order to describe and analyse the complexity of religious behaviour in a city like Madras, Singer decided to study the Great Tradition through concrete localized observable capsules of 'cultural performances'. Singer felt that through an analysis of cutural performances and their constituents e.g., 'the media and themes the place and occasion of performance, the performance and the audience,' it would be possible to infer the structure and organization of particular kinds of performances.

Then by tracing the linkages among these structures and organization, it would be possible to arrive at the more comprehensive and abstract constructs of cultural structure, cultural value system and a Great Tradition (Singer 1964, 1972. See also Singer, 1955 and 1958). Singer also felt that anthropological study of Great Tradition cannot be done exclusively on the basis of observation of ritual behaviour without reference to the meanings in the texts. He combines textual knowledge with contextual analysis of the "Social Organization of Sanskritic Hinduism in Madras City" (Singer, 1972). The structure and organization of Sanskritic Hinduism in Madras City were described in terms of its sacred geography, its sacred specialists and literati, and its sacred calendar of rites and ceremonies as observed in 'the domestic sphere' and 'the temple sphere'. Through these descriptive procedures Singer analyses the processes of transformation of Sanskritic Hinduism-'the cultural drift of orthodoxy', 'technical modernization of the sacred culture', 'transformation in the transmissive sysem' and 'the prospects of structural change'. He also deals with the problems of 'competing self-definitions of Sanskritic Hinduism: orthodoxy and the sects'. In a symposium organized in 1962 Singer brought together a number of anthropologists and textual scholars to present papers on various aspects of the cult of Krishna. The result of the symposium was the book, *Krishna: Myths, Rites and Attitudes* (Singer, 1966).

Ghurye's pioneering work on the *Indian Sadhus* (1953), Kapadia's *Hindu Kinship* (1946) and Karve's *Hindu Society: An Interpretation* (1961) combine textual knowledge with contextual sociological information.

In an important book *The Sacred Complex* in *Hindu Gaya* (1961) Vidyarthi describes how the pattern of interaction between patrons and sacred specialists in an important centre of Hindu pilgrimage has changed through history.

Nirmal Kumar Bose through numerous writings has suggested fresh lines of enquiry into the changing structure of Indian civilization. Perhaps his most important contribution in this line is the book *Hindu Samajer Gadan* (Bose, 1949) in which he brings into a broad canvas of time many dimensions of India's social structure and social processes; links with kingship, fairs and pilgrim centres; sociological analysis of norms of sacred and secular life in the ancient texts; and social and religious movements in response to Islam during the medieval period.* In another article 'The geographical back ground of Indian Culture', Bose writes about the various traditional cultural media which provided a mechanism through which the unifying thoughts and feelings of thinkers, artists and saints of India were brought to the door of the most distant communities and enabled them to share some common intellectual and emotional elements of the civilization (Bose, 1950). As Director, Anthropological Survey of India. Bose initiated some studies on the superstructure of Indian society through the study of important temples and *muths* and sacred roles of kinship (See Sinha, 1972: 10-11).

The Anthropological Survey of India initiated a series of studies during 1967-70 on the social organization of Hinduism in order to study the changing structure of Indian civlization (See Sinha, 1970: 87-145). Originally it was planned that the main focus of the study would be on studying religion in the sacred city of Kasi (ibid, 137-145). The unpublished report of Saraswati and Sinha on the Sadhus of Kasi brings into relief the sectarian basis of ascetic organization, their spatially far-flung organization and secular props, their composition in terms of caste and linguistic affiliation and trends of change from orthodox sectarian rural linked forms to new universalistic urban centred forms (Saraswati, 1970). Saraswati has completed an extensive survey of the Pundits of Kasi and is now engaged in organizing a research programme on the sacred complex of Kasi including the sacred shrines, Visvanath temple, the burning *ghat* and the bathing ghats. One of the significant features of these studies is the use of textual and contemporary native categories in guiding observations and interpreting data. The broad picture that is emerging is that while larger volumes of people are getting involved in sacred rituals, the rituals themselves are becoming simplified and standardized in order to cater to modern urban needs. Saraswati had also posited a universal scheme for classification of cultures on the basis of combination of three modes of transmission of knowledge: oral (*Laukik*), textual (*Sastriya*) and transcendental (*Nairvritik*), (Saraswati 1970a).

5. *Religion and Economic Development*: I have already mentioned Weber's thesis about the constraining role of Hinduism on economic development. The Weber thesis has recently been restated with some variation by Misra (1962) and Kapp (1963). The limitations of the hypothetico-deductive approach of the Weber-Kapp-Misra type has been discussed in detail by Singer in two papers (Singer, 1961 and 1966). M.S.A. Rao, in an interesting paper on "Religion and Economic Development", critically examines the Weber thesis and demonstrates the complexities involved in tracing relationship between religion and economic development and suggests that a fruitful line of enquiry wouldks be to compare reformatory sects of Hinduism with Protestatism rather than "Hinduism" as such (Rao, 1969).

6. *Secularization and modernity:* Srinivas has indicated how was contrary processes have been gaining in strength in modern India. Following the sacred path of 'Sanskritization' the lower castes and tribes are taking over the rites, customs and beliefs of the higher castes. But while the lower groups are increasingly sanskritising their lives, the higher strata are becoming increasingly westernized. Westernization is a multi-layered process, including the acceptance of Western technology, political, legal and social institutions and Western literature, philosophy and science (Srinivas, 1956 and 1968).

I have already mentioned how Milton Singer has critically reviewed Weber's ideas with reference to the process of modernization in India. In an interesting article on "The Modernization of Religious Beliefs" (1966c). Singer emphasises the process of "compartmentalized adaptation" of European and modern models. Whereas European models have been incorporated in the spheres of "factory" and "office", traditional Hinduism has been maintained in the sphere of home and social relatins. This compartmentalization has minimized direct conflict between tradition and modernity. The conflicts that have emerged from the co-existence of traditional and modern life styles tend to be resolved by abbreviating the timegiven to ritual observances, by delegating the responsibility for ritual observances to those who have time and by re-interpreting traditional religious beliefs such as the doectrines of *Karma, dharma, moksha* and *ashimsa* so as to make them applicable to the conditions of modern life (ibid: 65-66).

In his latest book, *When a Great Tradition Modernizes* (1972). Singer further elaborates his proposition that there is no essential schism between tradition and modernity in Hinduism. The chief actors in the modenization process are individuals and families (rather than castes and religious communities) who relate their modernizing activities to their caste and religious activities through various adaptive strategies. R.S. Khare's publications on the Kannya Kubja Brahmins and their social organization also emphasize the teme of adaptive adjustments in traditional cultural values of Hindusim (Khare, 1970. 1971).

7. Sociology of Hindu-linked religions: Sociology of off-shoots of has receive dverlittle systematic attention.

Although the different historicians and philosophers, there has been very little sociologicalstudyof either Tibetanor of Theravada Buddhism non the ground.

The most importan sociological owrok on th eJainsis by Sangava who finds the existence of numerous endogramous grous amogn them although the origionalteachers of Jainism envisaged "a society where in classes were not watertight compartments and complete freedom was granted to people to change to the class of their own aptitude"(Sangave, 1959: 67-70). Mandelbaum emphasises theree special characteritics of Jains--their propensity to ascrism, their indination towards trade, and their proclivity to extreme fission (mandelbaum 1970: 536).

Although there is a wealth of basis ethographic material on the Sikhs (Bingley, 1899; Gordon, 1904; Ibbetson, 1916: macauliffe, 1909 and Wilson. 1948). there are very few publications strictly belonging to the sphere of sociology of religion. The following studies, however, deserve special mention: "A Sikh village" (singh, 1958); "Religion in Daleke: A Sikh Village" (Singh, 1961) and "on being Unshorn" (Uberoi, 1967).

Nihar Ranjan Rays social history of Sikhism, The Sikh Curus and the Sikh Society 91970) brings into relief the social and economic factors that led to total involvement of Punjab peasantry in the growth of a well-knit militant socio-religious organisation.

8. Sociology of Islam: Although the 'Tribes and Castes' volumes do cover the customs of the ethic groups amogn the Moslems in differnet regions of India, the social organisation of Great Tradtion of Islam in India has not yet attracted the attention of social scientists in and on India. The ethnographic notes, however, indicate that converted Moslems have retained to a large extent the local cultural norms indiffernt regions. The immigrant Arabs and others with purer Islamic backgrouns have also adapted themselves to the local cultural milieu. Recently there have been a number of reports on the existence of caste-like segmentation and stratification in Islam in India, beginning with Ansari's pioneering work "Muslim Caste in Uttar Pradesh: a study of culture contact" (Ansari, 1960; see also A. Ahmed, 1965; I. Ahmed, 1965; Z. Ahmed, 1962; Guha, 1965 and Siddiqui, 1972). Siddiqui's report on the Moslem groups of Calcutta goes beyond th erealm of caste analogues and examines the role of sects and *Khanqueas* in social grouping among the Moslems (Siddiqui, 1972).

Pratap C. Aggarwal's report on the Meo of Rajasthan who widely shar eboth Hindu and Moslem traits indicates a recent trend towards asserting Moslem identity and consequent Islamization of culture (Aggrarwal, 1966)

It seems to me that the social organization of Islamic Great Tradition in India if properly mapped will give a much more lineally centralized picture than the tangled networks of Hindu social organisation.

9. Sociology of other minority religious groups: As in the case of Islam the other minority religions in India, have also made adaptive compromise to the superarching Hindu milieu, particularly to the caste idio,.

(I) Jews: Ther eare two major ancient settlements of Jews in India, one in Cochin and the other in Maharashtra. The Cochin Jews are divided into three endogamous groups and there is no interdining between the 'White Jews' and the 'Black Jews' of Cochin. Like th eCohin Jews. the Jews of Maharashtra, Bene Israel, are divided into Gora' (white) and 'Kala' (black) groups (see Mandelbaum, 1939 and 1970: 560-63; Strizower, 1959).

2) Parsis: The Parsis although forming a smal lcommunity of a little over 1,00,000 persons, have tenaciously stuck to their ancient Zoroastrianism while modernising themselves in secular life. The Parsis have also not split themselves into separate Jatis (Karaka, 1884; Mandelbaum, 1970: 563-64).

(3) Christians: As in the case of Islam, there is no systematic sociological description of the organization of Christian denominations and sects in India. The ethnographic accountont he Syrian Christians by Anantakirishna Ayyar deserves special mention for describing indetail the IJati divisions amogn them along denominational and territorial lines (1926).

Mandelbaum has adequately summarised the reports on the process of Indianization of Christianity, its compromises and rationalizations in adaptation to the dominant *varna-jati* milieu (Mandelbaum 1970: 564-571;s ee also Raj, 1959).

10. Recent Trends in Tribal studies: Radcliffe-brown's classic *The Andaman Islanders* (1922) based on his fiedl work during 1906 1908 maybe regarded as th efirst structural -functional interpretation of ceremonicals,myths and legends of a tribal group in India. As a matter of fact, since the publication of this great book, there has not been a single rigorous structural-functional study of religion of a tribal group in India during the last 50 years.

An evolutionary approach to the study of Tribal culture, including religion, was posited by Sinha in his particle. "Tribal Culture of Peninsular India as a Dimension of Little Tradition in the study of Indian Civilization; a Preliminary Statement" (Sinha,1958). In contrast to the `evolutionary emergent', `peasant'and the `urban' systems the tribal religions arehedonistic, pragmatic and are not loaded by ethical strivings (ibid., see also Sinha, 1965 1966).

In an important article 'Morals and Merits: A Study of Values and Social Controls in South Asian Societies". Furer Haimendorf writes: "Although some of the tribes also believe in a sequence of lives, and others set great store on the acquisition of *social* merit which raises the person's status in this life, in none of the tribal societies did we encounter the idea that moral choices affect a person's fate in future existence" (Furer Haimendorf,

1967: 168).

Perhaps the most significant book on tribal religion during the last two decades is Verrier Elwin's work on the Saora (Elwin,1955). Apart from detailed description of rites and beliefs in social context, there are three chapters on Saora Ethic.

In his book, *The Maler: A Study in Nature-Man-Spirit Complex of a Hill Tribe in Bihar,* Vidyarthi delas with Maler's approach to supernaturalism under four sections: conception about Gossaiyan, sacred geography, sacredks performances and sacred specialists (Vidyarthi, 1963).

Surajit Sinha has written a series of articles on the process of Hinduization of the Bhumij within the framework of tribe-caste/peasant continuum. In these papers the process of regional universalization and synthesis of culture within the social frame of indigenous states and pressures for social mobility, and the role of mediating specialists and culture performances have been highlighted (Sinha, 1953, 1957, 1959; 1962, 1966).

Recently the researchers of the Anthropological Survey of India have published a number of ethnographic monographs relating tribal religious beliefs and practices with social structure: (Bannerjee, 1968; Thusu, 1970; Hajra, 1970; Nandi *et al.,* 1971; Rajalakshmi Misra, 1971; Guha *et al.,* 1972; Thusu, 1972).

In 1965 two important books were published, both dealing with the problems of tribes responding to the pressures of the dominant section of the Indian population. Orans' book on the Santal is an account of how an encysted tribal group, surrounded by dominant groups, improvished a 'Great Tradition' in their political solidarity drive (Orans, 1965). Stephen Fuchs' book, *Rebellious Prophets,* makes a comprehensive survey of the published literature on the 'messianic movements' among the tribes and peasants (Fuchs, 1965). Edward Jay's interesting paper on "Revitalization Movement in Tribal India" may also be mentioned in this connection. Jay examines the revitalization movements among the Munda, Bhumij and the Oraon and analyses them as mediators between the Great and Little Traditions (Jay, 1961).

Suggestions for Priorities in Research

From the foregoing review we get an idea of the ground covered so far. It appears that we now have enough information to prepare distribution maps of religious customs and their association with ethnic groups. This exercise, however, needs to be systematically carried out. This will give a broad framework for studying inter ethnic and inter-regional linkages and boundaries. Resources of the Anthropological Survey of India, University Departments of Anthropology and Sociology and the I.C.S.S.R. could be mobilized for such socio-cultural mapping.

The theme of purity-pollution in relation to *Varna-Jati* hierarchy has received considerable attention and attempts have been made to construct 'grammars' of pollution. Such grammars of pollution based on classification of attributive symbols should, however, be supplemented with systematic observation of actual ritual transactions.

Religion has provided important basic materials as well as concepts for studying the cultural processes of Indian civilization. The concepts of 'universalization'and 'parochialization' in relation to the ideas of Great and Little Traditions have undergone considerable re-evaluation. We now need to study the social processes underlying the interaction of Great and Little Tradition and the cultural processes of 'universalization' and 'parochialization'.

During the last decade Weber's construction of Hindu ethic has gone through considerable critical re-examination and the complex adaptive qualities of Hinduism in the process of economic development and modernization have come into relief. Uncritical evaluation of Hinduism as a major stumbling block for modernization has been more or less discarded on the basis of recent research. The complex linkages between religion, ultimate values, behavioural norms and social institutions, however, have yet to be systematically worked out on a comparative basis. The practical implications of puritanical ethic in Jainism. Vaisnavism, Sikhism, and Zoroastrianism have not yet been studied systematically.

The process of 'secularization' of Hinduism also has received very inadequate attention. Linkages and confrontation of religion with secular ideologies like nationalism, socialism and communism are important uncharted areas of research. This will also involve study of the process of politicization of religions, sects and monastic orders.

It will be apparent from the foregoing survey that systematic coverage of the sociology of non-Hindu/non-tribal religions has been very inadequate. This is an area in which considerable research needs to be done. The emphasis should be equally on studying the social organisation of Great Tradition and of local syncretic adaptation in different regions of India.

The other major gaps in research areas which require attention on a priority basis are the following:

(1) Study of religion in relation to class stratification: how religion reinforces upper class in interests and also provides opportunity for the lower strata to mobilise themselves.

(2) Mapping out of the wider network of Great Tradition: how the different social strata and segments are involved in the social organization of Great Tradition.

(3) Sociology of inter-religious conflict and integration: Role of religion in regional and national integration and the divisive role of religion.

(4) Study of religion and world view in relation to basic pre-industrial livelihood activities: hunting and gathering, agriculture, fishing live-stock breeding and handicrafts.

(5) A comparative study of religion-based world views of the tribals and the peasants.

(6) Sociology of sects: progressive *vis-a-vis* atavistic role. Sects as products of solidarity movements of the socially marginal and deprived.

(7) Linkage of the emerging political leadership with religions and cults: reinforcement of sacred culture in the process.

(8) Relation of religion with different dimension of modernization: economic development, science and technology and political modernization.

(9) Role of religion in social revitalization in modern India.

(10) development of indices of 'secularization': comparative

study of secularization of religion and sects in different parts of India.

(11) The patterns of syncretism: Hindu-tribal, Hindu-Buddhist, Hindu-Jain, Hindu-Moslem and Hindu-Christian.

(12) Role of religion in the traditional pursuits of excellence.

Bibliography

Aggarwal, P.C., 'A Moslem Sub-caste of North India: Problems of Cultural Integration.' *Economic and Political Weekly,* 1966, 1, 159-167.

Ahmad, Aziz, *Studies in Islamic Culture in Indian environment,* Oxford University Press, Oxford, 1965.

Ahmad, Imtiaz, 'Social Stratification Among Muslims,' *The Economic Weekly,* 1966, 10, 1093-1096.

Ahmad, Zarina, 'Muslim Caste in Uttar Pradesh,' *The Economic Weekly,* 1962, 14, 325-336.

Ansari, Ghaus, 'Muslim Caste in Uttar Pradesh" A Study of Culture Contact',*The Eastern Anthropooogist,* 1960, 13, 5-80.

Atal, Yogesh. 'The Cult of Bheru in a Mewar Village and Its Vicinage,' in L.P. Vidyarthi (ed.), *Aspects of Religion in Indian Society,* Meerut, 1961, 140-150.

Ayyar, L.K. Anantakrishna, *Anthropology of the Syrian Christians* Cochin Government Press, Ernakulam, 1926.

Barnow, Victor, 'The Changing Character of a Hindu Festival,' *American Anthropologist,* 1954, 56, 74-86.

Bannerjee, S., *Ethnographic Study of the Kuvi-kandha,* Memoir No. 21, Anthropological Survey of India, Calcutta, 1968.

beals, Alan R., 'conflict and Interlocal Festicals in a South Indian Region,' *JOurnal of Asian Studies,* 1964, 23, 99-113.

Bhattacharya, J.N., *Hindu Castes and Sects,* Thacker, Spink, Calcutta, 1896.

Berreman, G.D., 'Barahmins and Shamans in Pahari Religions,' in E.B. Harper (ed.) *Aspects of Religion in South Asia,* Washington University Press, Seattle, 1964.

Beteille, A., 'A Note on Pongal Festival in a Tanjore Village,' *Man,* May-June 1964, 64.

Bingley, H.H. *Sikha,* Simla, 1899.

Bodding, P.O., *The Santhals and Disease: Studies in Santal Medicine and Connected Folklore,* Parts, I, II and III, Memoris of the Asiatic Society of Bengal, 10 (1, 2 and 3), 1925, 1927, 1940.

Bose, Nirmal Kumar, The Spring Festival of India,' *Man in India,* 1927, 8.

Bose, Nirmal Kumar, The Hindu method of Tribal Absorption,' *Science and Culture,* 1941, 7 (4).

Bose, Nirmal Kumar, *Hindu Samajer Gadan* Visva-Bharati, Calcutta, 1949.

Bose, Nirmal Kumar, The Geographical Background of Indian Culture,' in N.K. Bose (ed)., *Culture and Society in India,* Asia Publishing House, Calcutta, 1967a, 1-11.

Bose, Nirmal Kumar, 'Organization of Services in the Temple of Lingaraj Bhubaneswar,' in N.K. Bose (ed.), *Culture and Society in India,* Asia Publishing House, Calcutta, 1967b, 105-108.

Buchanan, Francis Hamilton, *Journal of Francis Buchanan Kept During the Survey of Patna and Gaya in 1811012,* (Edited by V.H. Jackson), Patna, 1925.

Carstairs, G.M., *The Twice Born,* Hogarth Press, London, 1957.

Carstairs, G. M., Patterns of Religious Observations in There Villages in Rajasthan,' in L.P. Vidyarthi (ed.), *Aspects of Religion in Indian Society,* Meerut, 1961, 59-113.

Chattopdhyaya, K.P., 'Dharma Worship in Bengal,' *Journal of the Royal Asiatic Society of Bengal, Letters,* 1935, 1 (3).

Crooke, W., *Things Indian,* John Murray, London, 1906.

Crooke, W., *Religion and Folklore of Northern India,* Oxford University Press, London, 2 Vols.

Damle, Y.B. 'Harikatha, a Studyin Communications,' *Bulletin-Deccan College institute, S.K. De, Felicitation Volume,* Poona, 1959.

Das, T.C., 'Sun Worship Amongst the aboriginal Tribes of Eastern Indian *Journal Department of Letters,* Calcutta University, 1927, 2.

Das, Veena, 'A Sociological Approach to the Caste Puranas: A case Study,' *Sociological Bulletin,* 1968, 17 (2), 141-164.

Diechl. C.G., *Instruments and Purpose: Studies in Rites and Rituals in South India,* Lind, Gleerup, 1966.

Dubois, Abbe J. A. And Beuchamp, H.K., *Hindu Manners, Customs and Ceremones,* Cosmo Publications, N.Delhi.

Dumont, Louis, 'World Renunciation in Indian Religions,' *Contributions to Indian Sociology,* 1960, 4, 33-62.

Dunmont, Louis, *Homo Hierarchicus: The Caste System and its implications,* University of Chicago Press, Chicago, 1970.

Dumont, Louis *Religion, Politics and History in India,* Mouton & Co., The Hague, 1970a.

Elder, J.W., Caste and World Views: The Application of Survey Research Method,' in Milton Singer and B.S. Cohn (eds.), *Structure and Change in Indian Society,* New York, 1968, 173-188.

Elmore, W.T., *Dravidian Gods in Modern Hinduism: A Study of Village Deities of South India,* University of Nebraska, Lincoln, 1915.

Elwin, Verrier *The Relion of an Indian Tribe,* Oxford University Press, Calcutta, 1955.

Farquhar, J.N., *Modern Religious Movements in India,* Macmillan, London, 1929.

Fuchs, Stephen, *Rebellious Prophets,* Asia Publishing House, Calcutta, 1965.

Furer-Haimendorf. C.V., The After Life in Indian Tribal Belief.,' *Journal of the Royal anthropological Society,* 1953, 83 (Part I).

Ghurye, G.S., *Indian Sadhus,* Bombay, 1953..

Ghurye, K.G., *Preservation of Learned Traditons in India,* Bombay, 1950.

Gnanambal, K., *Religious Institutions and Caste Panchayats, in South Indian,* Anthropological Survey of India, Memoir No. 18, Calcutta, 1972.

Gough, E.K., Cults of the dead Among the Nayars,' in Milton Singer (ed.), *Traditional India: Structure and Change,* 1959, 140-272.

Gould, H.A. 'Priest and Contrapriest: A Structural Analysis of Jajmani Relationships in the Hindu Plains and the Nilgiri Hills, *Contributions to Indian Sociology,* New Series, 1967, 1, 26-55.

Guha, Uma, Caste Among Rural Bengali Moslems,' *Man in India,* 1965, 45, 167-169.

Guha, Uma Siddhiqui, M.K. A. and Mathur, P.R G., *The Didayi,* Memoir No. 23, Anthropological Survey of India, Calcutta, 1972.

Gumperz, J.J., 'Religion and Social Communication in Village North India,' in E.B. Harper (ed.), *Aspects of Religion in South Asia,* Special No., *Journal of Asian Studies,* 1964, 23.

Hajra, D., *The Dorlas of Baltar* Memoir No. 16, Anthropological Survey of India, Calcutta, 1970.

Harper, E.B. 'Sharmanism in South India', *Southwestern Journal of Anthropology,* 1957a, 13, 267-287.

Harper, E.B. 'Hoylu: A Belief Relating Justice and Supernatural,' *American Anthropologist,* 1957b, 59, 801-816.

Harper, E.B., 'A Hindu Vilalge Pantheon,' *Southwestern Journal of Anthropology,* 1959, 15, 227-234.

Harper, E.B., 'Spirit Possession and Social Structure,' in Bala Ratnam (ed.) *Anthropology on the March,* The Book Centre, Madras, 1963, 165-197.

Harper, E.B., 'Ritual Pollution as an Integrator of Caste and Religion,' *The Journal of Asian Studies,* 1964a, 2, 151-197.

harper, E.B., *Religion in South Asia,* University of Washington Press, Seattle, 1964b.

Hein, Norvin, 'The Ram Lila,' *Journal of American Folklore,* 1958, 71, 279-304.

Hutton, J.H., *Caste in India: Its Nature, Function and Origin,* Third edition, Oxford University Press, Bombay, 1961.

Ingalls, Daniel, 'The Brahman Tradition,' *Journal of American Folklore,* 1958, 71-209-215.

Jay, Edward, 'Revitalization Movement in Tribal India,' in L.P. Vidyarthi (ed.), *Aspects of Religion in Indian Society* 1961.

Kane, P.V., *History of Dharma Shastras,* 5 Vols, Bhandarkar Oriental Research Institute, Poona,1958.

Kapadia, K.M., *Hindu Kinship,* Bombay, 1046.

Kapp, K.W., *Hindu Culture, Economic Development and Economic Planning in India,* Bombay, 1963.

Karaka, D.F., *History of the Parsis* Vol. I, Mcmillan, London,1884.

Karve, Irawati, *Hindu Society: An Interpretation,* Sangam Prakashan, Poona, 1961.

Karve, Irawaati, 'On The Road: A Maharashtrian Pilgrimage,"

Journal of Asian Studies, 1962, 22, 13-30.

Khare, R.S., *The Changing brahmans, Associations and Elites among the Kannyakubjas of North India,* University of Chicago Press, Chicago, 1970.

Kolenda, P.M., 'Religious Anxiety and Hindu Fate,' *The Journal of Asian Studies*, 1964, 23, 71-82.

Lall, R. Manohar, *Among the Hindus: A study of hindu Festivals,* Minerva Press, Kawnpore, 1933.

Levi-Strauss, Claude, 'The Bear and the Barber,' *Journal of the Royal Anthropological Institue of Great Britain, and Ireland,* 1963, 93, part I, I-II.

Mc.Cormack, W., 'The Forms of Communication in Virasaiva Religion,' *Journal of Amrican Folklore,* 1958, 71, 325-335.

McCormack, W., 'Lingaits, As a Sect,' *Journal of the Royal Anthropological Institute,* 1963, 93, 59-71.

Mandelbaum, G.G., 'The Jewish Way of Life in Cochin, *Jewish Social Studies,* 1939, 1, 423-460.

Mandelbaum, D.G., 'Form, Variation and Meaning of a Ceremony,' in R.F. Spencer (ed.), *method and Perspective in Anthropology* University of Minnesota Press, Minneapolis, 1954, 60-102.

Mandelbaum, D.G., 'Transcendental and Pragmatic Aspects of Religion,' *American Anthropologist,* 1966, 68, 1174-1191.

Mandelbaum, D.G., *Society in India: Change and Continuity,* 2 Vols. University of California Press, Berkeley, 1970.

Mandelbaum, D.G., 'Curing and Religion in South Asia,' in Surajit Sinha(ed.), *Aspects of Indian Culture and Society,* Indian Anthrolpological Society, Calcutta, 1972, 171-186.

Marriott, Mckim, 'Little Communities in an Indigenous Civilization, in M. Marriott (ed.), *Village India,* University of Chicago Press Chicago, 1955, 171-222.

Marriott, Mckim, 'Changing Channels of Cultural Transmission in Indian Civilization,' In vERNE Ray(ed,) *Intermediate Societies. Social Mobility and Communication,* American Ethological Society, Scattle, 1959, 66-74.

Marriott, Mckim, 'Cultural Policy in the New States,' in Clifford Geertz (ed,), Old *Societies and New State,* New York, 1963, 27-56.

Marriott,. Mckim, 'The Feast of Love,' in Milton Singer (ed.),

Krishna: Myths, Rites and Attitudes, East West Centr Press. honolulu 1966, 200-212.

Marriott, Mckim and Cohn, B.S., 'Networks and Centres in th eIntegratin of Indian Civiliztin,' *Journal of Social Research,* 1958 1, 1-9.

Mathur, K.S., *Caste and Ritual in a Malwa Village,* Asia Publishing House, Bombay, 1964.

Misra, C.R. Rajalakshmi, *Mullukurumbas of Kappala,* Anthropological Survey of India, Memoir No, 30, Calcutta, 1971.

Misra, S.C., *Musim Communities in Gujarat,* Asia Publishing House, Bombay, 1964.

Misra, Vikas, *Hinduism and Economic Growth,* Oxford University Press, Bombay, 1962.

Morris, Morris, D., 'Value as an Obstacle to Economci Growth in South Asia,' *The Journal of Economic History,* 1967, 27, 588-607.

nandi, S., Rajalakshmi, C.R. and Verghese, I., *Life and Culture of the Mala Ulladun,* Anthropological Survey of India, Memoir No, 26, Calcutta, 1971.

Nicholas, Ralph, 'Ritual Hierarchy and Social Relations in Rural Bengal,' *Contributions to Indian Sociology,* (New series), 1967, 1, 56, 83.

O'malley, L.S.S., *Popular, Hindusim: The Religion of the Masses,* Cambridge University Press, Cambridge, 1935.

Opler, Morris E., 'The Place of Religion in a North Indian Village,' *Southwestern Journal of Nathropology,* 1959a, 15, 219-229.

Opler, Morris E., 1Family, Anxiety and Religion in a Community of North India,' In M.K. Opler (ed.), *Culture and Mental Health: Cross-cultural Studies,* The Mac Millan Company, New Yrok, 1959b.

Opler, Morris E., 'Particularization and Generalization as Processes in Religion an Culture,' in E.B. Harper (ed.), *Aspects of Religion in South Asia,* 1964.

Orans Martin, *The Santal, Tribe in Search of a Great Tradition,* Wayne State Unviersity Press, Detroit, 1965.

Orenstein. henry, 'Towards a Grammar of Defirement in Hindu Sacred Law,' in Milton Singer and B.S. Cohn (eds.) *Structure and Change in Indian Society,* 1968, 115-132.

Patnaik, Nityananda, 'The Recent Kings of Puri,' in Surajit Sinha (cd.), *Aspects of Indian Culture and Society,* Indian Anthropological Society. Calcutta, 1972, 87-114.

Pocock, D.F., 'Inclusion and Exclusion: A Process in the Caste System of Gujarat,' *Southwestern Journal of Anthropology,* 1957.

Pocock, D. F., 'The Anthropology of Time Reckoning,' *Contributions to Indian Sociology,* 1964, 6. 78-95.

Raghavan, V., Methods, of Popular Religious Instructions in South India,' In Milton Singer (ed.) *Traditional India: Structure and Change,* The american Folklore Society, Philadelphia, 1959, 130-140.

Raghavan, V., Variety and Integration in the Pattern of Indian Civilization,' *Far EAstern Quarterly*, 1965, 15, 33-41.

Raj, Hilda, *Persistence of Caste in South India: An Analytical Study of Hindu and Christian Nadar,* Doctoral Dissertation, American University, Washington, D.C., 1959.

Rao, M.S.A., 'Hinduism and Economic Development,*Sociological Bulletin,* 1969, 18, 1-15.

Ratan, Ram. 'The Changing Religion of the Bhangis of Delhi: A Case Study of Sanskritizatin,' in L.P. Vidyarthi (ed.) *Aspects of Religion in Indian Society,* Meerut, 1961.

Ray, Nihar Ranjan, *The Sikh Gurus and Sikh Society,* Pariala, 1970.

Redfield, Robert and Singer, Milton, 'The Cultural Role of Cities,' *Economic Development and Social Change,* 1954, 8 (I), 53-73.

Redfield, Robert, 'The Social Organization of Tradition,' *Far Eastern quarterly*, 1955, 15, (I), 13-21.

Redfield, Robert, *Peasont Society and Culture: An Anthropological Approach to the Study of Civilization,* University of Chicago Press, Chicago, 1956.

Risley,H.H., *The People of India,* Second dition, W. Thacker & Co., London, 1915.

Robinson, S.M. and Joiner, L.W., 'An Experiment in the Structural Study of Myth,' *Contributions to Indian sociology,* New Series, 1968, NO.2.

Roy, S.C., *The Mundas and Their Country,* , Calcutta, 1912.

Roy, S.C., *Oraon Religion and Custom,* Ranchi, 1928.

Roy, S.C., 'Caste, Race and Religion: Inadequaties of the Current Theories of Caste,' *Man in India,* 1934, 14, 75-220.

Sangave, V.A. *Jaina Community: A Social Survey,* Bombay, 1959.

Saraswati, Baidyanath and Sinha, Surajit, *The Ascetic Organization of Kashi,* Unpublished Report submitted tothe Anthropological Survey of India, Calcutta, 1070.

Saraswati, Baidyanath, 'The Traditional Mode of Learning in Indian Civilization', in Surajit Sinha (ed.) *Aspects of Culture and Society in India,* Indian Anthropological Society, Calcutta, 1972, 153-170.

Sharma, K.N., 'Hindu Sects and Food patterns in North India,. *Journal of Social Research,* 4, 47-58.

Siddiqui, M.K.A., 'Caste Among the slims of Calcutta,' in Surajit Sinha (ed.), *Cultural Profile of Calcutta,* Calcutta, 1972, 50-60.

Singer, Milton B., 'The Cultural Pattern of Indian Civilizatin,' *Far Eastern Quarterly, 1955,* 15, (I), 25-36.

Singer, Milton B., 'Cultural Values in India's Economci Develop ment,' *Annals of the American Academy of Political and Social Science, 1956a,* (305), 81-91.

Singer, Milton B., 'India's Cultural Values and Economci development: A discussion,' *Economic Development and Social Change,* 1956b, 1,1-12.

Singer, Milton, B., 'The Great Tradition in a Metropolitan Cen Madras, Journal of American Folklore, 1958, 71, 347-388..

Singer, Milton B. (ed.), *Traditional India: Structure and Change,* The American Folklore Society, Philadelphia, 1959.

Singer, Milton B., 'Review: The Religion of India by Max Weber,' *American Anthropologist,* 1961, 63 (I), 143-151.

Singer, Milton B., The Radha-Krishna Bhajans of Madras City, *History of Religions,* 1963, 2, 183-226.

Singer, Milton B., 'The Social Organization of Indian Civilization, *Diogenes,* 1964, 45, 84-119.

Singer, Milton B., 'Religion an dSocial Change in India: The Max Weber Thesis, Phase Three,'*Economic Development and Culture Change,* 1966a 14, 497, 505.

Singer, Milton B., *Krishna: Myths, Rites and Attitudes,* East-West Center Press. Honolulu, 1966b.

Singer, Milton B., 'The Modernization of Religious Beliefs,' in Myron Weiner (ed.) *Modernization,* Basic Books, Inc. New York, 1966c. 55-67.

Singer, Milton B., *When a Great Tradition Modernizes: An Anthropological Approach to Indian Civilizatin,* Prager Publishers, new York, 1972. (Read particularly, Chapters— I. "Text and Context in the Study of Contemporary Hinduism", "Search for a great Tradition in Cultural Performances, IV. "The Social Organisation of Sanskritic Hindusim in Madras City", V. "Urbanization and Culture Change: Bhakti in the City," VI. "The Radha-Krishna Bhajans of Madras City." IX "Beyond Tradition and Modernity in Madras",)

Singh, A.K., 'Hindu Culture and Economic Development in India,' *Conspectus,* 1967, 3, 9-32.

Singh, I.P., 1A Sikh Village,' *JOurnal of American Folklore,* 1958, 71, 479-503.

Singh, I.P., 'Religion in Daleke" A Sikh Vilalge,' *JOurnal of Social Research,* 1961, 3, 38-43.

Sinha, Surajit, 'Some Aspects of Change in Bhumij Religonin South Manbhum. Bihar,' *Man in India,* 1953, 33 (2), 148-164.

Sinha, Surajit, 'The Media and nature of Hindu-Bhumij Interactions,' *Journal of th eAsiatic Society: Letters and Science,* 1957, 23, 23-37.

Sinha, Surajit, 'Changes in the Cycle of Festivals in a Bhumij Village,' *Journal of Social Research,* 1958a, 1, 24-49.

Sinha, Surajit, 'Tribal ultures of Peninsular India as a Dimension of Little Tradition in the Study of Indian Civilization,' *Journal of American folklore.* 1968b, 71-504-518.

Sinha, Surajit, 'State Formation and Rajput Myth in Tribal Central India,' *Man in India,* 1962, 142, 35-80.

Sinha, Surajit, 'Tribe-Caste and Tribe-Peasant Continua in Central India,' *Man in India,* 1965, 42, 35-80.

Sinha, Surajit (ed.), *Research Programmes in Cultural Anthoopology and Allied Disciplines,* Anthropological Survey of India, Calcutta, 1970a. [See: "Complex Religious Institutions and th eStudyof Idian Civilization: Preliminary Statement" (pp. 87-95), "Study of Sects in Hinduism (pp.

128-136) and "Study of the Sacred Complex of Kashi" (pp. 136-146).]

Sinha, Surajit (ed.), *Science, Technology and Culture, India International Centre,* New Delh, 1970b.

Sinha, Surajit (ed.) 'Is There an Indian Tradition in Social/Cultural Anthropology,' *Journalof the Indian Anthropological Society* 1971, 6, 1-14.

Singh, Surajit (ed.) The Temple of Kalikhat and the City of Calcutta, in S.C. Sinha (ed.), *Cultural Profile of Calcutta,* Indian Anthropological Society, Calcutta, 1972a.

Sinha, Surajit, 'Anthropology of Nirmal Kumar Bose in Surajit Sinha (ed.) *Aspects of Indian Culture and Society,* Indina anthropologycal Society, Calcutta, 1972b, 1-22.

Slater, Gilbert, The *Dravidian Elements in Indian Culture,* London, 1924.

Srinivas, M.N., *Religion and Society among the Coorgs of South Indian,* Oxford Unviersity Press, Oxford, 1952.

Srinivas M.N., 'A Note on Sanskritization and Westernization,' *Far Eastern Quarterly,* 1956, 15, 481-496.

Srinivas, M.N., *Social Change in Modern India,* Unviersity of California Press, Berkeley, 1966.

Staal, J.F., 'Sanskrit and Sanskritization,' *The Journal of Asran Studies,* 1963, 22, 261-275.

Stein, Burton, 'The Economic Function of the Medieval South Indian Temple,' *Journal of Asian Studies,* 1967, 19, 1633-176.

Stein, Burton, 'Social Mobility and Medieal South Indian Hindu Sects,' in James Silverberg (ed.) *Social Mobility in the Caste System in India,* 1968, 78-94, *Comparative Studies in Society and History,* Supplement II, Mouton, The Hague,

Stevenson, H.N.L., 'Status Evaluation in the Hindu Caste System' *Journal of the Royal Anthropological Institute,* 1954, 84, 45-65.

Stevenson, Mrs. Sinclair, *the Rites of the Twice Born,* Humphrees Milford, London, 1920.

Strizower, Schifra, 'jews as an Indian Caste,' *Jewish Journal of Sociology,* 1959, 1, 43-57.

Toothi, N.A., *The Vaishnavas of Gujarat,* Longman, Green & Co., Bombay, 1935.

Uberoi, J.P.S., 'On Beign Unshorn,' in *Sikhism in Indian Society,* Transactions, Indian Institue of Advanced Study, Simla, 1967, No.4.

Underhill, M.M., *The Hindu Religious year,* Association Press, Calcutta, 1921.

Vidyarthi, L.P., *The Sacred Complex in Hindu Gaya,* Gaya, Asia Publishing Houe, Bombay, 1961.

Vidyarthi, L.P. (ed.) *Aspects of Religion in Indian Society,* Ram Nath kedar Nath, Meerut, 1961.

Vidyarthi, L.P., *The Maler: A Study in Nature-Man-spirit Complex of a Hil lTraibe,* Bookland, Calcutta, 1963.

Weber, Max, *The Religion of India: The Sociology of Hiduism and Buddhism.* Translated and Edited by Haus H. Gerth and Don Martindale), The Free Press,Glencoe, 1958.

Whitehead, H. *The Vilalge Gods of South India,* Cosmo Publications, New Delhi.